Adventures of Coconut Woman

Also by Debbie Smoker

Turn on your Magic Eyes
Joy of Jamaica

Adventures of Coconut Woman

Debbie Smoker

Foreword by Dr. Dexter Russell

Book design: Keith Lippert
Cover design: Kari Held
Cover art: Detail of 'Angels Appear'© by Rita Genet from the collection of Evita's Restaurant, Ocho Rios, Jamaica

Printed in the USA

ISBN-10: 0-97187-919-2
ISBN-13: 978-0-97187-919-5

Library of Congress: 2006922859

The author kindly acknowledges permission to repro-
duce the photos contained within the book.

Joy Won Publishing USA

Helga K. Melichar   *Victor J. Melichar*

*I dedicate this book to my Mother
and Father with my deepest love and gratitude*

JAMAICAN NATIONAL ANTHEM

Eternal Father, Bless our Land,
Guide us with thy mighty hand,
Keep us free from evil powers,
Be our light through countless hours,
To our leaders, great defender,
Grant true wisdom from above,
Justice, truth be ours forever,
Jamaica, land we love,
Jamaica, Jamaica, Jamaica, land we love

Teach us true respect for all,
Stir response to duty's call,
Strengthen us the weak to cherish,
Give us vision lest we perish,
Knowledge send us Heavenly Father,
Grant true wisdom from above,
Justice, truth be ours forever,
Jamaica, land we love,
Jamaica, Jamaica, Jamaica, land we love

ACKNOWLEDGEMENTS

This book would never have been completed without the help and encouragement of many people. I wish to thank and honor everyone who is in the book for sharing and believing.

I also wish to thank, in particular: my mother, Helga Melichar, for her encouraging words and all the warm meals she cooked for me while I was busy writing; my brother Mathew Melichar for the computer he and mom bought me; my brother and sister-in-law, Richard and Judy McCue, for so generously allowing me use of their computer while I wrote the first draft; my father and step-mother, Victor and Betty Melichar, for constantly begging me to finish this ever since they personally experienced Jamaica for themselves; my sister, Vicki McDonald, for starting me journalling when I was ten years old; my brother, Mark Melichar, for motivating me after a psychic told him to tell me to finish the book; my husband, Keith Lippert, for his devotion, his brilliant technical assistance and his endless patience and love; my friend, Carol Swanson, for helping me find direction in life; Dexter Russell for his friendship and understanding; Suzzanne Lee Scott and Sharon Udell, for your guidance and support in Jamaica; Kira Henschel and Robin Willard for your editing and input; Tony Rajer for business advice; Rita Genet, for her magical cover art; Kari Held, for her lovely cover design; and finally, a special thanks to my spirit guides and all who helped me from the "other side."

If I have missed anyone, please forgive me. I love you all.

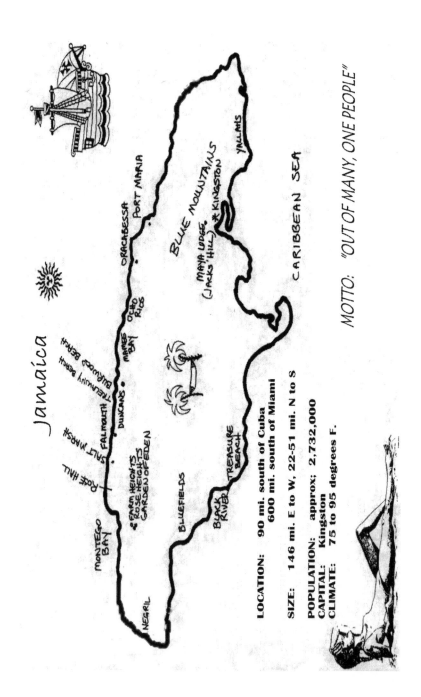

Jamaica

NEGRIL
MONTEGO BAY
ROSE HALL
SALT MARSH
FALMOUTH
TRELAWNY BEACH
Burwood Beach
DUNCANS
FARM HEIGHTS
ROSE HEIGHTS
GARDEN OF EDEN
MARCE BAY
OCHO RIOS
ORACABESSA
PORT MARIA
BLUEFIELDS
BLACK RIVER
TREASURE BEACH
BLUE MOUNTAINS
MAYA LODGE (JACKS 'HILL)
☆ KINGSTON
YALLAHS

CARIBBEAN SEA

LOCATION: 90 mi. south of Cuba
600 mi. south of Miami

SIZE: 146 mi. E to W, 22-51 mi. N to S

POPULATION: approx; 2,732,000
CAPITAL: Kingston
CLIMATE: 75 to 95 degrees F.

MOTTO: "OUT OF MANY, ONE PEOPLE"

VIII

TABLE OF CONTENTS

Jamaican National Anthem VI
Acknowledgements VII
Foreword by Dr. Dexter Russell XI
Introduction XV

1. WE'RE NOT IN KANSAS ANYMORE 1
2. VOICE OF THE PEOPLE 63
3. DREAMS AND PROPHESIES 99
4. THE OTHER SIDE OF PARADISE 127
5. REFLECTIONS 141
6. BIBLES AND DUPPIES 159
7. SPIRIT SONGS 209
8. HIGHS AND LOWS 227
9. PSYCHICS, RASTAFARIANS
                    AND CINDERELLA 251
10. THE FINAL HOURS 287

Eplilogue 301
Glossary 303
About the artist 306
About the author 307

FOREWORD

Several years ago I read Zora Neale Hurston's classic book, *Tell My Horse.* This novel dealt with voodoo in Haiti and Jamaica. Set in the 1930's Jamaica, the practice of obeah or voodoo was controversial then and although less visible today, the subject still evokes fear and a source of power in many parts of Jamaica.

When the privilege of writing the foreword to *Adventures of Coconut Woman* was extended to me, I readily accepted in spite of my busy schedule. Reading the manuscript brought back many memories of my childhood, growing up in the old Spanish colonial capital of Jamaica, Spanish Town. The topic of obeah was never discussed in my home and no one I knew ever admitted to believing in such nonsense. In spite of these denials there was always a sense of uneasiness when the word obeah was mentioned. I even recall taking the long way home from school in order to avoid running into the "black art man," as the practitioner was called.

I first met Debbie Smoker in the mid-ninties while living and working in Chicago, Illinois. She was a writer and book reviewer for a regional publication. I remember looking forward each month to reading her writing on spirituality and conscious living. She often mentioned Jamaica in her pieces and I was ever so curious how a person in Wisconsin possessed such intimate knowledge of Jamaica. In her previous novel *Turn on your Magic Eyes,* Ms. Smoker demonstrated an understanding of Jamaica, its people and culture that was quite remarkable. I have followed her career with a lot of interest over the years.

A life long visitor and part-time resident of Jamaica,

Debbie has developed a grasp of the subtleties of daily existence on the island. Her total immersion into the culture has not only enriched her spirit, but has given a voice of expression to a segment of the population that is very often neglected, or worse, ignored. She has an uncanny ability through her friendly manner to draw out the true essence of what is behind the expressions of her interviewees. It takes special talent and focus to resist being mesmerized by the stunning physical beauty of the island and connect with the people. Careful listening is an absolute must, as profound thoughts and insights are likely to come from the mouth of a street vendor just as easily as it could from a member of the elite class.

Jamaicans are a proud people and are skeptical of outsiders asking questions. Even when they are acquainted with you, their first response is often meant to extract more information before saying what they really feel. They don't reveal a whole lot until they establish the questioner's intent. Debbie is one of the few writers of her generation to break down this facade and put the speaker at ease. The people sense she is genuine and value what is being said. She will ask about their children and other family members. Often low on funds herself, she willingly shares food and drinks with the people she meets. It never ceases to amaze her how generous the people are to her even though they have so little materially. Day after day, Debbie demonstrated that she did not consider herself superior or better than those around her. This humble attitude endeared her to the people, thus gaining their trust and respect. Jamaicans truly believe actions speak louder than words.

It is interesting that Debbie's introduction to Jamaica was by way of the tourist industry where the main attractions are the sun, sand and the sea. At some point however, Debbie sensed that there was something more to this tropical paradise than the usual tourist sites. She has made this elusive factor a quest of discovery and is convinced that it lies within the people. That unseen aspect is what Zora Neale Hurston wrote about in *Tell My Horse*, the classic novel on the supernatural in Jamaica.

While Christianity is the dominant religion in Jamaica, it's no secret that some inhabitants will consult with the obeah man when they are desperate. Obeah, a quasi-religion brought over from Africa during the slave trade, still plays a powerful role in the spiritual landscape. Some see no contradiction in worshipping in church on Sunday while going to the obeah man on Monday. Many people Debbie interviewed freely talked about their encounters with obeah. Whenever the pressures of daily living become too much to handle, it's not unusual for some to turn to the unseen for help. Economic hardship and uncertainty dominate the lives of many people and they see the obeah man as part of the solution.

Debbie Smoker's newest novel will pull you into a world of intrigue and mystery. You discover how people's belief in the spirit world keeps them alive and hopeful, in spite of the destruction and poverty around them. They cry and laugh at their plight and are certain things will get better. How else could they face their day?

I admire Debbie's account of life in Jamaica. She doesn't hide or hold anything back. So much comes to you unfiltered. This is a novel about Jamaica and its people, but it's also a novel of self-discovery. Debbie does not hide how she is feeling at any given moment. Self-revelation and vulnerability are constantly running through her encounters. She has chosen to write about an area of Jamaican life that some might suggest would be better suited for religious scholars or anthropologists to explore. Some Jamaicans might feel uncomfortable seeing this part of the culture exposed. They might argue that obeah is evil and only the ignorant find value in this practice. This subject matter ought not be so easily dismissed. That which we resist persists. People's religious and spiritual beliefs play a crucial role in defining who they are and their purpose in this life.

Consciousness runs along a continuum. As humans we are part of a collective mind and indestructible memory. We are linked to our ancestors and our past and perhaps it's time to listen to other voices, views and opinions. No one person or group possesses the whole truth. There are so few certainties in life we cannot afford to dismiss what others feel by labeling them superstitious or foolish. I applaud my friend Debbie for embracing the culture of Jamaica and the many gifts it has offered the world, including its spiritual side.

Jamaica Love! Jamaica Live!

Dr. Dexter Russell
Naples, Florida
March, 2006

INTRODUCTION

In 1990, I backpacked through Jamaica for ten weeks, interviewing people all over the island in an attempt to capture Jamaica through the eyes and hearts of her own people. Although I was born in Wisconsin, I spend enough time in Jamaica to call it my second home. Living on the island for several years while working for a wholesale tour company out of Chicago, provided me with an opportunity to live with a culture vastly different from my own. For this, I am deeply grateful. It was during this time that a well known Jamaican singer gave me the pet name of Coconut Woman.

But my personal interest in Jamaica goes way beyond tourism. I've always been utterly fascinated with the island people, their beliefs and philosophies, life styles and folklore. I have an inner need to understand what makes them tick. My insatiable curiousity led me to do the backpack excursion. I knew that this adventure would be a spiritual sojourn as well as a physical one, and that in order for it to be successful, I must conjure up all my courage and be willing to also bare my own soul.

When I excitedly shared the news that I was going to do this, well meaning friends in Wisconsin told me that I "was crazy, would be raped or killed trapsing around Jamaica alone, and also that Jamaicans would not be willing to open up and share their true beliefs with me because I was just a little white girl whom they would have no reason to trust."

So, I left Wisconsin armed with one thousand dollars, a backpack and tent, notebooks, tapes, a camera, and a resolve to give Jamaicans everywhere a reason to trust me. I came with an honest and open heart, one filled with love, and a mission to honor these people who mean so much to me. Because of all the previous time I had spent in Jamaica, I already had several close friends there, but I knew I would also be meeting many other people for the first time.

Part of this journey would be experiencing the hardships of third world living for myself. I was often thirsty, hungry, moving around on blistered feet, and wondering where I would be sleeping at night. But the experience was worth any pain I went through. I was forced to look into the mirror of my own soul as I journeyed through the psyche of the island people.

What did I learn about and from Jamaicans? As I traveled, I heard many stories of prophetic dreams and visitations with spirits. I find many Jamaicans to be extremely intuitive and consciously living in harmony with the physical and spiritual realms. That in itself makes them unique. So much of the human race is very wrapped up in the physical plane, not yet recognizing consciously that we are simultaneously living in other dimensions.

I learned that pain and suffering do have a purpose. They serve as teachers if we let them. I learned the power of keeping a sense of humor. Jamaicans are always laughing at themselves and life. I learned how much I can learn by shutting my mouth, observing and listening. I learned the danger and folly of passing judgement. I learned that freedom is a state of being, not a place. I learned the power and value of meditation. Jamaicans taught me that we do indeed live in a world of illusions, but we can see truth through the eyes of our spirits. Life is vastly different when it's not perpetually invaded by the media and the tools of technology. The inner chaos we experience as a result of the violence and fear consistantly crammed down our throats is disempowering all of us. The fact that it's called news and entertainment speaks volumes about how unevolved we really are. The Jamaica that I journeyed through in 1990 was one where the people were deeply connected to themselves and nature. Entertainment was interaction with each other, not with a machine. Everyone I met and shared time with in Jamaica fascinated me. People went out of their way to help me and they blossomed like vibrant flowers when they shared the secrets of their souls. I worked with them, laughed and cried with them, danced and sang with them, and grew wealthy inside spiritually.

To any Jamaicans reading this, I say stand up and be proud of yourselves, your unique and precious culture and your astoundingly beautiful island and seas. Jamaica is a mystical place, one which is always gifting our planet. People too often speak of Jamaica as a violent place, but I experienced the phenomenal love and treasures existing there. And I humbly thank you for opening your arms, hearts and homes to me.

One Love,
Debbie
2006

1

WE'RE NOT IN KANSAS ANYMORE

"De three women work miracle, keep
down de world wid science and magic. "
-- Daniel God

Wednesday, January 10, 1990
It's 7:30 AM. I'm at O'Hare International Airport in Chicago. My flight for this long awaited journey leaves in one and a half hours. I feel at peace and somewhat out of body, as though I'm watching a movie. What I see and experience I will write about.

I'm taking a box of clothes, toys and books for my Jamaican friend Harris and his family. I'm also taking a backpack, a sleeping bag, a tent, a carry on with all my writing and recording supplies, my music and my books. I feel like a queen and will live the life of a Caribbean Gypsy.

Harris called me at 4:00 AM, just as I was getting ready to catch my bus to Chicago. He's going to meet me at the airport. At least I know I'll have a place to stay tonight. Everything will work out.

Yesterday, my dear grandmother asked me all about Jamaica and said she wished she could come with me. I resign myself now to the Higher Forces.

11:30 AM I'm starting my journey to Jamaica, my spiritual quest. I was

1

hardly aware of my body as I prepared these last few days. I know without a doubt, that I have Spirit Guides directing my physical being. I would never be this calm, collected and ready on my own.

Seriously, I can feel them and I can hear them. I was told by them to simply relax and to let it happen, then to write, write, write and observe. I've been guided all the way through this. First, the whole idea flooded into me at a time I least expected. Then, things seemed to fall into place for me, bringing me this far.

For a while I worked for a tour company, taking senior citizens on bus tours around the United States. This enabled me to save the cash that I needed. Then I lost my job, through what seemed to be a quirk of fate. However, in the long run I realized that it was a blessing in disguise because it enabled me to focus totally on this. With no job to come back to right now I can take whatever time I need in Jamaica, at least until my funds run out. I've got one thousand dollars.

While I was preparing for this, my friend Ron showed up unexpectedly with the gift of a tent and backpack. I was very touched, as that solved my hiking and housing problems. I was also able to get a round trip ticket to Jamaica for the unbelievable price of two hundred and nineteen dollars.

I really wasn't sure where I would end up tonight, so Harris's call was a relief.

Thursday, January 11

I feel like it's impossible to write on only the one page my journal gives me, so I'll also write in the notebooks I brought. Yes, I truly am home again. The magic flows within me and without me. I was greeted at the airport by many wonderful old friends, some of whose names I couldn't even remember. I have been away too long.

Harris was not at Sangster's International Airport when I arrived in Montego Bay. I found out today that he did come, but was told that everyone from the flight was gone. Actually, what really happened is that he showed up for the wrong flight!

It's hard to believe that I'm really here. Anyway, my friend and former co-worker Deedra (who is also a Resort Rep for the company I used to work for) happened to be working at the airport when I arrived. We had a joyous reunion and she invited me to spend the night at her little apartment. I graciously accepted.

The Reps had all been invited to a free event, and since I'm a former Rep I was allowed to come. So my first evening back in Jamaica was spent touring Rose Hall Great House (a haunted, historic plantation home) in candlelight. Some of the local people refuse to enter the building at night, for fear of seeing duppies. Duppies are Jamaican ghosts or spirits of the deceased.

There was a full moon last night, which just added to the magic in the air. We also enjoyed food, drink and live music. A dream. A mystical energy hung everywhere, in the trees, the air, the glowing sky and the sparkling sea, in the song of the tree frogs, and in the gentle, soft-spoken people.

This morning, I rode out to the parish of Trelawny with Sara, another Rep. I thought that I would feel nervous and uncomfortable, but I knew that I had to face it. While repping, I had lived at Trelawny Beach Resort for about eight months. I fell in love with a local man from the nearby village of Falmouth. His name was Denton, and he's one of the people who will live in my heart forever.

That's where I was living when my company suddenly and unexpectedly transferred me to Acapulco, Mexico. It was extremely painful for me to leave. It broke my heart, shattered it. I knew that I had to go back now, to bring my life there to some kind of closure.

This morning, I really felt like I was only dreaming as we drove through Falmouth. So much of my spirit and soul and self was still there. My first reaction, as I wandered through the resort, wasn't one of longing as I expected it would be, but a sense of peace that I have moved on.

The beach. Ah, the beach... with its foamy aqua waves... its soft sand... its jungle vegetation. That pull... that elusive yearning... was still there, on that beach...that intangible thing that I need to understand and make tangible, so that I can share it with the world. It's still there, very heavily there. I don't understand it.

It's something spiritual and I already know that I must spend a good amount of time there, listening to it. Because something will be revealed. There is some kind of spiritual force there and I know that I am receptive to it. It's almost like a spot in the world that has a door to the dimension beyond this one. I was close to opening that door when I lived there. I feel like this time I will be able to open it, if I stay here long enough and if I listen.

I must not, at any cost, close myself, my intuition, my awareness of spirit. I feel that I may be frightened for a time and tempted to blot it out, but I must see it out.

I'm living in a much higher plane now than I was when I was here before. I am listening and I was told by my voice to follow my heart and relax. "Don't try too hard to make anything happen. Things are happening. Your job is just to observe and be aware of that. Your job, be assured, is to record all that you observe from your spirit."

So, that's probably why I wasn't nervous this morning on the beach. I wasn't conscious so much in my physical being as I was in my spirit. I was deeply engrossed in a conversation with five Jamaicans about how I wanted to understand their souls. In truth, I never intended to tell them I was writing a book, but I followed my instincts and it just happened.

Suddenly I looked up and saw Denton, my old lover, walking toward us. He was coming from Burwood Beach, the local beach where I spent several months and learned so much about Jamaican culture. I turned to him, smiled and said hello. I could tell that he was very uncomfortable, wondering how I felt about him now and how I would treat him. Our lives had moved on and Denton was now living with another woman. I had almost quit my job rather than transferring to Mexico. I wanted to stay and live with Denton, yet I knew that it would be next to impossible to earn a living in Falmouth. Denton makes beautiful coral jewelry right there on the beach and sells it to tourists, but he didn't earn enough to support both of us and his three lovely daughters. Our paths had forked in different directions.

I was amazed at my own feelings now. I felt calm, controlled, peaceful and loving. I had expected chaos inside and pain, afraid that seeing him would recreate a desire to pick up where we had left off.

Denton smiled his beautiful smile that seemed to cover the whole earth and shyly said hello. He looked much taller than I remember, otherwise the same. Then he stood about six feet away from the rest of us, looking down and listening intently to what I was saying. When I finished, I waved brightly and said good-by.

Next I headed down to Burwood Beach to visit my old friend Sonny, the local lifeguard. I purposely hadn't given myself a chance to talk to Denton. At that moment, it seemed like the right thing to do. Seeing each other had been shocking enough and I was feeling vulnerable.

On my walk down the beach, I stopped to visit old Sam, a caretaker at a nearby house. Sam was sitting primly on a tree stump, wearing a bright yellow shirt and a baseball cap. He said that what I am doing is good and that he will sit and tell me stories.

The sea... As soon as I touched it I became One with it. We merged and floated into each other.

Sonny runs a local refreshment stand on the beach. Hurricane Gilbert flattened his old place, but he had rebuilt it. It's small, modest, all wooden. Every night he loads up everything in the shop (liquor, soft drinks, candy, buns and cheese) onto a little cart, and wheels it down the road to a place where he can lock it up. And every morning he wheels it back. This is his life and how he serves the people.

Although Sonny is the official lifeguard at Burwood, he hurt his knee and can't even swim. He buys his lifeguard license for JA $1800 a year. Denton has taken on the job of watching the beach and helping those in need, as he is a very strong swimmer. The title of lifeguard is not important to him, but taking care of people is. This is a prime example of how Jamaicans work in harmony. Everyone here is happy.

My reunion with Sonny was sunny. "Debbie Girl" had come home. We laughed and chatted about old times. It was somehow comforting to realize that even though I had changed so much, this very special place had not.

Denton showed up later and we finally had a talk. When I got transferred to Mexico and had to leave so unexpectedly, we devised a plan which we hoped would reunite us in the future. I was hoping to save enough money so that when I came back we could start either a taxi (tour) business or a jet ski rental business. Well, it never happened. I got very sick in Mexico, quit my job and moved back to Wisconsin where I found work in a restaurant. I couldn't save any money at all on my wages. Denton didn't understand this. Most Jamaicans don't understand that although wages in the States are much higher than in Jamaica, so is the cost of living.

We wrote, but in time Denton came to believe that I was just putting him off. Meanwhile, I sadly watched our dream blow further and further out to sea. We discussed this today and I realized that our communication had suffered in other ways, too. Clear communication is so vital in life.

It's really quite humorous now. Denton enjoys smoking his ganja (marijuana). I had written him a letter stating that if he was going to be driving the tour taxi, I felt he needed to clean up his act a little bit. All that I meant was that he needed to curtail his smoking. What I didn't know until today, is that Denton thought that I was asking him to cut off his dreadlocks! I would never ask anyone to cut his hair for any reason. I believe hair is a personal reflection and I know that hair has religious significance to Rastafarians. Denton was angry and hurt when he thought I was asking him to cut it.

Denton

I felt sad when I realized that he thought that I was able to, but just didn't want to, help him financially. I knew that he had always shared everything he had with me and had tried to make me as comfortable as possible. He never had very much, but he would share whatever he did have.

Anyway, it felt good to talk to Denton and clear the air. As painful as it was, I had to let the dream go. I knew now that I had other things that I came to Earth to accomplish.

Friday, January 12

Denton and I took a walk down the beach in Trelawny this morning. I still care about him and I know he still cares. I also know that I'm going to be very careful not to get involved again. I don't want to interfere with the new life that he has going for him. Until yesterday, the last time I saw him was a couple of years ago.

See? Everything is unfolding. I've had no problems so far finding places to stay or getting where I want to go. And everyone seems very happy to see me. That touches my heart deeply. Also, everyone is very happy to be interviewed for my book.

Farm Heights

I'm already so far behind in recording my experiences. It's 4:00 PM and I'm now on Market Street in Montego Bay. Harris and I are waiting for a taxi to take us up into the mountains, to an area called Farm Heights, where he lives. I'm going to spend a few days there.

We've been waiting an hour now. This is typical in Jamaica. I can't imagine people in the States having this kind of patience. We are always in such a blessed hurry. Why? We run so fast that we forget why we're here. We run so fast that we kill ourselves from the stress of it.

This is no problem. We just stand on the corner. I love watching the people. All the dear children are out of school now. Their songs and laughter ring in the air. It fills my heart with joy and I want to join them in their play.

7

Later: Earlier today, Deedra dropped me off on Union Street, which is a local area of Montego Bay. Harris is a security guard at a place there called the Western Wheel. I had given him a box of clothes, some of which he was wearing. "Quit whining" was written on his T-shirt and he had on grey denim jeans.

He was also wearing a necklace that I had given him. The chain holds a small golden image of a Gucci bottle and has red and green stripes on it. It looked very Jamaican and he wore it proudly.

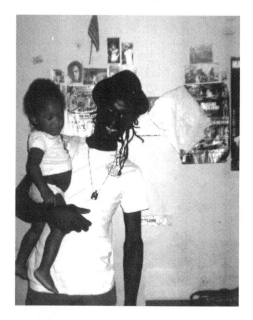

Harris and Kimoy at home

He is about six feet tall and weighs about one hundred sixty pounds. Harris has dreadlocks which hang about six inches below his shoulders, but are now piled precariously into a dark brown suede hat with a suede roping band. He has dark brown eyes, smooth dark skin and sports a moustache and a goatee. One of his front teeth is missing, but he has a great smile and sincere personality.

His favorite thing that I bought him is a little purple battery operated radio, which he'll probably carry around like it is a limb of his own body. Definitely a cool dude. He looks adorable, even more so when you know him, know his kind, gentle spirit and his quiet, shy way. He relates his simple life to what "de Fodder" (God) expects of him.

Today we waited two hours and ten minutes for a local taxi to his home. Ours was a typical Jamaican style taxi, a dilapidated, green Lada with a rusty skeleton of a roof. Seven passengers were crammed in. On the rusty, rippled dash there was a blue silk rose and a button that said "Bob Marley is the King." It cost us JA $2 (about 30 cents US) to ride. The car sounded and felt like it would fall apart any second as it rattled up the road and swerved around the potholes. I enjoyed the experience though. It was a "Lada" fun.

I was anxious to explore Jamaica, to talk to the people, to go to the very local, local places. So I met some friends tonight and we went out. We started at Thrillers Discotheque, then went to Gloucester Tavern. Then Harris took me to a place called The Spider Web, which had dancing girls. The sign on the outside of the building said, "Dear good customer, please pay as you are served. No credit. Thank you."

I want to begin to understand why I am so attracted to all of this local stuff. Harris went into The Spider Web with me and asked a female bartender to take care of me. He had to leave for a while, so here I am alone. What a place! I'm in a medium size room. The walls are painted black with spider webs all over them. There are seats and benches around the room. In the right corner is a stage and on it is a bored looking dancer clad only in boots and a bra. But I sense her feeling of power. There are men everywhere, pretending indifference, but really very intrigued by her. They are behaving as most Jamaican men do, "just cool."

I should really feel out of place here, but for some reason I don't. Harris's daughters fixed my hair tonight and I was told I look fourteen years old. I have braids and ponytails and bright ribbons and barrettes and combs all over my head. But I was honored that they cared and tried to make me look pretty, so I wore it that way anyway. They love me so much and I love them. This is Jamaica. This is the real Jamaica. I'm getting a taste of how most Jamaicans live.

As I sit here, my mind drifts back to earlier in the evening. As we approached Harris's house, he told me that he had a surprise for me. It turned out to be a beautiful one year old baby girl, his latest daughter. She waddled

9

up to me and reached up to hug me, stealing my heart away.

All of his children, all of those girls, hold secrets that I will learn here. Harris also has a wonderful son named Prince. I've known this family for years and I love them dearly. This evening, they all sang and danced and modeled for me, and they laughed freely and joyously. They hugged me and kissed me and loved me as though I had never been away. And the oldest one, Coreen, who is thirteen, told me about her life.

Back to The Spider Web. It's now 1:00 AM. Harris has left me for an inexcusably long time. I'm sitting in a corner writing and I feel like I could write forever. People are looking at me with a lot of curiosity and fascination. I'm sure I do look out of place. This is a typical Jamaican hang out and here I am, a white woman. Not only are white women not normally seen in places like this, but here I am sitting in a corner, madly scribbling in a book. Some people have asked me what I'm writing.

Think I'll go outside and look for Harris. He seemed shocked that I was curious about this place.

I'm outside now, and feel a bit irritated with Harris for not coming back for me. He told me he was going to get some jerk chicken and would "soon come." But he's been gone a long time.

Harris has one major problem which is interfering in his life in a big way and it makes me very, very sad. But, Harris is here to learn his own lessons. He has been doing a lot of drugs lately.

Well, some part of me can't believe that I'm sitting here on a stoop in a very third world part of Jamaica. But here I am, so white, sticking out like a sore thumb even though I'm trying to be invisible. I know better. All the men that hang out here are eyeing me curiously and I just pretend not to notice them.

A bar patron just came out to tell me that Harris is across the street where he works. Somehow, he has been mistakenly locked inside the gate. The security guard is locked in. This is getting funnier and funnier by the moment. Someone is supposed to be coming to get him out. Harris has himself locked into the place he's supposed to be guarding.

I just crossed the street and hollered to Harris. He came to the gate and is vexed because he is locked in. He wants to try to climb the fence to get out, but he's afraid that this will attract the police. So, here I sit, waiting for him. Now it's 2:00 AM.

Union St., Montego Bay

I'm wondering if he'll come around. If he doesn't, I'm stuck here on the street with all the night crawlers. Ha, the things I go through to write a book.

Am I afraid? No. Do I care what these people may be thinking of me? No. Why? Because I know that my intent here is pure and good and that is all that really matters.

Oh no! Harris just wandered right by me and headed into The Spider Web looking for me. I was just talking to him for Pete's sake! Now I know that he is ozoned on drugs tonight. This is very sad to me. I must not judge. I'm here to be objective, to observe, not to become involved. It's very important for me to stay focused on that. But, it's difficult. I am here to learn that I can't change someone who doesn't want to change.

Oh, the moon is so beautiful and almost full tonight... The energy is very different when the moon is full. My emotions intensify and so does my desire to create. My passion flows torridly through my veins, and I long to dance wildly by a fire or the sea, singing, howling and celebrating life. The full moon awakens my primeval self. I honor it, because it is a part of me.

Well, Harris just found me and took me inside the gate. I've been to this place before and it holds many memories. What a strange place. Harris took me here when I first met him. This place has two walls, no ceiling, pipes and boat ropes hanging all over. And inside, there is yet another small room.

Why is this place locked up anyway? I can't figure this out at all. And Harris is supposed to be a security guard here? For what? Something just doesn't seem to fit...

Anyway, Harris brought me in here, laid a newspaper on a stair and asked me to sit down. Then he disappeared again. Now what?

The drugs have definitely taken control of this man. I found him hunched in a corner and asked him what he was doing. There was a jar that was covered with foil. He said it was weed mixed with gum, (whatever that means).

Western Wheel, outside the "cell"

Well, so much for staying uninvolved. I lost it. I told him that he's being rude to me and irresponsible to his kids and to himself, and I asked when he was going to grow up. He calmly looked at me and said that I simply misunderstood it all, that the Government owes him house repairs and he's waiting for the zinc to come. (The roofs of the houses are made with zinc).

What did I, should I, could I have expected of all this? I don't honestly know. I see that Harris is finding excuses not to be responsible. He doesn't know which way to turn, because of the poverty in Jamaica. My heart goes out to him. Here's my opinion getting in the way again, but I believe that turning to drugs is not the answer. I feel so sad for his children. Harris is kind and gentle, but he escapes in his drugs. This I see very clearly.

In his own odd way, he thinks that "God" doesn't mind. Maybe "God" doesn't. Who am I to judge? I'm trying to see things through Harris's eyes and the eyes of other Jamaicans. In a way, I understand what they are going through.

When I stop and think about where I am right now and what is happening, I realize that I must have pretty tough skin to follow this project through. I do have tough skin, because I am going to follow it through at any cost. It's so hard, yet it's so important, to be an impartial observer of all this. Whew!

Later: I was walking around Montego Bay and saw a little outdoor vendor. Everyone names everything in Jamaica. They call them "pet names." We call them nicknames. This one is named "Mr. You Wayside Shack." The menu says "stewed beef, chicken, cow foot, cow mouth, fish, oxtail and roast beef."

As we're walking, Harris tells me that one of his basic philosophies of life is "each one teach one." It makes sense, because we learn from each other. It's a nice thought to carry in our minds.

Well, here we are back at the gate. Across the street, on the second story, is a local bar called Sir Candles. Dawn, the "baby-mother" of four of Harris's children, works here. She is a lovely lady. Dawn hollers down and asks me to come up and talk to her.

I do, and we have a great talk about the worth and potential of her children. We also spoke of Harris and both agreed that he should be more responsible. We both care about him and see his potential. I was saying, out of frustration, "Grow up boy!" when he walked in, causing Dawn and I to giggle.

Harris pulled up a chair and went into a long spiel about politics, which I didn't fully grasp. But I know he feels strongly about his beliefs, and he has a very personal relationship with his God.

Someone in the bar suddenly said to me, "You're not white. You're an Indian, like an Apache or someting." How odd that he would say that. I'm Bohemian and Norwegian. Then he said, "We's all one blood, same color. We's all sweet people and life is sweet." That's a typical Jamaican attitude. The motto of the country is "Out of many, one people."

It's now 4:00 AM. Harris says it's good that I'm writing this book.

Saturday, January 13
Harris, Dawn and I finally taxied home at 5:30 AM, after Dawn closed the

13

bar. Music was blaring loudly in the taxi but it didn't bother any of us.

Harris offered me the only bed in the house, but I chose to curl up on the living room floor in my sleeping bag. There was ample space, as the room has no furniture in it, just posters on the walls.

After four and a half hours of sleep, I opened my eyes and found five beautiful smiles staring down at me. I realized that was all the sleep I was going to get and forced myself into a state of semi-coherence.

The girls fixed my hair and offered to do my laundry, which has to be done by hand. One year old Kimoy waddled in and gave me a big smile, hug and kiss. I feel so loved.

The girls have been clinging to me all morning and are now very patiently waiting for me to finish writing. I'm sitting on the porch. This house is located on top of a mountain. Across the street is a field and the view is breathtaking. Goats, pigs and cows roam the streets. It's so peaceful and serene. This side of the yard has lush vegetables and trees everywhere and I can feel their energy blowing around me.

The children use the front porch as a stage to play. One by one they are modeling now. They have great moves and very flirtatious expressions. Where did they learn this? They all applaud and cheer each other on. They don't cut each other down and compete.

Now they are dancing. Once again, they take the stage one at a time. The others are singing loudly and clapping their hands to make music. How did they learn such rhythms and sexy movements? Even little Kimoy has a natural rhythm. It's wonderful, joyous, spontaneous... seems inborn.

I had much more to write last night, but I was just too exhausted. I dozed off at Sir Candles finally, knowing that I was safe there. Dawn was bartending. Harris was just hanging out. And there were a few other interesting characters that I wanted to record, but I was just too tired.

I did converse seriously with Harris around 4:00 AM, standing on the balcony under the full moon and glowing clouds, overlooking Union Street and Mo-Bay. I enjoyed watching the city finally settle down for the night. A man was sleeping on a bamboo bench across the street.

Harris gave me a good synopsis of his basic philosophy of life. Again, I was too tired to record it, but he said he'd be happy to tell me again, for my book.

The girls want me to walk over to Dawn's house to meet Grandma Sweet and Grandpa Dudley, who are Dawn's parents. So, I'm on my way.

Later: What a warm welcome I received! The first thing Grandma Sweet said to me was, "I love you so very much and I am so glad to meet you. De children, dem love you very much and dey were so hoppy last week when dey hear dat Debbie was coming. Dey just jump and shout for Debbie, Debbie, Debbie! For a whole week, dem don't slept. Dem just shout, cuz Debbie's a comin' to Jamaica!"

We had a wonderful visit and I made plans to go to church with all of them tomorrow. Grandma kept telling me how proud she is of all her grandchildren. I can see why. Dawn has two other children that I had never met, Dolly and Carlton. They are very young, very shy and very sweet.

While we were talking, Grandma Sweet's son strolled up. She said his name is John Wayne and asked me if I would take his picture by the coconut tree. The family also has a dog named Lassie.

When I asked Grandma to tell me about her life, the first thing she said was, "My life? I'm a Christian." She was born in the parish of St. Elizabeth, in a village called Newmarket.

Grandma eventually moved to Montego Bay and worked in the "fly kitchen" at the airport for eight years and eight months. It was here that she met her future husband. Grandpa Dudley also worked in the "fly kitchen." They cooked food to serve on the airplanes.

One day Grandpa cleared the empty food trays out of an airplane and took them to the kitchen, where he discovered a huge pile of money that someone had left sitting on a tray. He never thought of keeping the money, but immediately called the airlines to inform them. Sure enough, the people who had left the money had phoned and were frantic. It was returned to them and Grandpa's reward was a warm and ongoing friendship with the people. It made him happy to be able to help.

Grandma says, "Honesty is the best policy." She understands that important cosmic law. Whatever you put out will come back to you.

As we are talking, I can hear the chickens and roosters crowing outside. I call them Jamaica's alarm clock and smile as I reflect on how pleasant it is to wake up to their song every morning. It makes me feel so much more in tune with life than waking up to one of our traditional alarm clocks.

Jamaicans like to sing, and while I was visiting, Grandma sang me this song, "Why won't you hold me in the palm of your hand? Hold me in the palm of your hand? Hold me, Jesus. Hold me, Mighty God. Hold me in the palm of your hand. Thank you, Jesus."

Everyone took his turn singing and we had a great time. Dawn sang an interesting song called "God is Not Dead." "I feel him in my hands. I feel him in my feet. I feel him all over me."

What a special afternoon this has been! I don't remember ever getting together with my friends back home and singing joyfully about our spiritual beliefs. No wonder I'm so drawn to Jamaica.

Earlier, as we were walking down the road towards Grandma Sweet's house, I noticed a small stone room behind a fence. This room turned out to be the home of a man who calls himself Daniel God Ferguson. What really made me curious was the sign that hung on the wall of his home. It said:

Daniel God

Daniel God will deliver you if you believe it. How do you do? The missing link of man. A clean hand. A clean heart. Me see God today.

I stopped to read this and soon Daniel God himself appeared around the corner and started talking to me. Daniel is about five feet, nine inches tall, has short greyish black hair, is very dark skinned and was wearing a white T-shirt and beige pants. I found it impossible to guess his age. Both his face and voice are extremely intense and expressive. When he speaks, his whole face moves excitedly and his eyes seem to look deep within me, far beyond my exterior. I found it a bit unnerving, but I tried to hide this fact from him. The eerie part is that I felt like I couldn't hide anything from him. I was intrigued by this character and I ended up making several tapes on him.

Daniel saw me copying down the words on his sign and told me that the reason I was doing that is because I have a spirit. He invited me into his sacred space, which he calls the Garden of Eden. I was amazed at what I saw. He had carved bible quotes and pictures all over his lawn with his machete! When I asked him why he had done this, he went into a long speech about who he is and what he believes.

"I was born wid de spirit, to fulfill de work of Daniel God, to show mon dat God is inside of mon. And mon are to seeks God first, before he seeks de woman. Odderwise, you condemn your wife. Seeks ye first de kingdom of God, and all odder tings in his righteousness shall be added unto you. If you doesn't seeks God first, you smash de earth.

"I'm not one of dem. I separate myself. I was afflicted for thirteen and a half years and dere is a spirit grow up in me to do all dese tings.

"Dese are three cross. One teef, two teef. Dat teef say when he on de cross, 'Fodder, when thou goes to de kingdom, remember me.' Christ said to him, 'I will meet you in paradise.' Dis one says, 'If Christ call yourself God, take me off de cross, dat I come back and sin again.' He go to hell! De odder got pardoned, just as de Christ. He died, dat we might be forgiven from sex. Widout God, is death. Roman said, verse one, 'He suffered dat we might be forgiven. He died to make us good.'

"Now, Daniel God come back to represent de spirit of truth dat hide from de world because of sex in de Garden of Eden. Dis is de Garden of Eden. But my own blacks forsake me. Just as Jesus says, 'I come unto my own and my own receives me not.'

"Don't pick de fruit. Don't look wid love on de woman widout God. You will disfigure de baby. Our Fodder, which art in heaven, all de way be thy name. Jamaican mon crush God and mash up de children. Dem and de women. We crush dem cuz we doesn't see God first. Sinners, sex and God shall reconcile. For God so loved de world, he gave his one son.

"I call dis little garden heaven. I don't get no sex. I'm a barren for de Lord. If you's not of de Lord and you's try come through de gate, I don't let you come through it."

He carries on, stating that man's body is a temple of God, but chaos has resulted because of disobedience. Daniel told me I am one of the chosen ones. He talks about the commandments and then gets off track.

"De law of God, Job, 21, 'Woman, you kill baby? Where's de milk? Start rotting your bones inside.' "

Next he rambles about the dangers of money and what can happen. "You know, de money took away to buy de flesh, and get dese children wid no protection. Dis is why God is vexed. It's better you hung a millstone around your neck, Daniel, and throw you in de deepest sea, dan tell a woman, 'I love you baby! I give you a baby.' Odderwise you be like de Virgin Mary, if I never come and tempt your body."

I don't know what to think at this point. I'm certainly surprised by Daniel God. He's obviously in his own world and his own reality. It's clear that he has some kind of hang up about sex. He's trying to live very spiritually. In spite of his unusual way of thinking, I find that I am very touched by this man who lives in his own Garden of Eden way up on a mountaintop in rural Jamaica. He is connected to his God.

I find it amusing that he only allows people that he perceives as clean and holy into his garden. How he decides who is, I don't know. I'm tickled pink that I was allowed in.

At this point, someone hollers into the yard. Daniel goes and speaks with him for a moment, then comes back and says to me, "I'm glad to meet you. It's de end of time. My body is de temple of God in de four cornerstone. Can we go in de garden a little?"

We walk in further. "Tank you. You see de girl who wear de trousers?" He was referring to one of Harris's children who was sitting with us.

"She's abomination unto de Lord! God says to encourage and enlighten. De woman doesn't put her and de mon apart. Neither does de mon put him and

18

de woman apart, you know? Dese are tings dat de daughters of Zion doesn't know, and he needs de mon to seek de pants."

"So you're saying that woman should wear dresses?"

He whispers, "Yeeeeeessssss! Later on de spirit will teach you. He will tell you in your own heart. Your own heart will teach you, because of de spirit dat is dere to fulfill, you know."

He points to a cement slab in the middle of his garden. "Dis was a little church, you know, but Gilbert blow it down. Yeah, a church and a school. I got a Basic School for little children. I got a drum and all. I got Bible School, you know. But de church is fighting against me because I'm not of de flesh. I abandon dese little children." He sounds sad that his church is gone.

Daniel starts talking about sex again. "I taught dem not to do dat. Dey must come of age. Strong tings belong to adults, but not to children. Dat's why we have so much children. Children, children, children. No papa! Psalms 190: 'Dey shall be fodderless and modderless.' "

At this point, I break in and tell Daniel how lovely his garden is. "It's de Garden of Eden!" he says. "Have one of dese." He plucks a grapefruit off of a tree and hands it to me.

We wander around his garden for a while and then he suddenly shouts, "Sit down baby!" I notice some posters that Daniel has made. He holds them up and explains them to us, then goes into a long sermon about the missing link of man. It involves a number of bible quotes and his own very unique interpretation of them. Eventually he gets into speaking of obeah and experiences he is having right here in his garden.

"Right now I catch Revelation 16: 'De three woman work miracle, keep down de world wid science and magic.' I got her in de garden down here. She bring me right down in de garden, down to bare bone and skin, suck me out, dat I may come wid de gospel, dat she may catch me to kill my spirit! I bound her in Revelation 20. I lock her up. She's behind me."

I'm not sure what Daniel is talking about here, as he is mixing bible quotes with some kind of personal experience he had. I let him ramble on, as I want to understand.

"One day, I showed a black woman, 'Jezabel, Mother of Harlots,' Revelation 17. I catch her! I caught her in de garden. She come to trick me and I catched her and tied her up! And she get piece of de garden now, over dere!" Daniel points to another side of the garden.

I'm stunned. "You caught her and tied her up and killed her and buried her?"

"No, no! She is alive. She and her family and—"

"— But you've got her tied up over there?"

"I have her tied up in de garden. You know, when somebody come and tell you lie, and God make you find out de truth. Maybe de boy come and say, 'Darling, I love you,' but de boy was a devil! When you catch part of de—"

I was recording our conversation and here my tape ended, but what Daniel was trying to convey to me was that he believes that when someone has sex with you they take part of your soul. By the time I put in a new tape, he started preaching bible quotes again and speaking of the evils of sex without marriage. He said the children of such unions are evil and condemned. Harris's girls were huddled around me in fear, their huge eyes glued on Daniel. Their parents are not married. One of them decided to leave at this point, and the interruption broke Daniel out of his reverie.

He turned his focus directly on me. "Say, um, God sent you here, Debbie. De spirit of God is inside you. When I say God sent you, I mean de spirit of God is inside your heart, from your Mom and your Dad, dat you may meet Daniel God.

"And now wid dese truths, after leaving me, dere is someting dat going to talk to you all de while. You have a comforter, a husband, a real husband of God. He's going to walk inside you now. No harm shall come to you now. And anyting dat isn't right inside you, he is going to tell you come out. And you's body going to come out. Says, 'Come body. I want dis little body for de Lord.' Whedder you red, whedder you black, your body must be holy before we tell de story. It's a living sacrifice. Dat's what God word. He called de Virgin in its virginity."

I'm not certain, but I think what Daniel God was saying here is that he's calling out any evil spirits that are inside of me, and that I will have a spirit guide walking inside me and protecting me for the rest of my life.

There was more sermonizing and then, "In de beginning was de word and de word was wid God, and de word was God, not Selassie I. He's de serpent!"

Haile Sellasie I is the late emperor of Ethiopia. Some Rastafarians consider him the Black reincarnated Christ. Daniel points to a drawing on his chart. "Dis is de natty dreadlock. He give de little boy de ganja spliff. He said, 'He have dem half naked,' Isaiah 2. Catch dem! Dey don't put no clothes on at all, because dere modder play de harlot. Isaiah 2 say, 'I shall strip ye sons and ye daughters naked as de day dey born.' "

After another rampage, Daniel says, "God made us de way he wants to made us. Dat night when Mom and Dad gettin' it on, we could be invalid. We could be blind. You know, we became holy children, but de world's passion stole us away. Because de woman has no husband. Daniel God is de—"

At that point, my tape became unclear, then —

"I came back. I'm going to go out, and from back to de bible, broadcasting from Jamaica, as a missionary towards who I'm about. And, over dat side, it's called a new Jerusalem. If you sex, only you could sex and go over dere as you got de spirit which no person has.

"De boys head out and parade around and don't make sex come in dis big yard. Dis is true. I saw you readin' de sign. I come to you. I said, 'You've got a spirit!' I saw you readin' dis sign, Debbie. If you don't got no spirit, you afraid of me. You afraid of de garden. You walk along.

"Whenever you got a spirit from your modder, you come up to de sign and take a look. Sometimes I hear de girl callin' to de boy, saying 'Come take a look. Let's read de sign.' Boy keeps pushing along. I call to de girl, tell her, 'You's along wid Satan! He's movin' you away from God, young lady. Be careful!' She said, 'Yes, it's true you talking. De boy is un-Godly, you know.'

"I say Debbie, you got a spirit. You know, dat's why de Lord sent you walk up wid dese little birds around you." He was referring to Harris's children. "So, do you live up in Farm Heights?"

"No. I lived in Jamaica for two years when I worked for a tour company. I've known these children for almost three years. I came back here to write a book."

Suddenly, I had an unexpected and overwhelming urge to cry. I was spiraling, flooded with emotion and tears. I had no idea where they were springing from. I tried desperately to compose myself, realizing that sometimes I just feel so lost and frightened because I really have no idea what I'm doing. I'm just following the inner voice that sent me here.

The next thing I experienced was a sensation of floating out of my body.

21

I looked down at it and thought, "Oh, you poor little girl! You're so lost and scared. What are you doing there? How can I help you?"

I re-entered my body and told Daniel, "When someone asked me why I was going back to Jamaica, I realized I didn't really know. I wasn't sure where to go, or where to look, but I just knew that I would be guided. I knew that I had to trust that, that somehow it was part of the reason I came to Earth."

"Your faith make you whole, baby! Mary, de first modder. I wrote your name in de book. You was de first daughter. A hundred and twenty princess's Mom went and visit me. You was de first one, Debbie. You work wid de Virgin Mary. You going to write a book to all de world have to listen to your tales. Just like yourself from up to now on. God sent you to de right spot.

"See? God is movin' in mysterious ways. His wonders to perform. He plant his footstep. You come to de right seat. We going to get togedder. De world wants dis book now. De world wants to calm down. But not until dey find de spirit of truth. Dat your Mom and your Dad born you one night to come to dis world, dat you may hunger and thirst of de righteousness. Now you are filled. At all times you are going to find tears come to your eyes. You have someting to cry about, baby.

"If God come to de stranger, should have received de spirit of truth. But I have come to my own black people up here and my own receive me not. Thirsty, dey poison me. Hungry, dey give me no bread, you know. And, dey nail him to de tree of God for wickedness.

"Which month you born, Debbie?"

"I was born in November."

"You under de water sign. You must find Daniel God. I am your pauper. I am your husband. I am your fodder. I am your savior. I am your friend. I am your guidance. As long as de sun shines, my spirit got to guide you all along wid a message. De world must bow when Papa Dan gots to speak dese words. You see, if you don't wicked, tears run from your eyes to know I speak dese words from your heart. And, dey are true, to comfort de heart.

"A woman, after seeking God's truth, to took down into de world. Where's de mon? Dey are just lookin' for flesh, baby! And because of de flesh, de spirit can't abide wid mon. You have to take away from de flesh to give de spirit away.

"See? When you keep away from de flesh, de mon, den de spirit gets to

22

teach you. When you go to bed, you gets visions and dreams. Your body be hoppy wid de spirit inside it. In odder words, you got your own mind. You got your own body wid de spirit."

I cut in, "Can you tell me more about that lady you were talking about? You have a lady tied up here, Daniel God?"

"Yeah, yeah!"

"Where is she?"

"You going to tape her?"

"Have you got her here?"

"Yeah, is behind. Dere was a day I was at de garden three years back. I went out to Farm Heights to her home and I come back. I saw two women standing at de gate. De gate was locked up for three months and I couldn't find de key. De spirits locked de gate, said nobody must come through dat gate unless you clean yourself of de flesh.

"So, I open a place in de bamboo and come through. One of de ladies asks me, 'Are you named Daniel?' I said, 'Yes.' She said, 'God sent me to you.' I said, 'Come along. I glad to hear you.' I was glad to have someone because I had someting to say. If you bad... stop you from bad. If you good, you got de spirit of good. I'm going to give you de same power all to de world and control mon. All rulers are king. Listen to your wives from now on, not beggin' dem. Dey gonna listen. Dey wants to hear you. Dey gonna beg you more to hear.

"Say, I talks to her. She say she Modder Heart from Mount Salem. Say dat I was locked up in de garden by witchcraft and iniquity. Dey grudge me in de garden. She said dat God sent her to warn me dat some obeah woman tie her head wid cloth, working miracles about people. Is against me! Want to spoil de garden, because I am truthful. I'm against dem witchcraft, island powder, mixing it up. You know?

"So I listened to her. I opened de gate and lets she come in. I sit her down and we talk. And from she catch me spirit and know dat I represent de spirit of truth dat hide from de world. And I come to catch up de black woman dat control de whole world. Revelations 16 and 13. Three of dem working miracles. She catched my spirit and I loved her.

"She never come too long. She never show me dat she wants me. She just come and show me dat say, 'You got de spirit of Daniel inside you and de whole city is against you.'

"I say, 'Yes, how you know dis?' By dat time one of me neighbor tell me, said she come to catch me spirit because she want to come into de city to work de iniquity, de miracle. But if I'm around, she can't do it.

"I'm a sinner. I wake up in your bed at night baby, and make you repent of dis blood baby. Whedder you want a prayer behind you or not, I'm gonna pray! I'm a dangerous boy! I got de spirit to control Satan."

Daniel is very emotional and his eyes spook me.

"Say, and she hold onto me and make me love her. And she been visiting me for three, four, maybe five months, you know, and she catch me spirit. And dere are some bad rings of boys dat want to sell out dis land you know. Set de boys on me. Said I must sell out de place over dere to people, de garden, dat people come live inside it.

"I tell dem, 'No, I'm not selling de land!' And dese boys were tormenting de garden, because it captured land, you know. Over dere is not my own by law, you know. After dese boys, I get rid of dat. But she pay one of de boys five hundred and fifty dollars to torture me.

"Meanwhile, she catch me as his son, say God sent him. And you know, when I turned half de garden, all dose breadfruit trees and tings. I haf to give it to her you know. Nice piece of land! When I give her dat, I find she work in miracle!

"So, Saturday night I went to bed on de Sabboth and I was mourning. I never be good. And de angel came to me in de night and said, 'Teacher Dan, you see de three women who come to you?' I said, 'Yes.' He said, 'De three of dem work in miracles. Wake up!' I got up. He said, 'Look, Revelation 16, verse 13, Daniel.' So I sit and read it. I said dese three women walking togedder is working miracles. Dey has de spirit of frogs. Frog spirit is dangerous! Dangerous women! She keeps from everyting dat good. Dangerous!

"She say you got a mongoose work wid de miracle. Have on a necktie. Dat is his conqueror, duppy who sent out. He works wid de Fallen Angels. He sent three Fallen Angels. For eighty day, eighty night I inside. I could eat nothing at all."

What Daniel God was saying here, is that this woman who came to see him talked him into having sex with her. Jamaicans believe that when you have sex you give away part of your soul and spirit, and the other person captures it. So, of course this frightened him a lot once he came to believe she was an obeah woman. He had a dream one night that an angel woke him up and told him to read certain bible passages. When he did, he understood that these women were obeah women.

So then I asked Daniel, "She sent duppies on you?"

"Yes, yes, Fallen Angels! She work a miracle! I prove it to you one day."

"What are Fallen Angels as opposed to duppies?"

"Said ghosts, a human being like yourself, dat gone to de grave already. She catch de spirit of dem and send dem out to suck you. You know? She got a way to mix it up. De Laurence teach dem dese tings."

"Dealerance? What's a dealerance?"

"De Laurence is a science, mon! Don't you hear about it in de States? Dey work witchcraft and iniquity, change demselves into different creatures, and came back and change dem."

"Do they live around here?"

"Yeah, dey, de black people, got de book from America."

I had no idea what he was talking about, but I asked around and later found out that there is a man named De Laurence. He is considered the most powerful obeah man in the world. He is from Chicago and has written and published several books on obeah. These books are considered so dangerous that they are not legally allowed in Jamaica and have been smuggled in. [1]

Daniel said, "Dey use dis book wid island powder to do each of de evil. Were it to have power over you, I'd have to keep you down. Dat is what keeps down God's righteousness, work wid island powder, Egyptian perfume. Whedder you wants to be in love wid de boy or not, he makes you be in love wid him widout your consent.

"Powder, oil, Oil of Love Me, Oil of Hate You, oil to turn you down, oil to change your countenance. Boy use de oil to trick girl."

---

[1] NOTE: When I got back to the States, I did finally manage to track one of these books down. Just out of curiosity, I wanted to see what was in them. I had a difficult time getting one even in the States. I was told that even most public libraries don't keep them, for two reasons. The first is because people who understand the power of this black magic always end up stealing the books. The second is because other citizens try to get the books banned because they feel they are unfit for public libraries because they are so powerful. Many people fear them.

I finally managed to find a bookstore in Butte, Montana that was able to order one of them for me. It's a pretty frightening book. I say this based on my own understanding of the power of thoughts and energy.

"So basically, to do their witchcraft?"

"Yeah, to perform de witchcraft! De boy rub de oil on his body and when his hands touch you, you must has to give all you have to him. He use de oil, rub his hands in his kerchief. He takes his hands and he holds you. Every little ting you have, he took away. Everyting from you! You just have de order to give him everyting you got, and he cares nuttin' about you. If he cares about you, he don't doubt de truth. When someone cares about you, trust de truth. Only de truth shall set you free!

"Just like I catched dis witchcraft woman by de heart you know. De truth, de truth, only de truth."

"So you've got this woman here, Daniel?"

He looks at me like he realizes that I'm just not getting it and says slowly, "I tell you, I catched de witchcraft woman, who is Modder Heart! Three of dem work in miracles. I catched de three of dem, but I scattered two of dem, and I tied up de head of dem, who is Modder Heart. She is in de garden.

"You see, God tell me dat dere is a she goat, a bad red girl. She do lesbian and sodomy. God say I must catch her. De three women got de frog spirit. Dey turn de frog in time, too, and come back and turn somebody. Right now, I catch her. You see, dis time last year, September, when I was in trouble wid her, she wants to kill me because I condemn her!"

"This was last September? Was it in 1989?"

"Yeah. On de Monday mornin' I asked God if he doesn't show me a sign, because de woman I catch - is around twenty of dem come on me - she come and talk to me, and bring a posse of people after dat, all be known to me, bad children, all bad, bad children! You know?

"And I tell God, if God don't show me a sign wid her, de Monday morning I'm going to do someting evil to dem. Because I was suffering a lot of pain from dem. And, by de night, God sent a storm, and you see from dat, dat anytime I ask for earthquake, because of de spirit of truth —"

I cut in here. "Are you saying that this happened last September or when Hurricane Gilbert hit?"

"Gilbert! Gilbert!"

"So that was in 1988. Okay."

So, basically what Daniel God is saying here is that God heard his prayer and sent Hurricane Gilbert to Jamaica at that particular time as an answer to his dilemma. Gilbert was one of the most devastating hurricanes to ever hit the island.

"Gilbert! Dat Monday morning I asked de Lord for a sign to keep her cool, to cool her down, because she wants to hurt me badly. And I'm of his spirit. I'm not of wickedness. My spirit, my flesh is not of wickedness."

"In other words, you were a threat to her because of your good spirit, right?"

"Yeah, yeah! And de Lord answered my cry, and Gilbert came in de night, down in sheets and destroyed some lovely trees, pear (avocado) trees and fruit trees on de land. I had gave dem to her and she took dem and took control of me. God blew dem out de root, and even dat mango tree dere. Dey cussed me for it, and God dig out de mango root, too.

"God answered me, said, 'Daniel, I sent a storm to answer you. From now on, whenever you asks me for a cause, I'm going to answer you.' And just like yourself today. From now on you're going to asks for tings and God answer you back. When any person around you kept you from doing de will of God, God promise, say whenever anyone at all come and bug me, come in de way, wid de spirit of truth you shall never escape death.

"Like I say, if she never wicked, God wouldn't send me. Well, God said she is de woman in Revelation 17, de modder of iniquity and of witchcraft. God said I must catch her and bound her for a thousand years. And I catch her two years before dat thousand years.

"God pleased wid me. God said in de last 1990, am going to catch Satan in de Revelation 20, and bound him down de bottomless pit. And I catch dis witchcraft woman and her husband Satan two years before de time expired! Dat's why God give me so much power to go along. De people fire me. When I talk, baby, dey fire me.

"And when you find de Lord, all mama will against you, too. De bible says dat. Your brodders and sisters will against you. Say, when you find de truth, people fear you. Dey fear de truth because dey are evil. If dey are not evil, dey don't fear to answer you."

What Daniel is saying is that he eventually ended up giving Mother Heart part of his property. It had breadfruit, mango and pear trees on it. When he realized that she was into witchcraft and obeah, he regretted what he had done and asked God to help him. God sent Hurricane Gilbert and Gilbert ripped up

27

all the trees on her property. Daniel saw that as an answer.

"Daniel, I have a question about this lady. I'm trying to understand why you gave her trees."

"Yeah! When she first come along, she did want to catch a part of de garden, and to catch me to be her husband, to capture de spirit of me. Say, she fell in love wid me spirit, wid me heart. But if you don't catch de body, you can't catch de spirit. But de moment you give him your body, he catch de spirit.

"Say, she couldn't catch me body. God make me find out, after she come up here runnin' around me. You know? I'm lonely up in dis place. Dere's no one around to come along and let me talk about de spirit as you did. You know, dey cussing. Dey swearing. Dey leading a bad life. Adulterers, fornication, you know. I keep away from dem. It shows dem dat God is inside me, you know.

"And she comes along as a grandmom. She tell me she stop to see de flowers. She's an old ma'am. I said, 'Go ahead.' She said, 'Yes, you is de Daniel God. De city is against you.' I say, 'You is talking de truth.'

"It is de first I ever saw her. She catch me spirit and she trick me spirit. And every time she come back and look for me, me love her good. But she want to kill me spirit baby, to condemn dis spirit of truth, dat she, de witchcraft, may take over and kill all God's children. But after dat, I gave her half de garden, all de mango. I have de breadfruit trees for ten years."

"But you didn't know at the time that she had evil purpose."

"Noooo, I never know! If I had know, I wouldn't have touched her. God made it like dis so I was to catched her. I give her de big breadfruit tree, pass up thousands of dollars. See dem dere, de tree? She took everyting.

"Say, de spirit been talkin' to me. You know how dat does feel good. So she was carrying dinner for me one Sunday afternoon. I never asked her for it, but she was carrying it.

"So, de Saturday night I went to bed, and de Angel Gabriel woke me up and said, 'Daniel, look up at de light.' I said, 'I look.' He said, 'One black woman coming and a red woman. Dey having dinner for you. Don't take it! Stop her by outside de gate.'

"Dis is de way I stop her. When she come along I say, 'Modder Heart, why you never tell me you work in miracles? Over six months you been coming to me. You take half of me garden and you trick me.' And I bust out crying and I say, 'Why you never tell me? Say you are, Modder Heart, working de land, keeping down children. Lord, God, you make me mad now!' "

"How did you understand that she was doing this?"

"De spirit. De angels wake me up on Saturday night! Tells me dat I must read Revelation 16, verse 13. I get up from de bed and read it. It said, 'Is three women dat has frog spirit and work in miracle.' Angel said, 'Yes, is de black woman dat bring de two women dat come here in de night. So come on Daniel, wake up! You got to lock her up and tie her up! Wake up mon!'

"I say, 'God, is it true?' Say, 'Yes! Dey keep down every human being under de sun. Me sent her to you, Daniel. I will make you head of de lamb.' I said, 'Jesus Christ, I understand!' I sing for de whole rest of de night, until daylight.

"You see, dis Sunday when she come along, she look for de spirit. Say, 'On my mind is to look for Daniel first. De comforter, you know.' She come and look for me, and as an old mama, I never knew dat an old mama would do all of dese tings."

I had been recording our conversation and at this point my tape shut off. As I put in a new tape, I couldn't help reflecting again on how incredible it was that I was sitting here up on this mountain top listening to this man. Who is he? What led me here? Here he was, very seriously telling me his stories about how the angels appeared to him at night to warn him about the obeah woman that was coming to hurt him. Listening to him was like walking through many dimensions of time, space and realities.

When I turned my tape back on, Daniel was saying this, "I been tinking dat, what a friend, you know, God is. He say dat Modder Heart coming Sunday morning to look for me. Say dat I must turn me back on de dinner. And de spirit come, wake me up and say dat I must stop her at de gate.

"If Modder Heart did know dat she couldn't manage me, she wouldn't have took de garden. She find out dat I find out dat she is a serpent. She's de old Modder of Evil! She set her own kind of evil, turn me down, you know. It's not my spirit to go to any scientist, because de rest of de modders is just like she.

"If I sick in dis vineyard, I wait and I heal it myself. I don't go no places. Sick, bad, down on me knee, and it's God who better me. I don't go to somebody to ask him for me. Your faith can make you whole if you trust in de Lord and in yourself. And dat is what happened to me.

29

"So I been tinking, 'What must I do now?' And de angel said, 'When she comes in de morning, burst it out of her! Discharge out de part of de garden left in her name down dere!'

"So early in de morning when she come along she said, 'Teacher Dan, how do you do?' I said, 'I'm bad, Modder Heart!' She say, 'What's wrong wid you?'

"Den anodder girl, she come to me as a young, pregnant girl and she and me did talk. And she come in here and buries herself in de flowers spot. She just come and she look for me. She bury iniquity dat I may not turn her out of de garden."

"She buried what??"

"Bury someting in de flowers spot. Said she planting de flowers, and she bury obeah inside it! Evil! Someting she picks up in a paper. Buried it down herself, in de flowers spot."

He points. "Right over dere. It's not dere now, you know. She bury it cuz she in love wid me. I have a garden where she want a home. She would have liked be wid me, you know? So her modder taught her de way to bury herself down in de mon's place. But I know what she do, so she don't catch me.

"But dis ma'am now, when she comes I bust out and cry, 'Modder Heart, you deceive me in de garden! You done wid de lies! Come out of de garden. You leave me alone!' She start to talk. I say, 'Leave me! Get out of de garden, please. You deceive me! And de spirit you have got, de spirit you walk, achieve you own wizard.' And she stepped out, got out.

"And baby, for eighty days and eighty nights, I inside is sick. You see, when I duty, I has to call a stranger to clean up. I too sick. Stink like a dunder! De whole of me insides is a rotting out!

"God sent a lady come here from a place dey call Mount Zion. She say, 'God sent me cuz I know you're sick.' I say, 'How you know me from?' Say, 'God sent me here. He say three vampire bat feed you.' I said, 'Modder, did you know for eighty day, eighty night, I cannot eat nothing?'

"She said, 'How you feeding your guest? Who is dis woman who tie her head wid a piece of cloth?' I say, 'Dat is anodder science, obeah woman, just like yourself.' She come to me, said God sent her to me because me sick bad, got de whole of me inside eaten out."

I was trying to understand what was going on here, so I said, "So, in other words, it was really another obeah woman that came to you?"

Daniel God said, "Yeah! She was anodder obeah woman, just like she. But not as wicked as she. She come to help me. God sent her. She come up here now."

"So you think obeah can be good or bad?"

"Yeah! Dey work obeah! And you who are not an obeah woman cannot take off de obeah."

"Okay, okay, okay! So only another obeah woman can take off the spell of the first one."

"Yes, only anodder obeah woman can take it off me. When dey witchcraft, you ask de Lord to help you. God cannot help you. Him say you must seek anodder obeah woman. Harm no mon, and let no mon harm you. Dat's what God says. He knows dat somebody will harm you widout a cuz."

"Okay, so if one obeah woman comes and puts a bad curse on you then God can't help you, but another obeah woman needs to come and take it off? Is this what you are saying, Daniel God?"

"Anodder obeah woman will come. And he knows what she do. He moves de demons and feel your body good again. I said, 'Tank God dis woman help me from my demons!' And she tell you who did it, and why she did it, you know?"

"How does she know about this?"

"She? Well, how did you know to come here dis morning, Debbie? Is de spirit sent her, of course. Just like how she come search me out and call me at de gate. Tell me God sent she.

"You got some lying angels and you got some truthful angels. You have boys who tempt you wid de truth. You have some come wid lies to get what dey want."

Daniel tells more bible stories here and then says, "And de more you read dose books, God find you out. No matter where you go wid your secrets, Daniel God want to know. He and his children want to know. We coming out dere. We going out dere to make de world happy later. Who for happy, happy. Who for sad, sad.

"But you got de power dat you're lookin' for. You got it now. De world have to listen to you. You're not begging. It's so sweet for dem dat dey are going to like it.

"I had no power to fight Modder Heart, but I said, 'All right God, must be you who sent her here. It's not me who call her. All right God, you tell me how I can manage her now.'

And God really tell me, said, 'Just relax, Daniel. She gonna work out all de evil to get you down. But I be wid you all de way.' And God did deliver me. For three years she got me down under de foot. She did want to hurts me bad. Den sit and make up wid him.."

"Do you mean that everybody around here started to say that you were bad, and nobody would come to you? Is that what you are saying?"

"Say, if de child is disobedient and wander through de gate, unless papa or mama carry her come, dem, de parents, de mom and dad commit adultery. Sex widout marriage. I don't appreciate dem in de gate until dey try to do better, so I just stays like dis, because I represent de spirit of Daniel God. I must be God and God alone. Not a God offer de flesh, but a God offer de spirit."

Daniel points to Harris's children who are huddled around me.

"Say, dis school dat I got for dese little ones, dem mom in a wedlock. Around me, dese children born late. I know dere dad, a disobedient and ruly mon! Of course dey are disobedient. He got dese babies not even married to de baby modder. Dem all go about on de land while he goes on yonder. Who are you pleasing? God?"

Daniel was, of course, referring to my friend Harris. Suddenly Daniel went on another bible quote rampage about the evils of babies born out of wedlock. He ends by screaming hysterically about twenty times, "Dem bad! Dem bad! Dem bad!"

I'm trying to hide a smile. "Have you ever talked to their dad?"

"He's my pal! When he came here, he was my pal. Respect me. Killer." Killer is Harris's pet name.

"Yeah, he was my pal. He move along wid me. He call me Papa Dan, you know. But he just go along and got de babies widout trusting me. I know him a long time before he start having babies. A long time!

"Over sixteen years I live in dis place. I live alone on dis mountain over here. Pure pasture for two years. Leave de church and build a school up dere. I tell you den how dey just cut de land and get some houses coming. Killer, dey were wid me. And after dat, he got a baby wid a girl I know. I say he should have marriage and make de baby holy. You know, he just after de flesh. And

32

tomorrow de baby just out in de street doing everyting dat is wrong.

"Who's going to give account for de mom? And de woman who born dem, too? But de woman, she cracked you know. From a woman leave her baby fodder, she can't be a clean woman any longer.."

Daniel made the family sound like monsters, and I know them all to be just the opposite. But, in Daniel God's book, Harris was a fine and holy man for many years, but as soon as he impregnated a woman he was bad. The entire family was unclean and unholy. He believes that the babies are cursed.

I was pretty astonished. To me that doesn't make any sense. How can you take an innocent baby and think that the baby is condemned because of the acts of the parents? Daniel's reality and mine clash here. I know all of the family to be God loving, gentle people.

Next we heard Daniel God's own version of Adam and Eve in the garden of Eden. "Adam and Eve is in de garden. Eve left forward wid de natty dreadlock, which dey call de serpent. Go pick de fruit and call it sex. She come back pregnant, widout God's consent. God said, 'Adam!' Adam said, 'Yes, sir?' God, 'Dis woman is a garden. But in de middle of her garden dere is a fruit tree of good and evil. She has many odder trees in her body to partake of dis young lady, beside de tree in de garden. But dare you touch she widout my consent, you surely damned!'

"Dey call it pussy out here. It's fruit, fruit, Genesis 2, someting like dat. And de mon have stick. None of dem is sweet until you call it stick and fruit. When I say fruit, I respect you. Your body feel nice, because it is a spiritual person talking to you.

"You know, from dey call it sex and romance. Dat's not de way God terms it. And we must term it de way God did from de beginning. So from de beginning, so to de end, de world is going right back where it coming from, baby! Youth, no money, nor no garment, nor no university could reward you out dere after you got de calling."

The girls ask me when I'm going to leave. I tell them soon and Daniel launches into a prayer for me and my mission.

"Tank you Lord, for dis lady dat you sent to me. I've come to my own in dis Montego Bay, dis Sodom and Gomorrah what I am going to turn upside down wid de spirit of truth. And dey deceived me. But you have sent a stranger to me, which have received de spirit.

"Do you know de reason why you have sent her here? Because she has de desires to fulfill. And no odder pleasures in de world could fulfill dis young lady's pleasure, until she found de truth dis morning on de Sabboth day, which is not her approval to keep holy because Papa never has de spirit to teach her.

"Den, wid her power de time will come. She going to write dis book. Dis book going to be de greatest book ever come out in de world! And de word begin, de missing link of mon. Say, woman has de power of de Earth, and I'm de God of Daniel come down. Redeem woman wid de power in which she got from de tomb to Thomas, and from de well wid de living water of life. De word of your mouth is de living water of life.

"Lord, may your spirit guide her in dis unclean Montego Bay, Jamaica. Wicked, murdering place, where dey kidnap, rape. Police inspect everybody. De land, de lass, slack and unclean. De lass slapping de children. De mon no teacher. Dem buy drug and black up wid de ganja and de coke.

"But Lord, put your spirit in dis young lady. May your soul redeem her cuz she has a soul to gain in de body. She gonna gain your soul too, cuz you have sent her to de tree of life, de Garden of Eden, de fountain of de fountain of water dat she was looking for. De word of her mouth is de living water of mon.

"May your spirit wake her up from all tings dat she was moving around which was not right since she came along. She has met de narrow road dat she was looking for, not de wide road dat she was looking for, to climb dis hill wid Calvary's cross. So remember, she's a burden bearer. She has tears to shed for Christ.

" May your power now go to dis young lady's Modder and Dad in any part of de world dey may be dis afternoon. Bring forth rejoicing, and Gabriel and Michael to guide de parents at dere home, until she return back to dem wid glad tidings of great joy to de world dat is tormented.

"She has found Daniel God, not in her vision, or a dream, but in reality. Her spirit lead her right to de Garden of Eden, de highest vision, Mount Zion. May Gabriel and Michael, two angels, guide her before and after from up to now on and forever more, until she return again to dis garden in peace. My peace I give unto you."

I lost all sense of reality while Daniel prayed. Something inside of me kept screaming, "Is this really happening?" I wondered what my parents were doing at that moment as Daniel God prayed for them. It made me aware that we never know who is praying for us and when. What would they think?

I kept thinking, "Oh, if my friends could see me now!" It's Saturday morning. Is it possible that I'm sitting on a mountain top in Jamaica in the Garden of Eden, listening to a man pray for me and my parents? Calling angels to guide and protect me? Telling me that, yes, I must write this book? I believe his prayers were strong and powerful. They shook me to the core of my being for some reason that I could not explain.

I wasn't sure what I believed about the incredible things that Daniel God was telling me. But one thing I was sure of is that everything he said was definitely reality to him. And who's to say what reality is? There are many realms of reality. We each live and experience our own.

I was absolutely fascinated by this colorful character. I have never before, or since, met anyone like him. Where are you now, Daniel God?

I thanked Daniel for the prayers and he said, "He dat believe in God believe also in me. Dis is de truth of why I live in de garden, why God's power not in mon today. I want Jamaica to wake up and realize dat dere is a God to serve mon.

"It's not of works dat mon should boast. It's a gift. You get a gift. Dis is de first time, but we gonna meet a second time. When we sit down and ready to sign de bargain, you going to write me. Every Reagan, every German, every Russian wants dis. Say, what time do you have left in Jamaica?"

"I'm going to stay as long as my money holds out. I want to get as much information as I can for the book, and then I'm going to go home and try to put it together."

"Say, um, you reach dis top. Just after dat, you go settle now. And den you find a lot of angels come down inside you. You're not gonna need any outcome, baby. Yeah, you're gonna find legions of angels to help you speak about what your heart desires. You know, when you go home now, and your flesh and your heart and your mind be made up, when you feel de feeling you will tell me de feeling dat come down. Den one day, you come along and we get togedder to set your business in order. And when you go walk, when you ready to go, your task is finished. Den you go work on your task now."

I assure Daniel that I will be back, and ask him if I can go see the obeah woman now. He seems frightened and suggests that maybe she is gone to the market. I'm confused because I thought he had her tied up.

"Say, de woman now, I'm going to show you her."

Stone cross the in Garden of Eden

We walk over to a huge cross that Daniel has made in his garden. Composed of stones, it stands about two feet high, is about twenty feet long and fifteen feet wide. It looks majestic standing on that mountaintop and Daniel obviously feels that it provides him with great protection. I'm awed by the time and care that he put into making this. Where were his mind and heart as he labored for so many hours on this?

Daniel picked up a smaller cross that he had made. It was about eighteen inches tall, a foot wide and was painted white. He said, "I'm holding onto de cross, nutting but de cross, de cross of Jesus. You see de piece of wood? It is a cross, mean truth. You see, evil, obeah." And here Daniel's eyes grow huge and he whispers, "Dey afraid of de cross! De obeah people, dey are afraid of de cross! If you hold it, de cross in your hand, de demons cannot get you. So I hold my hand on de cross. Come here!"

I find myself spinning deeper yet into another reality as Daniel and I walk toward another part of the garden. I can physically see and feel fear bristling all over him. He is very nervous and he clings to his wooden cross, holding it out in front of him as he tells me about Mother Heart, how she studies the book of De Laurence. It's a science by which one learns to call up the dark forces.

Daniel told me that Mother Heart killed one of her fourteen children and supposedly tied the spirit of the child in seven yards of red cloth, which I can now see tied up high in a banana tree. This way, she has access to work with the spirit whenever she needs it. Even though Daniel was frightened, he took me there so I could see for myself that this was really going on.

I said, "Okay, so the evil spirits can't come here while you are holding the cross. Is that correct?"

"Yeah!" Daniel looks up and points. "You see dat banana tree up dere? She's got seven yards of red cloth. You see dat cloth? She bound it so tight up dat tree! Can't you see dat must some evil over dat place? She look at banana tree when she got someting to eat, and she took dat seven yard of red cloth. You see de way she wind it tight and tie it, and keep down de whole city, bloodshed and worry!"

Daniel obviously believes that Mother Heart's obeah practices are contributing largely to crime, drug use, babies born out of wedlock, etc. He is convinced that she has great powers which are causing the people of Montego Bay to behave in such a manner. So, of course this is extremely frightening to him.

"In de seven yards of red cloth is a demon. And she have seven yards of white cloth. She's got a young children. She keeps down young children. She's de miracle worker. She's de one I catch! Is over dere she lives. See all de breadfruit trees I have planted? Dere were pear tree and odder tree, but Gilbert knock dem down. If you's a mommy and I give you tings like dat, don't you would be pleased for dat young mon who give you dese tings?"

"Yes, of course."

"Dat is de only ting she got. She is de miracle worker. I catch her. She have a long pole put up down dere. She tie de demon's spirits in knots in de red cloth and use dem for her Obeah!

"I draw de banana tree for you, and I draw de red cloth[2] tied around it and let you put it in your lesson to fulfill Revelation 16, because we catch de serpent! Revelation 17 and Revelation 20.

"Satan is a Black mon and his wife is Jezebel. You know, dese is two

---

[2] NOTE: Later Daniel did actually draw this scene and he gave it to me to take home. I still have it. Even though it frightened him, he felt that it was very important for people to be aware of what was happening up there.

people who make trouble in de world today. Now you know, he catch down people and he hold down righteousness. So de government want to know about him, too. So we hold him, because after hour de righteous will have de freedom and de wicked will has de last pain for destruction.

"Say, dis whole bit of land is mine. And when she come to me, she come to me like—"

There was a sudden loud rumbling on my tape recorder and I couldn't hear what Daniel was saying. There was no logical reason why the tape should distort here, and at this point even I am wondering what kind of unseen powers are at work here. The energy is incredibly strong. I feel like I've crossed a threshold and entered another dimension, leaving the Earth realm behind.

Daniel is saying, "She have all thirteen kids."

"She's not married?"

"Yeah, she married to an old mon."

"She got fourteen kids. She kill one to have one to work wid! Yeah, she killed her daughter."

"Why?"

"Say, when dey study de DeLaurence book, it say you have to destroy one of your firstborn to get de spirit to work wid. So he sent out de spirit to her, to who he wants to call him up and talk to him, you know. We'll get dis fully later you know."

It's pretty obvious at this point that Daniel is done talking about obeah for today. He has shifted back into his bible quotations. I suddenly realize that I am absolutely exhausted from everything that I've been through today. I feel like I need to be alone to think about and sort out all that has happened to me so far. I bid Daniel good-by and spend the rest of the afternoon resting.

This evening I went out with my dear friend Birgitta, (another Rep), her boyfriend Howard, and Harris. It was Saturday night in Montego Bay and the mood had shifted completely from that of the afternoon. We sat outside at a little place called Tony's. The air was sultry and everyone was in good spirits, ready to laugh and have fun.

What a switch of energy. We found ourselves discussing some bikini swim trunks that Birgitta had given Howard. He was afraid to wear them on the beach because he thought he might get raped by a gay guy. We all laughed because we know he is not shy. In fact, he modeled underwear at a lingerie party that I had in the States once. He looked so good that even my then ninety-one year old grandmother was applauding him. Howard insisted now that the only reason he felt comfortable modeling and hamming it up was because he didn't know anyone there.

I told Harris and Birgitta that Janesville was a city of almost totally white people, but my friends adored Howard. Here he chirped in, "Yeah, I figured most of dese women never see a black mon before and want to see what de big bamboo is all about. So I figured, 'No problem.' "

We all laughed heartily at this, and Howard continued, "But it's true, you know. I knew it consciously, Debbie, dat even though I was dere, dat this was more to dem, because a lot of dose people, dey are not like you. It's like somebody new coming to dem and dey hearing of dis news for a long time, like dere was a lot of anticipation dere, you know. People just staring at me.

"I knew when I was dere dat I was like an ambassador for Jamaica. At de same time dere was a lot of tings dat I was tinking of. You know?"

"Howard, you're quite the diplomat! I love you."

Our conversation moved on and somehow we found ourselves discussing cats. Harris said, "One ting wid me. If you told me you was a friend and I come to your home and see a cat and it come up against me, I will kick it hard!"

I was surprised, as I had never seen this side of Harris. "You don't like cats?"

"Give me a dog! Give me millions and one dog, but don't give me de cat."

"Why don't you like cats, Harris?"

"When I was a kid around fifteen years old, I have one. And we have a straight post dat we nail some nails on to really sun de fish. All right, I come home and I hanged up de fish dat I caught on de post, de smaller one on de bottom and de bigger one on top. I went to de shop to go buy oil for cooking. When I come back, I go round back and focus my eyes on de pole. I see de small fish at de bottom, but de big one dem gone!

"So I go into de house. I searching for kitty and I can't find him. I come at de door and I say, 'Sweee, sweee, sweee.' And when I look I see him come out wagging his tail. So I say, 'Okay, it must be you who eat up dose fish.' When I look up de house better, I see half of de last one dere and it's uneated.

"I hold onto him and I start to beat him wild! And when I'm beating him badly I see his eyes start to change a lot, and in myself I feel scared. I say, 'If I let him go, he going to be dangerous to me.' So I has to do away wid him. I ties him up and beaten him!"

"You did that to a cat?"

"Yeah, cuz I feel so grieve about my fish!"

Birgitta says, "But cats love to eat fish! It's like if someone put a bowl of bananas in front of you and you hadn't eaten in two days."

"Yes, dat is true. But de reaction of how de cat behaved, dat's what I get ignorant about. Cuz he passed de small fish down at de bottom and go way up to de top to take away de biggest one!"

"Well, wouldn't you take the biggest one?" Birgitta is staunchly defending the cat. We all convulse into laughter. "If you had your choice, wouldn't you take the cow with the most meat?"

"Well yes, but as a youth I never really look into dose tings. I just react at ignorant temperature. I go to buy flour now to come back and fry my fish and so find dat dis best one is gone. So I just start to beat him. And den I see his eyes start to get a different color and every lick of him I see move at me."

"Well, he's defending himself!"

"Yes, so you see normally I just get a piece of stick and just give him one lick, and I see he just—" Here Harris imitates how the kitty acts. "—and shake out, and I just take him and threw him in de gully. Like two day after I don't see him anymore. He just disappear away. From dat day on, I don't like dem!"

I was sympathetic. "You worked hard to catch that fish, didn't you?"

It's no joke to Harris. "Yeah! But you know if he take from de bottom I would grieve, but not so grieve. But de biggest one. You know? So it just get me upset to really move at him to know dat he should never do dat."

What Harris was saying is that he wouldn't have minded so much if kitty took the smaller fish, but he was really vexed because the kitty took the biggest fish he had, the one that he was looking forward to having for dinner. In his anger he hurt the cat, and then feared that the cat would hurt him back, so in order to protect himself he decided he had to destroy the cat. The story still upsets him to this day and that's why he doesn't want to have a cat for a pet.

Then Harris starts talking about black cats. "You know black cat is a dangerous ting. Cuz normally, if you have a kid and leave a black cat alone in de room wid your kid, dat kid will die. Dat cat will put his mouth on de kid's nose and suck out every blood of de kid."

I'm shocked. "Do you really think a black cat would do that?"

"Well, I don't really figure more less, but I know dat de black cat is de dangerous one. Most of de time dat any people work in iniquity dey work wid de black cat. I know an old lady in Jamaica used to have a lot of cats. Don't have any husband. One morning dey wake up and dey don't see she come out. And dey attack her door and dey kick it off. When dey go in dere, it's a cat dat killed her! When dey go in dere dey see all of her face and her neck claws up, and dere's no blood left in her."

"So you think the cat killed her?"

"Yes! Not tinking, I know! Cuz it show. You can see de imprint. You can see de impression by de crying of de cat who done her face and her neck and all dose places."

"Where was this at?"

"In St. James here. Dose tings really get me annoying against cats. Sort of like by Annie Palmer's house. Dere's some large cats out by dat house. And normally she used to work wid dose tings, especially de black cats. De people who work in obeah work wid black puss."

Annie Palmer used to live at Rose Hall Great House and was known as a witch.

"Harris, what do you know about obeah?"

"Not much. I just hear people talk about it. Like say dere was a boy who wanted to obeah somebody to really die like. Someone obeah you to a car lick you down or obeah for you swell up or someting like dat.

"But still, dey say dat who believe in dose tings it affect dem more dan dose who don't believe. Cuz normally den, you believe dat, bam! You can look at dis beer bottle, and your mind force make de beer bottle jerk like how I jerk it wid my finger a while ago. It will happen, okay? But if you don't have de belief dat your mind force can make it move, den it can't. So if you have de belief dat someone can obeah you, it will take you. But if you have de belief dat it can't happen to you, if someone really tried at you, it's very hard to attack, you know?"

"Because you've got your mind closed to it. You're not receptive."

"Yeah, yeah. You don't open your mind for it to take in. In Jamaica you find a lot of people say dey are working obeah on people, but it just sometime a trick. Sometime it just a fraud to make money off people.

"If you stray your mind toward dose evil tings, it will take hold of you. But if you totally have your mind so where it just can't happen, then it just can't happen. You just work by your mind force. Dat's what controls. Yeah!"

"Harris, what do you think of duppies?"

"Normal, spiritual bodies goes away from de earth, exits. Some people can't pick up dere powers. But like if someone is born wid a caul, someting dat covers over de head to de shoulders, dey more can see dose spiritual tings."

"How do you know? Did you feel it when you were born?"

"No, my mama told me I was born wid someting come over my head and shoulder. From I coming up from a young lad to a big mon now dey told me dat kids what born wid dose tings can easily pick up or see dose spiritual tings."

"That's very interesting! So have you ever seen a duppy?"

"Lots of times."

"Where?"

"All around Jamaica duppies are about. Dere's dat place on Union Street. I hear him more time at night. He goes upstairs, walking up de steps. But true, we don't tink it for nutting, because we are not afraid of him because we are really used to it."

"Do you think it's someone who died right there?"

"I don't tink. I know."

"It was a mon die around four years ago, before we really control de place. But his spirit still moves around de place. He doesn't harm us. Cuz normally a mon on earth is armed more and more expert, but a spirit is only a spirit, so I not afraid."

"What about Rose Hall Great House? Do you think there are any spirits there?"

"Well, I guess so, cuz one of my friends died in a van accident. Tore up dem. I sure it was Annie Palmer come down for her New Year blood. I sure of dat. It's a straight road. You can see a mile ahead of you. No cause for accident. Lots of accidents dere. Thirteen people die dere dis year. No reason. Annie Palmer control de area wid her witchcraft."

Harris's attitude about all of this is very matter of fact. It's just part of life. Birgitta then told us about her trip up there one day with a bunch of tourists.

42

All of their cameras malfunctioned while at Rose Hall, yet resumed operating normally as soon as they left the area. This is so common in places where any so called paranormal activity occurs.

I asked Howard what he thinks of duppies.

"I feel passive when it comes to dat, because I don't know if I've ever seen any. But I sometimes feel dey probably exist. Biblically, dey are a spirit dat went to de grave and came out."

Here Birgitta interrupts him and asks him to tell us about the lady from his church who the pastor pulled the demon out of.

"Dat demon is not good."

"What's the difference between a demon and a ghost?"

"Demon is someting dat comes from if you practice Satanism or Devil or any cult. Demon take possession of de body. It can tell you to do tings. And even though you're still Debbie or you're still Howard, you're still under dat influence.

"For me personally, I've seen one girl who had three demons in her. Someone usually asks de demons what is dere name, because demons have names. If dey can recognize what kind of a demon dey are dealing wid, den dey can know what kind of method to apply.

"What happened is dat dis girl down and dey try to hold her, but she got away and run toward a car coming her way. She tried to run in front of de car to get killed. Now, she was not doing dat by herself. She was doing dat because she was possessed.

"And de church people hold her and dey was praying and praying over her and shouting and screaming. One ting I must tell you is dat if you are not spiritually inclined, do not go near someting like dat when it happening because it will do damage and destroy you. It will make you want to take a knife and stab yourself to death.

"So, dat I can say. I have seen dat and it is real. De demons is real. I tink de difference is —"

Birgitta cuts in, "What happened to the girl when the demons came out?"

"Well, she foam a lot. A lot of tings come out of her nose and mouth. I saw dis. She rasps and her eyes start to go up and down, up and down, and she say, 'Who are you? Who are you?'

"Now, dis is somebody who is a bank clerk, all right? So we're not talking about somebody who is not intelligent. And she usually act normal until dat particular morning. Everyone was shocked.

"Dere is a guy in de church who can see into you, see tings you don't even know, and he could tell you if you have a demon. I mean you and I may have. We don't know, because it's someting dat possess your body and it will do tings. It will let you do tings dat sometimes you don't even know why you do dose tings. It is because you are possessed."

He's quick to add, "Not dat any of us are!"

"Dis guy can tell just by looking into your eyes. And sometimes you just fall onto de ground and start to react. It's not you. It's just someting dat possess your body.

"To answer de question of de difference between a demon and a duppy, a demon is satanic and from Hell. A ghost, in my opinion, and I do tink dey exist, is someting dat come back after death. When you're sleeping and dreaming it's dere. It's a spirit dat leave de body and go on a search and dat is what you pick up from your unconscious state. Dere is a spirit dat leave de body when you're dead. When you're alive it does too, while you're sleeping. So I tink de difference is dat one comes from you de person, whedder you are alive or dead, and it's one dat communicates wid God, and demon is someting dat comes from de devil. Demon is someting dat destroys. Dere is nothing positive about it."

I ask, "Now, what church is this that you're talking about?"

"St. Bascal, in Coral Gardens. De mon dat see into you does not always come to service. But if you come and do not take dis seriously, is very dangerous. If you giggle and do not believe, dat is de time you are opening yourself up to be possessed. Because what de spirit does is dat it will possess de vulnerable one. Dis is very real.

"So for me personally, I never usually stay dere whenever dey do dat, because I'm always scared of de unknown. I'm scared."

I ask Howard to tell us about his experiences while visiting us in the States. He stayed at my brother's house, which was built in 1911. It was a huge old place with plenty of atmosphere. Several people had seen a spirit roaming there. We didn't tell Howard this, but he also had a rather strange experience.

He told us that he felt a bit uncomfortable simply because the house was so huge and occupied by so few. He was used to being in an environment where several people occupied a small space. So he felt a bit uneasy as he climbed into bed in Matt's guest room.

"When I lay down in de bed, I was like tinking and looking through de window and closet and I was tinking weird like dat somebody might climb up through de window. Dat is not what I was scared of.

"I went to sleep and den I could have swore dat somebody pushed de door, came in, looked at me as if de person want to know who I was and what I was doing dere. De person stood over me for about thirty seconds. After de person stood over me, I couldn't move. My modder usually call it trance.

"But it also happened to me in Jamaica. Someone came into my apartment and stood dere looking at me. And even though I felt a being or spirit was dere, I couldn't look at de person. I couldn't move. I couldn't do anyting. I knew somebody was dere, but it was like I was paralyzed.

"So anyway, when I was lying dere at Mac's (Howard calls Matt 'Mac'), I finally gather back my strength and I flip up, and just as I flip up de person went toward de closet. Den I stood up for about fifteen minutes trying to recollect everyting dat had happened. Den I just fall back asleep."

I enjoy hearing these stories. It makes me think. We understand so little of the universe that we live in.

The subject shifts to lighter matters for a while. We discuss different fruits of Jamaica, local bands and entertainment, stuff like that. Presently, a friend of Howard's named Sam joins us. Howard asked him what he thought of duppies.

"Demons. Demons are de ones dat dey say possess people. It is an internal problem. Dey is talking internally, like mentally. Most time is de mind. People dat are crazy are supposed to be demon possessed. De duppy is anodder fairy tale dat you can always hear from time to time from your grandparents."

"In other words, you don't believe in duppies?"

"I don't believe in duppy. To a lot of people it is so real dat dey can actually feel when dey are near to dem. For instance dey will tell you dat when a person is dead, den for a couple of days de spirit roams around. And of course it is dangerous to human beings at dat time, to living human beings. So dat is de difference between demons and duppies."

Howard asks, "Sam, have you ever had an encounter wid anyting like de

45

unnatural or de supernatural? You know what I mean mon?"

"Well, de demon possessed a person. I have seen it. Demon possessed a girl at one time. Natural setting. Dis person was at church one Saturday morning. It was a prayer breakfast and all of us were dere. We were praying and singing some music and, you know, getting down in some tings. We were really worshipping.

"And suddenly we saw somebody walking outside. And a brodder got up and went outside to see what was wrong wid her. And I saw dem coming into de back of de church. De guy was praying and de girl was crying. It went on for about five to ten minutes. And den de girl was dumb and she lie flat on her back!

"And de guys were praying to God, dat God would deliver her from demon dat inside of her. And from about two to three hours dey were dere, doing a whole lot of praying and tings. Den dey asked de demon to declare himself and to go. And of course de name dat de girl call should be de name of de ting dat was inside of her. It was Fret and Strive or Stride or someting like dat."

"And dey left! Dey left her and she could talk again! She spoke again. After dat, she was a little bit weak and dey give her what we call glucose water and she get a little strength."

"She is a popular girl, you know. She's around town, so she's well now. She's no crazy as before. So I believe dat dere are demons."

Birgitta is wide-eyed."So what happened to her when the demons came out?"

"She, she, she, well, after a while she was weak. Den dey give her someting to drink because she not have much strength. After de demons came out, she became whole again."

"Did anything physically happen? Did you see anything happen?"

"Well, she screamed. Dat's all. She was dumb. Dere was one odder instance dat I saw a person. And de lady vomited. About five times she vomited. And den dey put de *Gleaner* newspaper on de floor, and each time she vomit dey would spread anodder sheet over. And after de five vomiting, dey took de *Gleaner* outside and light it wid a match."

The *Gleaner* is Jamaica's largest newspaper.

"And dat was de first time I saw water burn like gas, because de vomit should have been water. And it burn like gas! It catch on fire so fast and it disappear very, very quick! It was very scary to me.

"Dat was someting I saw dat was unnatural. Dat was de second encounter. But de first one was more scary, because de first one took a lot of time and a lot of energy, and I could not understand what was going on."

This pretty much ended our evening. We gave Howard a ride home to Flankers. Flankers is a small area on the outskirts of Montego Bay. It is composed of tiny wooden homes which have zinc roofs and often have no windows, electricity or plumbing. It is one of the most impoverished neighborhoods of Montego Bay and is even more noticeable than most poor neighborhoods because it is surrounded by the glitter and glitz of the fancy resorts. Most of the people who live in Flankers either work at the resorts or are higglers, which are peddlers. I always feel at home in such areas, maybe because the people who live there live so intimately with the earth.

Harris and I said good night to Birgitta and Howard and headed back downtown. It felt great to walk in the sultry air, observing the tropical vegetation everywhere. The night hung heavy with romance.

Same night, 1:00 AM:

I'm very tired. I only had three hours of sleep this morning. Harris slept all day and is wide awake, so here we sit on Union Street again. Harris is a security guard for Western Wheel, which is a company that makes floor tiles and does masonry. I asked him what security guards do, and he said they guard the office upstairs, supposedly the machines and money. Harris's friend, whose pet name is Pearl Harbor, also works here. These men cover for each other when one wants time off.

So here I sit, in what I call the 'sort of room' room, because this room is in a building most of which has no roof. It's a small, stark room with a barred window. Cardboard is taped over the broken glass. Furnishings include an old chair, table and bed. A bright bare bulb glares down from the ceiling. Men's clothing is hung from the bulb's wiring and also on the gate. The clothing is clean and immaculately pressed and looks out of place in this dark, dingy room. This room is too dirty looking for my comfort. It has grey stone walls. Old, black boots and shoes are piled in a heap in the corner.

At least I can rest here. Harris is busy right now at the table, mixing something smoky with water, some kind of drug I am sure, so he can get his nightly fix. I want so much to ask him not to, but I can't. I am here to observe and record the facts, the life around me, not to tell him how I think he should live. But it's hard to remain silent. I am, after all, intruding on his world, as it has been for years and probably will be for years to come.

The table is covered with a ribbed plastic cloth designed with bowls of tropical fruit. On it is a small TV, an old tape recorder, an empty bottle of Wreys and Nephews over proof rum, a spool of rust twine, a spoon, knife, plate, flashlight, plastic white bowl and a padlock. In the windowsill is a bar of red soap, a broken mirror and a blue tube of something. Mosquitoes are chewing up my ankles.

Later Harris brought me a mosquito coil. Think I'll sleep. Harris is wandering around. He showed me an invitation that he got to his boss's daughter's wedding. He seems very proud to have received it.

I hate to think about how many people have laid on this filthy bed, so I won't. I'll just do it, because I really need to sleep.

There's a stairway outside of this room. Harris says there is a duppy which often climbs them. He's seen it. He thinks it's the spirit of a man who died here about four years ago.

Sunday, January 14

7:30 AM: This morning I am going to church with Dawn, Grandma Sweet and all the children. I want to experience first hand their religion. We are going to the Full Gospel Church of God, run by Pastor King.

LaVerne washed my blouse for me yesterday and ironed my blouse and skirt this morning. Since they don't have electricity, she has to heat the iron up on the gas stove. She insisted on doing this, saying that I must look crisp for church.

There is electricity in one room of the house, the room that Harris rents to his tenant, Angela. The rest of the home is lit with oil lamps and consists of only a few rooms. The living room has no furniture in it at all. Harris's bedroom has one shelf, one small table and a single bed in which he, his girlfriend Pauline, Kimoy and Trudy all sleep.

The bathroom has a pipe for a shower. Water runs slowly out non stop. I can never flush the toilet, so I try not to use it. To make things easier, I eat and drink very little.

Dressed for church

Later: I enjoyed the short walk to church. There was an incredible feeling of peace, bliss and love, so much natural beauty as we walked down that dirt road on that mountaintop. Soon we could see the church, or what was left of it. Hurricane Gilbert did a lot of damage to it.

The church is basically some pieces of zinc on a frame. It has a stone frame outside and a stone floor inside. The adults sit on the left side of the church and the school age children on the right.

When we walked in, the first thing I noticed was that all the ladies were wearing black skirts and magenta blouses and hats. I felt a little out of place since I was wearing a red skirt and a white blouse. The girls had fixed my hair, so I was sporting three ponytails and lots of ribbons. It was basically a child's hairdo, but I wore it anyway as I didn't want to offend them.

All of the children were very dressed up. Most of them have only one good outfit and they wear it every Sunday. The two teachers present filed in and out, keeping an eye on the children.

The front of the church held a platform with a magenta skirt around it. Magenta is obviously an important color to these people. There is also a podium on the platform, and a drum set on the left and two electric guitars and a table with flowers on it on the right.

Walking to church

The table has a white lace cloth and a roll of toilet paper on it. I couldn't help but chuckle at this. Only in my sweet Jamaica would this seem absolutely normal. There is also a huge bell on the table.

A message is written on a zinc wall in front of the church. It says, "He will save you now." As we walked in, everyone introduced themselves to me. Chris, who is one of the leaders, gave me a pillow to sit on and a bible.

These people were so wonderful. They went out of their way to make me feel welcome.

Chris said, "It doesn't matter that you are a different color. If we cut ourselves, we all bleed red. Welcome, sister!"

When he said it didn't matter that I am a different color, I thought he was talking about my clothes, the red and white as opposed to the black and magenta that the other women wore, so I said, "Oops, sorry!" When everyone started giggling, I realized with embarrassment that he was referring to the color of my skin. It was something that I seldom thought about, as people seldom mentioned it.

I am writing here in church now. I can see a light shining from everyone's eyes and faces. I feel all spirit here. Everything in the air is spirit and beauty. The topic for this morning is Jesus speaking to his disciples. The memory verse for today is from Matthew 5, Verse 6: "Let your light so shine before Me that they may see your good works and glorify your Father which is in heaven."

The children recited the memory verse and then everyone applauded. The ceremony progressed with a lot of bible quotes and singing and clapping. I soon realized that the services go on for hours and hours. No wonder I was told we could arrive at any time.

Somebody behind me is holding a small baby. The baby throws up. In front of me is a tiny boy in grey dress pants, a white shirt and a bow tie. He's too young to sit with the children on the other side of the church. He's adorable, but his behavior isn't. He keeps turning around and beating me with his bible. I smile politely even though it hurts.

After much singing and praying, the children are finally sent outside to take a break. Some of the adults move to different pews. Then, more prayers and singing led by Pastor King. She sang loudly and shouted out, wanting to make sure that God could hear her.

On the board up front someone wrote: "Record attendance = 118 people; Attendance today = 86; Offering taken up = $74.10; Bibles = 33; Visitors = 3." Next a choir came marching in, dancing and singing with soul. There was a bible reading that was interlaced with a lot of singing, clapping and tambourine playing. One of the choir members gave me her song book. This song was sung over and over, getting louder and louder each time and more frenzied as people got into it:

"Send the Light, the blessed Gospel Light. Let it shine from shore to shore. Send the Light, and let it radiate and be. Light the world forevermore."

When the singing finally stopped, the visitors were asked to introduce themselves and we were welcomed. Then there were announcements and more singing, clapping and music. A little girl danced uninhibitedly around the church and everyone just ignored her. I heard many spontaneous shouts of "Praise de Lord!" When people were moved, they would jump up and share experiences and visions they had had during the week.

The lady next to me jumped up and with a sense of urgency she delivered a message that had come to her in a vision in last week's service: "Fast and pray! Fast and pray or tribulation will come to you! God gave me this message to give to the church!" She is literally screaming this out.

People started filing up front. The guitars were making a lot of noise, but not playing any particular tune. The baby beside me fell asleep and I wondered how this baby could possibly sleep through all of this noise. There were very few men at the service, mostly women and children. As everyone swayed and swooned, Pastor King shouted the final prayer, which was called "Christ Died of a Broken Heart." Then more frenzied singing and shouting by the congregation.

It's 1:30 PM by now, and the morning speaker is about to come on. I have all I can do to not fall asleep myself by this time. The heat is stifling. I decide I'm going to sneak out as soon as possible. More songs. I'm leaving now. It's 2:00 PM.

Church was interesting and I was very touched by the warmth and beauty of the people, but holy cow, they must rock and sing all day long! Back at Dawn's, everyone wanted to know how I enjoyed the service. We talked for a while and relaxed.

I felt faint and disoriented as I stumbled up the hill later to see Daniel. He insisted that he had had all kinds of visions about me since our last visit, and he was so happy to see me.

But he did ask me to take my earrings off, saying they were sinful temptations to man. I recorded two more tapes this afternoon. Some of what Daniel said spooked me, but I found most of it amusing. I was touched at how he prayed for me.

When Daniel found out that I have no children, he assumed that I am "pure." I wasn't going to burst his bubble. I liked having my ego built up.

In part, here is a prayer that Daniel said for me. "Jesus Christ say dat dis woman is a messenger, a servant of God. Just be patient. Your heart will fulfill what your heart desires. Whatever work she came down here to do Lord, let she do it wid all her heart and mind and soul. And let no serpent change her mind. Dere shall be guidance and protection all along wid her, by Thee. All along dis Jamaica dat is rough and tied up wid dese three iniquity workers. May you strengthen her and guide her and protect her, and send angels to guide her, so she return back to her home land wid new spirit, new heart. De world gonna see dat she changed from what she were before. Dis young lady born again. May your angel control all dese spirits and demons.

"Please ma'am, tank you for de day you came along. Your spirit sent you here. De spirit of God is inside you. And de God you meet is Daniel God, wid a mon's spirit inside him."

Daniel rambles on about the problems of Jamaica caused by obeah and witchcraft, how they must be overcome. He was very concerned about the fact that I am a likely candidate for those who work in iniquity, since I am here to bring light.

Daniel has a really strong grasp of the fact that we all have God within us. I think that is why he calls himself Daniel God. Think of how we would feel and perceive ourselves and each other if we all put God as part of our names. How about Debbie God, Harris God and Dudley God? I love and respect my parents, but I have a new perception of them when I think of them as Helga God and Victor God.

Daniel clearly recognizes the power and energy of the Creator, and the truth that we all have the same God qualities in us. It's up to us to take responsibility in this life to do the best we can and to acknowledge that we are love. We came here for a reason and we have the choice and power to live the God qualities or to be destructive.

All of this is so intense for me. Hour after hour after hour of intenseness while I talk with these people in Jamaica. It gets to be overwhelming at times. I feel like I need to get away to think and reflect on it all.

It seemed like Daniel never came up for a breath of air today once he started talking. A lot of what he said sounded repetitious, but he was dead set on getting his point across. His message basically is that we are more of the spirit than of the flesh. He believes that we need to tend to this so that God will give us another body at another time. He's very, very concerned about the power of sex. He's also very concerned about the powers of obeah. He believes that the evil powers have manifested in the form of Mother Heart.

After hours of ranting, Daniel thanked God one more time for sending me, his little sister, to come to the Garden of Eden. He told me that I never knew I had a promise to fulfill, but a thousand years ago the Lord said that I would be coming to fulfill this promise and writing this book. Where Daniel God got this stuff I have no idea!

"When de time come for she to step foot wid her promise, her body gonna be happy, her spirit gonna be alive and her soul will rescue from dis world corruption. Tank you for your presence, Lord."

Daniel said that last night the angels came to him and told him all about me. They told him why I was there and that I have a very beautiful spirit. They also told him that I would be tempted by a Jamaican man and by other men, and that these temptations would get in the way of writing my book.

Daniel also told me to always put a glass of water by my bed at night. He said if I did this, then the angels would always watch over me as I slept.

Gate to the Garden of Eden

He also said that he is trying to speak only the truth to me, and that later if I found something to be untrue, then I would understand that at the time it was said, it was Daniel and not God speaking.

Daniel told me that I must not eat pork because the bible says that it is unclean. I never could understand that one. If God made all animals then how could pork be unclean? I don't buy the vegetarian thing either. Personally, I believe that we need a balance derived from eating all kinds of food. The secret is to eat in moderation.

It was clouding up and turning chilly and I was very tired, so I finally told Daniel that I was going to leave. His eyes burned right through me as he gave me a strange little smile and told me that I am a sunbeam.

I enjoyed the walk back to the house, soaking up all the beauty and enjoying the songs of the roosters and the gulls. Pauline was at home when I got there and we had a nice talk. She told me that she is really glad that I am staying with them. Her sincerity warmed my heart.

I had to get away for a while and sort out my feelings. I hadn't been alone for a moment since I arrived in Jamaica. The sweet girls have been clinging adoringly to me. I'm used to a lot of time alone, so this has been difficult.

I decided to walk into Montego Bay from Farm Heights, but this upset my friends. They warned me that for sure I would be "tieved." Dawn, who has very little money, even offered to pay for a taxi for me, which touched me deeply.

But as always, I wasn't afraid. My point in walking was that I needed exercise and solitude. It was a lovely walk, and as I neared town I suddenly realized that I hadn't eaten or urinated in over twenty-four hours. Not a very healthy thing to do. I walked down to Gloucester Avenue and actually managed to find a clean bathroom. For once, I needed to get away from all the local stuff.

I bought a tangerine and a fresh pineapple, which the vendor chopped up into bite size pieces for me. It was juicy and bursting with flavor and sweetness. Next I hit one of my favorite outdoor restaurants, the Pork Pit, for a Red Stripe beer. The scent alone of jerk food is enough to take me to heaven.

I'm really tired, but I must walk down to Union Street now to find Harris or Dawn. I know that Dawn is working tonight. I really don't feel like taxiing home alone, but maybe I'll try. It'll be nice to get to Bibsey's in Oracabessa and feel more settled. But I still have so much more business to finish here. I need to record Harris yet, talk more to Daniel, go to a children's school, and I haven't even gone to the beach yet!

Later: As I was walking, I remembered some experiences that I had had in my past. I remembered the first time that I had ever seen Harris's house. It was just a tiny house with a zinc roof and yet it felt so serene and peaceful. Houses hold energy, and this one spoke clearly to me of its occupants.

I was exhausted as we had been out late. So I laid down on Harris's little bed and fell asleep. I woke up hours later and saw something very strange. In my foggy state, I saw Harris standing over me, staring intently at me. He was holding a lit match and waving his arms wildly. His long dreadlocks cast magical shadows on the ceiling behind him. It seemed like he was performing some kind of ritual. I found out later that he was merely trying to kill the bed bugs, trying to take care of and protect me. Bless his heart! Even so, the side of my body that I slept on had a red rash for the next few days.

I remember getting a letter from Harris one time when I was back in the States. He asked me if I could possibly afford to send him two dollars and fifty cents to buy a new bed. Someone must have offered him a good deal.

Harris has done a lot for me. He can be credited for teaching me to dance reggae. I really enjoy watching him dance because he certainly has his own rhythm. After a while, I released my shyness and let the rhythm become a part of me. I picked up all the different moves and tempos. I became part of reggae and danced my way through the rest of Jamaica. What a joyful, glorious and fun way to express my feelings about life! The dancing provided me with a way to actually feel the culture.

I am most alive when I dance. For years, I studied ballet, jazz and mid-eastern dancing back in the States. Dance, to me, has always been a form of prayer, a true communion with the Creator. When I dance, I feel a transformation of my physical self into a being of pure energy, and I move in harmony with all of the energy around me. I can ride into other dimensions and gain understanding and insight.

As I was walking, I also thought about the fantastic sense of humor that Jamaicans have. It's a main ingredient for survival in a land where meeting the basic needs of life takes up most of their day. We take so much for granted.

For instance, the laundry isn't something they throw into a machine. Doing laundry is a day long event. Clothes are washed by hand in a bucket or taken to the river. First they are soaped up and laid in the sun, which works as a bleaching agent, then they are rinsed and hung to dry. One of my favorite sights in Jamaica is a woman knee deep in the river, happily scrubbing clothes on a rock, while her children frolic around her, enjoying their swim. Often on shore, they will have a dutchee pot of dumplings cooking for lunch.

I ended up not taxiing home alone tonight. I visited with Dawn for a long while and did a lot of reading and writing. I'm going to sleep at the Western Wheel again.

Monday, January 15

This morning was beautiful, so I hiked up the mountain. The girls greeted me and did some of my laundry. The tenant, Angela, and the girls and I are the only ones here now. I really like Angela. She has goals and ambitions. Her great sense of humor erupted as we talked.

She told me that Harris and Pauline, who is Kimoy's mother, are now more like brother and sister than lovers. She also said that Harris talks about me a lot and that he was really looking forward to my visit.

Harris and I did have a nice talk last night. He told me that he loves me very much and that I'll always be very special to him. It made me realize how much I also care about him.

Now is a very special time for me... being here... living this. Leaving this wonderful family will break my heart. I love them so much!

The girls didn't go to school today. Coretta told me she studies Math, English, Religion, Spelling, Gym, Art and Science. They have one teacher for all of these subjects. I find it interesting that religion is taught in public schools here. This reflects the awareness that Jamaicans have of our spiritual beings. When I asked Coretta if she has a boyfriend, she giggled and said no.

I asked the girls why they didn't go to school today. They told me it was because Dawn was sleeping. When I explained how important school is, one of them said, "But we didn't have no money to go!" Another one said, "It's raining out!"

I suspected the truth was they didn't want to go because they figured they would miss a visit with me. No one was there to make them go, so here they were. Normally, the girls love school.

I was about to head off towards the beach this morning, when we had a sudden tropical downpour. The after effects of Hurricane Gilbert are still being felt even though the storm occurred in 1988. Harris is still waiting for the zinc that the Government promised him so that he can rebuild his roof.

Today I realized the extent of the damage that was done to the roof. Almost every room had waterfalls tumbling in. We ran around with buckets, trying to catch the water. I loved the feeling of this, the coziness, and the sound of the rain beating on the roof and the banana trees outside. I loved looking out and seeing everything blowing and the clouds moving so quickly over the mountaintop. Everything was so alive.

I was very at peace in the midst of this, for I was surrounded by the love of the children. The girls are having a grand time. Right now, they're out on the porch, scrubbing the walls and giggling in delight. The rain is something to celebrate here. It's providing cool relief from the intense sun, as well as nourishing the vegetation.

I really would enjoy living here for a while with Harris and the kids. It would be such fun to make it look a bit homier, to paint it and put some furniture in the living room. If I had enough money to do that and to turn on the electricity, it would be a perfect home for me.

Harris's house   Catching rain water

The tenant's room is really cute. It has furniture, photos and electricity. Angela has a boyfriend who supports her well. She is also trying to save money and obtain a visa to the United States so that she can work in an old folks home there. I think the reason that she has more in life is because she demands more. It's all an attitude.

Angela and I discussed religion this morning during the rain. She said she doesn't like to use her brain to think about religion, but she would rather just sit quietly and know. She said, "Like last night, I was sitting on my bed when suddenly the whole room was filled with the spirit of God. Find God there, not in the gospel church rantings."

Her two sons live with her mother and they are all Seventh Day Adventists. She doesn't go to church now that she is on her own, but she told me she would if she had a Sunday dress to step out in.

Angela believes that all men are created equal and she just can't understand prejudice. She wishes that God the Spirit would make himself visible again, because she just knows that he is Black. If only people could see that, then they would realize that Whites aren't superior to Blacks.

Then the subject reverted back to Harris. Angela wants me to marry Harris and help him because he is so nice. She thinks he needs a woman's gentle nudge and guidance. She said that Pauline doesn't care about anything.

The sun came out later and I hobbled down to Doctor's Cave Beach. It was a long, very, very hot walk. At about 3:15 PM, I arrived at a little restaurant called Chicken Man and I sat down to write this. It was a nightmarish walk because I had my heavy bags with me. My feet were blistered as it was, and to make matters worse, one of my bags ripped open on the way.

I haven't eaten or drunk anything for twenty hours. My entire body hurts and I'm parched. It's extremely hot. I need to find a place to shower. Plus, the phones aren't working anywhere.

I finally hobbled down to the beach and fell exhausted into the sea. It was heaven! I'm not exaggerating. I honestly was stumbling. My entire body ached from all the hiking of the past twenty-four hours, and from carrying such heavy bags, and from all the huge, ugly blisters peppering my feet. I felt totally exhausted to a point where my mind wasn't even functioning right.

The soft, clear water massaged me and cooled down my body temperature. What relief! Then I laid on the soft sand and fell instantly asleep. I sure wish I had more time here, but the beach is closing and I simply must shower first. Cold showers are certainly better than no showers at all.

I'm curious. That thing that I'm yearning for... What is it? It's here. It's here at Doctor's Cave Beach. Yet it's still elusive to me. I feel total peace and total fulfillment, a connection with life in a very spiritual energy form, a total merging with everything. It's incredibly blissful.

I understand my wholeness. The idea that we are separate, that we are alone, is an illusion in life. We are never alone. We are One. Jamaica is a place that I can connect with that energy and experience that Oneness. There are no words for knowing.

Tuesday, January 16

I went on another Rep excursion last night. We went out on a glass bottom boat after dark. It was equipped with an underwater light, so we were able to view the coral reefs at night. It was a magical experience and I felt really pampered.

Afterwards, we went out for dinner and dancing and had a great time.

I stayed at Deedra's house. After sleeping in, we sat by the pool at the Rep house. I needed a good rest after the week I had been through.

Talk about going from one world to another in seemingly an instant. It was a strange sensation for me. It made me wonder, "Who am I, that I have this choice, this option?" This is not even my country, but many Jamaicans don't have the same options. They live in this country, yet are locked into poverty and struggle for the most part. They don't even know how to help themselves out of it.

I come here and I choose to live with them in their poverty to try to understand their struggle. Yet it is different for me, because all of the time that I am suffering I am also aware that I have a way out. At any time, I can call up the Reps and go live the life of luxury. It feels very strange to move back and forth from one extreme to the other like that. Of course, what I am referring to here is material and physical comfort.

Each way of life serves a purpose. I think the contrast was put into my life to teach me. What is it teaching me? It is teaching me values. It is teaching me about life, about my brothers and sisters on this planet. It is teaching me a whole lot about myself. Sara, Deedra and I went up to Harris's at sunset to pick up my sleeping bag. The house appeared dark and locked although I could hear the little radio that I gave Harris blaring from his room. We had passed Coretta on the drive up and she came running over now. After pounding on the door and calling through the windows, we came to the conclusion that no one was home.

Coretta ran around and discovered that the back door was wide open. We entered and opened the bedroom door, shocked and horrified to find five year old Trudy sound asleep on the bed with one year old Kimoy lying across her looking at a book. We couldn't believe that the small children had been left totally unattended. The tiny porch off the back door has a ten foot drop off with no railing on it. I shudder to think what could've happened had one of the tiny tots wandered out there.

Sara was almost hysterical. "Welcome to the real Jamaica, Sara," I said quietly. Up to this point, Sara had only experienced the tourist land of Jamaica.

Picking up Kimoy and hugging her, we headed outside and sat on the porch, waiting for someone to get home. Night fell and still no one came. Sara commented that she wondered what would've happened if the girls woke up alone there in the dark. Thirteen year old Coretta said, "Don't worry. Trudy can light the oil lamp." We all screamed then.

Kimoy had wet her panties so we went in, lit the oil lamp and changed her. Some of the other children wandered over and we sang and played. We also got them some food. Sara called me "Mother Teresa of Jamaica." I laughed hard at that one.

When Pauline finally showed up we asked her if she was concerned about how the children had been left. She said, "Well, yes, but what can I do?"

It seems that Harris is the one who left them that way. He told Coretta when he left that afternoon that he would "soon come." (Coretta and the other children live at Dawn's house now.)

Before we left, Pauline told us that she will take us to a Pocomania ceremony tomorrow night. I'm really excited! We drove down to Union Street and found Harris lounging lazily on someone's car trunk, hanging out and being "just cool." For this he left his little children in peril??? Sara lit into him and he giggled and said calmly, "No, Sara. Dat is de way we in Jamaica do it." She told him she charges $10 JA an hour for baby sitting and he really laughed hard then.

It's true that the children here learn to be self-reliant at an early age, but this particular instance was too much to swallow. Those beautiful, innocent babies...

2

VOICE OF THE PEOPLE

*"I never travel, but I know by teaching and talking
to people dat dis country is one of de best, as a
blessed Almighty God dat create heaven and
earth country."*
— *Harris*

Wednesday, January 17
I went out to Trelawny this morning. It was wonderful. There were huge winds and strong seas, my favorite kind of weather. It's so alive! I could feel all of the energy of nature flowing.

I saw Denton at the taxi stand in Falmouth, so we stopped to say hello. Sara is getting the biggest kick out of meeting the local people. Granted, my friends are all real characters.

Anyway, Denton said he's going to come to Oracabessa to see me. I wonder if he will. This will be interesting. I still hold him dear in my heart and I always will. We had such a rare and special thing together. It hurt to have to move on. But move on I must.

I'm at Doctor's Cave Beach right now, going to write and swim until the girls get off work. Then we're going up into the hills for a Pocomania ceremony.

63

Whenever I ask anyone what they really know about Pocomania, I receive different answers. Many people believe it is used for evil reasons. Through dancing, drumming, singing and praying, spirit possession takes place. The leader supposedly can control and use several spirits. This is about all I know of this somewhat secretive cult. It has an air of mystery about it, and many people seem to fear it. Should be a very interesting evening.

The "cell," Sara, Harris, Prince, Deedra

Tonight I'm planning on sleeping on Union Street, so I can catch the early bus into Oracabessa. The bus stop is only a half a block away. Harris promised to be there to make certain that I get on the bus at 5:00 AM.

I'm finding it hard to leave Montego Bay, even though I know that I'll be back. Farm Heights certainly is a place for the sharing of spirits. People move slowly at their own pace. They move through life following their own body rhythm. Here there is lots of singing, dancing, praying, laughing, "hanging out" and people watching.

American society tries to tell us when we should be hungry and tired and how we should behave and feel. No wonder we're all stressed out. We have no sense of our own needs and personal rhythms.

Same day, 11:00 PM
Pauline didn't get out of work in time to take us to Pocomania. What a

disappointment! Anyway, we played with the children again. I'm always so amazed by them, their joy, their self-reliance and their beauty. They are born singers and dancers and they are so perceptive. My love for them is spilling over again tonight.

Harris had promised to get me a room for tonight but was unable to, so here I am at the "cell" again. The cell has opened its doors to me and I'm so glad I had the courage to enter. I'm finding that when one has nothing materially the only place to turn is inward. I recorded several tapes here tonight.

I'm feeling very joyous right now. Harris and Pearl Harbor's boss just came around and invited me to his daughter's wedding and reception. I feel honored and really want to go. I just realized something quite amazing. These men are opening their hearts to me. My experience has been that generally men close themselves off. Women are thought to be the emotional beings.

I let these men express themselves because I knew they had so much to say. I've got a gold mine of spiritual treasures now to share with the world. Open up your hearts. These people have so much to say, and no one ever wants to listen.

I really thought that my tape recorder would stifle them, but it didn't. I think it would make people in the States very self-conscious. Here it seems to have the opposite effect. People feel that this is their chance to make a statement that perhaps will be heard.

Sometimes I wonder why I fit in here so well. Physically, I certainly don't. Somehow I feel that when I get back to the States it will all come together for me. How very special these moments are! Please God, don't let me ever forget that. So, so special...

I love the spirits of these men so much. I still don't know how they perceive me, but I really don't think about it much. Jamaica, my Jamaica... a world and a universe unto itself. So much oppression. I clearly emphasize with the underdog and believe that the underdog always has something valuable to teach us.

I feel like a rebel with a cause. The human race is evolving. (Oh no! Am I beginning to sound like Daniel God?) I've lived with the poorest of the poor materially to the so-called rich men, who are often only rich materially. Contrast and duality are teachers.

Life really is so wonderful and so easy, but it appears to be so difficult sometimes. I'm sitting here on this dirty little bed. A huge roach just ran across and for some reason it doesn't bother me. It's just a creature. There is a tropical rain pouring out of the skies now. To me it feels safe and happy. It's very romantic.

I had quite a talk with Pearl Harbor tonight. He's a local character who has had to struggle as hard as the next guy to get by, but he has a good heart and soul. His appearance shows his hard life. I would be very frightened if I ran into him in a dark alley and didn't know him. His face is etched with a lot of anger, fear and pain, but also with love and compassion.

I'm so glad that I didn't just pass him by because I discovered a very sensitive, intelligent man behind the frightful exterior. He told me that he first noticed me when I was sitting on the stoop writing the other night. It seems that everyone was wondering who the "mad woman" was and where she came from. I found this most amusing and asked him why they all thought I was crazy.

"Because it's not a normal ting dat happen. Yeah, you see people sitting on de street, but not sitting and writing. Maybe dey sit and read a book, but sitting on de street writing? And looking? Writing? Looking? Dere is someting dat is definitely wrong.

"Now, most of de people who know me, know Killer." Killer is Harris's pet name. "Dey know dat you are reaching us. So dey say, 'Killer's white girl is mod, mon! I see her mon, and she was writing, writing a book. Me no know what she is a writing in de night. Must be letters she write.' And me say, 'No, me not know what she be doing.' Him say, 'What become of de vibes? When seen de vibes, it come like I am a spirit. I just feel it mon!' I wasn't here when dat was happening. I still hear about it.

"And now, now I am being de one who is in de book. I have brought fire in de sands. De first ting looked on when dey want to test a mod mon, a person who is insane, is dey look at dere eyes first. And dey look at de terror in dere eyes and dey know dat yes, someting is wrong. And dey start to investigate it. But you can't just look at a person. Me ignore dose tings. Me listening and hearing.

"Like tonight, you come and tell me you is writing a book, and den I see tears drop, and I look in de spirit. Plus de presence of mind. Dem reflect. Den de brain side just come back quick at de front to me tinking of what you was saying just de odder night. And now of what you say tonight.

66

"I know dat some people tink I am a mod mon or a fool. Dem tink I on opium all de time. Dem don't see wid de spirit."

We talked on and on. Pearl Harbor spoke of how so many people move and communicate in the spirit in Jamaica. They communicate in their senses, their intuition, their feelings for each other, more than through mere words.

He spoke of how Bob Marley gave a wonderful gift to the world. Through his music he was able to express his philosophies of life and convey the beauty of life.

Pearl Harbor told me that by looking through the eyes of his spirit he knew he could trust me. It mattered little to him what others around him were saying about me. He's very tuned in to his own spiritual nature.

I later had a long talk with Harris. When I asked him how he developed his philosophies, he replied. "Normally, it's just a reality feeling."

"What were your parents like?"

"Well, my fodder never growed me up. My modder alone to grow me up. My mommy is very an ignorant lady right now. Both of us can't agree, okay? When we talk to each odder it's just an ignorant talking to each odder. She hurt my feelings by saying certain tings. She's my modder. She should be more calmer to me, okay?

"People say, 'Bwoy! How do you go through dat?' But dis is de reason why I cope and go through it. She is de one who brought me up. And she brought me up in a manner dat very much good. Respect her for dat. She brought me up not to steal, not to do tings dat wrong. She brought me up how to cook, how to iron, how to clean.

"She brought me up how to know dat I am a mon. Whenever I have a lady dat I living wid, if I come home and she cook de meal, I supposed to know when I is eating if it is palatable enough. She taught me dat as a kid coming up to be a mon to wash my own clothes. Dat when I come up, if I have a wife and she washes my clothes, and I take it from de hanger and put it on, I is supposed to know if it is washed properly or not. She taught me how to iron."

"But didn't she teach you that you should help to do it?"

"Yeah! Cuz at de time, as a kid, I has to do it also. And if I don't do it properly, she lick me in de head and say, 'Come back and do it over!' And now my kids, from Prince right on down, you see, dey can do everyting. And I'm not bragging or boasting. Behind my back you can ask de mommy. It's not she who learned dem. It's me who learned dem to do dose tings.

"Because normally when I gots to leave to gets some money, Prince is de one who gots to cook for all de smaller ones. He gots to really look after dem. Dey take de burden off."

I told him that I am very impressed with his children, and that little Sharon did my laundry the other day. He beamed with joy, and then expressed sadness that things aren't the best for them right now. I told him that I have observed that they are very happy regardless of the poverty.

He said, "You see, when dey was smaller, de energy was den put into dem, so right now dey grow up wid de energy. So if de energy is not really generating to de maximum at dis time, at de age dey are in, dey can really go on til de energy picks back up. Cuz de energy already come from de smaller age in dem. If dey didn't have de energy from smaller coming up, dere would be no energy now, in dis problem dat we are all in. You know?"

I commented on the fact that every time I see the children they flood me with positive vibrations. It's phenomenal.

"Dat's what I'm showing dem right now, de tings dat really get tings going in dis little country here. I never travel, but I know by teaching and talking to people dat dis country is one of de best, as a blessed Almighty God dat create heaven and earth country. Cuz normally we don't have no really bad tings taking hold of us in dis country. De baddest ting dat we have dat really took away is Hurricane Gilbert. We don't have no volcano, no big disease dat would kill eighty hundred people.

"Normally, in our little politics, we don't have tings like, you'd find people fighting for like six months, firing nuclear weapons. Yes, people die, but you know all over de world people gots to die. But in Jamaica right now, tings is not out of hand no matter which government is taking position.

"But you find some people don't really know how to manage dese tings, and don't really know how to look towards odder countries wid enforcement from Jamaica. Right now de system running is slow up de country a lot."

"What did you think of Seaga when he was Prime Minister?"

"Well, you see his brain is good enough to rule any country. He have a real brain piece. I don't say no one is perfect. De one person who is perfect is de Almighty who create everyone who is on dis earth. But I know dat if dat mon continue to rule in Jamaica at dis time, Jamaica would be a more brighter standard. Be better for de poor, de middle class and de rich.

"You gots to look at tings dis way. You can't come from de bottom to go to de top in a certain way. You gots to help de big mon come down. Seaga did help de rich and de middle class, and dis was de time now for he to help de poor at last. Most of de poor class didn't see dis and voted him out. Like, you plant a tree and de tree grow up. And when de tree grows up it blossoms. And when it blossoms you cut it down. Well, dats what de people in our country do right now to Seaga. Cuz if dey did put back dat mon right now, you surely see I'd be driving a car. You'd surely see a lot of people more and more modern style."

"How do you feel about Manley, the current Prime Minister?"

"I don't say I'm against Manley, okay? As a personal mon, okay? But normally his philosophy toward his people dat works under him, well, he can't manage dem. Like if you're a boss, you're supposed to know dat if I take up de cup, it's supposed to help me and my followers. Den you take up de cup and tell your followers it will help. You must be de leader. Like a captain, you must steer your crew out to sea. De crew members gots to hear what de captain says. So, if he say, 'I'm going through dere' de only ting de crew members can say is 'Be careful'. De captain must have de steering. So dat is Seaga. He try someting and if it doesn't work he use his brain and try someting else.

"But Manley is a mon who make a choice to move into battle, but if his followers down de line say, 'No, don't move into battle' right away he halt. A leader must be strong and powerful. If you are a leader and you are not strong and powerful, you can't lead.

"Dat's what soak us right now, Debbie. I know a lot of people right now is saying, 'Bwoy! We shouldn't never have do dat. Look what we have done to ourself. We had a mon who could really do tings dat we wanted to do to build our own self. Now we can't build ourself.' "

Harris went on to say that Seaga basically turned his back and allowed the number one crop in Jamaica to flourish. The largest crop was marijuana. It used to be much easier to smuggle out of the country. Manley has evidently put a halt to that. Why grow the crop if the buyers can't get it? I'm sure that it has hurt the economy of the island, but there are obviously issues other than economic growth which were looked at here.

Harris still believes that the island could be in much worse shape. Yet he told me that I haven't seen real poverty yet. He said if I was alone moving on the street then I would constantly run into beggars.

I told him that I've run into plenty of beggars, but I have a difficult time figuring out which ones really need money and which ones make a game of begging. I asked Harris what he thought about this.

"Well, you see in Jamaica dat is our only problem. We don't have no else problem. You see dat mon Seaga? Dat mon has every else country wrapped around his finger because of his education toward financing tings. He could go to any country and say, 'Look, I need fifty million dollars for Jamaica,' and he don't have to go through no hard protest to get dat money. Dey know dat he knows how to manage it, even though he going to take some of it for himself. Cuz a leader isn't going to go on de street and get ten dollars and give away back de whole ten dollars to de followers. If I a leader, no I wouldn't do it. I have to keep back two dollars for myself and spend eight dollars.

"Manley is a good guy, but his leadership strength is weak. It is weak to both his workers in dis country and to all de odder states around de world."

Harris went on to say that he is generally pretty happy. He has freedom to come and go as he pleases with no harassment. He has a lot of friends of all ages who love and respect him. He and Pearl Harbor are like blood brothers and will always be there to help each other. He said that the greatest thing in life is to have a roof over your head and shelter, and the Father has helped him to have that. He said he thanks him every minute of every hour of every day.

He said he knows the Father will help him find work because he has two trades. He is a painter and a plumber. He used to be known as 'Killer the Craftsman' because he did ceramics.

"But really de ting dat I would like to do in dis here Jamaica now, is to open a cook shop, because I know dat food is an essential part of life. People got to eat everyday, so dat is my main aim right now. I used to help out a brodder towards a cook shop and every night I put a lot of money in his hand. And people don't complain. Dey say my food eat good. I know dis can happen, because I don't reach too far in age yet. I can still make my life. As long as you have health and ambition den age doesn't matter.

"I'm praying to de Fodder day and night to answer dat prayer. I know dat he will, because I'm not getting myself in no problems. It will happen."

"Do you think your kids know how you feel?"

"Yeah! I want to have tings to my standard dat de kids can be really happy. I explain it to de bigger ones. I tell dem I would like to have a car so dat I could drive dem to school myself at morning time, and come at evening time and take dem back home.

"We don't have enough room right now and dat's why some of dem are by dere modder. As soon as tings get straightened out den dey must be back wid me, all of dem."

It was so obvious to me how deeply Harris loves his children and how it pains him that he can't offer them more. I always knew he loved them, but I never realized the depth of that love until tonight. I told him there was something I wanted to say, and I hoped that he would listen with an open mind, because maybe, just maybe, my perceptions were wrong. He was extremely attentive as I spoke.

"There is something elusive about you. You know how close I am to your children. I somehow think that they don't really understand how much you care about them. Whenever you're around, their eyes shine and they giggle with excitement at seeing their daddy. But I have never once seen you hug them, except for the baby.

"Everyone of them is so special and I feel like they need your hugs. Maybe the reason that I am so sensitive to this is because when I was little I adored my daddy, too, and still do, but I secretly wished he would've hugged me more. I always felt that he truly loved me, but only when I grew up did I comprehend just how much!

"I believe that your children would be so thrilled if you sat down with each of them and asked them things like, 'What makes you happy? What makes you sad?' And then pat them on the back and hug them and cheer them on. It would mean more to them than you can probably dream."

"Dat is true, Debbie, but listen. I know dat dose kids know, cuz I'm de one dat really grow dem out of de slums situation. Dey normally was wid me, but now dey know dat I am in certain difficulty and dat is why dey are wid dere modder. Dey know dat if I could cope wid dem and bring dem out of dis dark into de light, I would do it. At dis time right now, dey know dat tings is not balanced de way dey should be. So dey don't feel no way. Dey understand."

"Harris, you are such a loving and gentle spirit. That's why it surprises me that you aren't more physically affectionate with your kids." I thought about

71

this more, and decided that maybe it has something to do with Harris's own self-esteem. I think the hugs would be just as healing for him as for the kids.

We talked on and on for a long time. Late into the night, I was suddenly aware of how tired I had become. And at the same time, the realization swept over me that I had been stuffing and hiding a lot of intense emotions. Once again I felt awed at where I was and why I was there.

Feeling overwhelmed, I asked Harris to listen to me as I tried to sort out my feelings. Suddenly tears were spilling out everywhere. It felt good to release them. I was feeling overwhelmed with love, so happy to be in Jamaica, and also physically frustrated from the pain of trying to get around on my severely blistered feet.

I told Harris all of this. He held my hand and listened intently. Then he put his arms around me. Hugs do heal. I hadn't consciously realized how much I needed one. I found myself speaking about the love and caring that we have had for one another all these years. Even though our cultures and life styles are so different, we've been able to communicate well.

It shocked me when Harris gently asked me why I am afraid of myself. A friend recently asked me the same question in one of his letters. I didn't know I was afraid of myself, but it sure was obvious to others. This was an uncomfortable thing for me to look at. What are they seeing that I am not?

This provides countless reflections for me to look at. Do I mask my needs and desires from myself, yet wear them on my sleeves for others to see? Have I not learned to be honest with myself? Do I somehow feel invalid and unworthy of love? Am I ashamed of who I am? What exactly am I afraid of? I think I am afraid of rejection, and of the depth of my passions, and of my true potential.

All I could focus on now was my tremendous love for Harris and my extended Jamaican family. I knew it would be unbearably painful to leave them when I had to return to the States. I also ached with a desire to be able to help these people learn to help themselves. I've received so much from them. Their spirits shine right through me and somehow enhance my own spirit. I feel strongly like they are all part of me, and I feel somehow more whole and complete in their presence.

It seems strange to me to be so drawn to these people in the hills, in a country far from mine. But I came here to face this head on and find out whatever it is that I need to learn from them. I was led here by my spirit, so I'll quietly listen and trust. When the time is right, it shall be revealed to me. Actually, it is being revealed all along, isn't it?

Thursday, January 18

Harris walked me to the bus at six o'clock this morning. I was glad to have help with my luggage, even though it was only a short walk. As the bus rolled away, he turned and waved and smiled. By then I was feeling good. I knew he felt as serene as I.

My thoughts turned to my upcoming adventures. I was off to a local village about eighty miles away to see my dear friend Bibsey. I sat back to enjoy the bus ride, wondering what today would bring.

It was exciting to be back in Oracabessa. I hopped off the bus on Coloraine Street and hiked up the hill, where I found Bibsey in an outdoor shower. The water had run out and I found her standing there with soap all over her. More often than not, there is no water here now. Evidently the water tanks are now being shared with another nearby village.

Once again, I couldn't help thinking about how most of us in the States would react to such a situation. We would be in an uproar, impatient and angry, demanding that something be done instantly to remedy the problem. We do need our creature comforts.

But here was Bibsey, just taking it all in stride. She wasn't about to get all bent out of shape over something she could do nothing about anyway. I'm sure that her attitude plays a major roll in keeping her healthy.

What a beautiful sight! It's always such a joy to see dear friends after a long absence. And here was my Bibsey, a dark, robust woman with short, black curly hair, large warm brown eyes, and a huge happy smile. She was standing in the yard, clad only in a towel and a shower cap.

I've known Bibsey for a few years now. One day when I was out exploring around Port Maria, I met Bibsey's boyfriend Max. I gave him a ride home and we've all been close friends ever since.

Max works on a cruise ship now, so they seldom get to see each other. Bibsey is holding down the fort, waiting for the day when they can finish building their home. Max is working hard to build a future for them. He sends Bibsey money, and is also buying furnishings for the house.

Max and his brother were running a little bar called the Seagull, but other family members have taken it over. Bibsey and Max are building a home on the hill right behind the Seagull. Ever since I've known them, they have been living out of the one room that is completed. I must say, they are building quite a nest for themselves and have a lot more than many of their countrymen do.

I'll never understand the logic of Jamaicans. Bibsey is busy collecting all kinds of electrical gadgets, yet won't spend any of the money Max sends her to have electricity turned on. The room that she and her son Devon live in has a TV, a boom box, a VCR, a huge fan, and yet it is lit with a huge oil lamp.

Well, this is home for awhile. Bibsey wants me to stay as long as I possibly can. She has always mothered me even though I am older than her. The room they live in has two double beds. Devon will sleep in one, and Bibsey and I will share the other. I do feel welcome and at home.

Bibsey's house, Oracabessa

A few moments ago I went down to the Seagull to use the toilet. The bartender was vicious and told me to go use the bushes. I discovered that the relatives resent Bibsey because they want the money that Max is earning. They're trying to make her so miserable that she will leave, but it's not going to happen. I seldom see this kind of attitude in Jamaicans, but people are people, I guess. I realize I'm going to be treated the same as Bibsey simply because I am her friend.

No problem. That toilet is so decrepit that I actually prefer the bushes anyway. They seem safer. My years of being a camper are paying off now.

I love being in Oracabessa. To me it's like going back in time a hundred years. Bibsey has already introduced me to everyone around here. She always proudly says, "This is Debbie, my white friend," as though no one can see with their own eyes that I am white. Every time she does this, I roll around inside of myself laughing. It's things like this that I find so endearing about Jamaicans.

Sunshine's house, Sunshine, Bibsey

Hey, I just found out that Bibsey's neighbor, Sunshine, has a toilet. She has kindly offered me the use of it. I'm moving up in the world fast here. The gods are surely smiling on me today.

Friday, January 19

Last night Bibsey and Sunshine wanted to celebrate my arrival so we went to the village hot spot, a fenced in outdoor bar called Helsinki. Bibsey was as proud as a peacock because her sister is a go-go dancer there. Go-go dancing is very popular in local Jamaican establishments.

Bibsey's sister, Gilette, is very fat and yet was totally unself-conscious dancing around in her little bikini. I found that intriguing because most people in the States who are overweight would be too shy and insecure to do something like that. Sometimes I wish I had the guts to dance like that, but it'll never happen, not in public anyway. The other two dancers were slimmer, but Gilette stole most of the applause. Jamaicans love heavy women. I think they see it as a sign of affluence.

I remember one time in Kingston when I was heading out of the airport to board a little plane. One of the ground crew ran up to me and said, "Mmmm, how come you're so fat?"

I knew he thought he was paying me a compliment, but I was furious. I spat back at him, "How come your mama never taught you any manners?" He laughed uproariously, which made me even angrier. I'm older now and if the situation came up again I would calmly say, "Honey, if you don't like it, don't look at it."

I wish I was more comfortable with nudity. Last night at bedtime, I was trying to figure out what to do about getting into my nightgown. Devon is sixteen years old. I'm a large breasted white woman who is concerned about his libido. I realize that families who live in one room dress in front of each other all the time, so he may not think anything of it. On the other hand, it just may cause some problems.

What to do? I realized that I would be terribly uncomfortable undressing and dressing in his presence. And I soon realized that he wasn't about to leave the room. I was so grateful that I happened to bring along a huge, long, baggy nightgown. It turned out to be the answer to my prayers. I threw it over my head and used it for a dressing room.

Bibsey has a chamber pot under her bed. She and Devon pull it out and use it during the night. Of course I was too self-conscious to do that, so I snuck out to a tree last night to relieve myself. I tried to be quiet, yet managed to awaken them. Bibsey insisted that I learn to use the chamber pot. They think it's very funny that I'm embarrassed about normal bodily functions. That makes me even more embarrassed. Yes, I am embarrassed to be bare assed in their presence. Enough said. From now on, I'll make sure I don't drink anything in the evening. That should solve my problem.

Funny what I'm learning about myself on this adventure. Guess it's not all spiritual, ha-ha.

By the time I woke up this morning, Devon had gone off to school, so Bibsey and I got dressed and headed down to her father's house in Race Course. After standing at the bus stop for a few minutes, I asked Bibsey how far we were going. When I found out that it was only about a mile, I suggested we walk.

It seems that Bibsey normally walks there, but once again she was looking out for me. She knew my feet were blistered. I assured her that they were healing well and that I preferred walking. I know how Jamaican busses are. We could easily have waited up to one and a half hours for a bus.

The walk was beautiful and Bibsey explained everything we saw en route. Once in Race Course, we turned down a little dirt road, passed a few houses, and found ourselves at the home of Bibsey's father and step-mother. They welcomed me and I soon had two new friends.

Mr. Lindsay is a musician who plays guitar in a band called the Calypso Ticklers. They have played in the United States and Canada, as well as in several major Jamaican resorts. Music is always heard at the Lindsays.

Three months ago while doing a stint at Sans Souci, Mr. Lindsay developed heart trouble. Then while he was off recouping, he developed some kind of infection in his leg. So he has been off work since then.

Bibsey's step-mother has also been feeling ill, so Bibsey's daily routine is to go down and cook breakfast and dinner for them. She also keeps house and does the marketing and laundry. She is glad to be able to help them out and would never think of complaining about it.

I love this modest little home. It has two bedrooms, a living room, a kitchen and a bathroom. Curtains are hung in the doorways. A lot of time is whiled away on the front porch.

Bibsey's dad took me on a tour of the yard, proudly showing me the two chicken houses and all the fruit trees. They have papaya, gungo peas, coconut and bananas. There are cats and dogs frolicking around. What a pleasant environment.

Inside the house are several photographs of the family, as well as several religious pictures. The family is very religious. In fact, the first thing they asked me when they met me today was, "Are you a Christian?"

While I was there, a friend who is also helping to nurse them stopped in. Her name is Ms. Williams. We inevitably began discussing spiritual beliefs and somehow got on the subject of speaking in tongues. I asked her what she thought was really going on when that happens.

"Well, some people, some churches, might say when you speak in tongues you don't speak to mon. You speak to God. But my bible told me if dere's no interpreter, you's to keep silent. Because in odder countries, every country is talking different languages."

"So when people speak in tongues, they don't understand the language?"

"No, no!"

"They can't normally speak the language, but when they get into spirit possession what happens?"

"Dey can't come back and tell you what dey said!"

"So how do you think this happens? Do you think another spirit comes in and talks through them or what?"

"Well, maybe it could. Dey say dey get in spirits. Dey say dey are talking by anodder spirit, because dey are a spirit of God. Can talk into anodder world, in anodder world. Remember, you have God's will and you have Satan's work. Satan can approach you in any situation."

"Yeah, we have to be careful not to be vulnerable. Do you personally feel like you have ever talked to other spirits?"

"Yeah, I hear voices like somebody calling to you or somebody talking to you. You can start to do a ting, and somebody says, 'No, no! You don't have to do it dere!' But you turn back and don't see no one.

"You have a good will and a good mind, you can hear good spirits talk to you. Because a good spirit never tell you de wrong ting. He tell you someting dat right. If you listen to someting dat is not good minded, you can't heed to dat. Temptation is sin.

"I am a different person of de world. I am in de world, but I am not of de world. Dere must be two inner minds working. One will say yes and one will say no. De real tings you know. Dere is a sign in your heart."

I agree with Ms. Williams. "Yes, people have to learn to listen to their spirits. A lot of people don't know how to do that. Why don't churches teach people this very important thing? I believe that parents have an obligation to teach their little children to do this, and to encourage them to do this as they are growing up."

We both start jabbering excitedly here. I finally shut up and listen to her.

"God is dere wid you. He never leaves you alone. Because I was a person who was sick. I walked wid a stick. I never know dat I would come back, dat

I would be able to even move around. And I pray to God and ask him many tings.

"But he said, 'You must go into your closet and pray.' Bible tell you when you is going to pray you must go into your closet and shut de door and pray. Not getting from here and going around dere into dat closet. If you went in dere and you feel de fear, you pray. But where he's talking is here." She points to her heart.

"Because what you say in here, de Devil can't read it. He don't know what you say. God understand. He's a peaceful mon. God is love. He's not deaf and he's not blind. Yes, ma'am, God is good! He's a good, good guy! So your religion, what is it, Catholic?"

"It was. I don't practice Catholic anymore, because the old school nuns raised me on concepts of fear and guilt, not love. I was just a little girl and they would come at me in those scary nun outfits and say, 'Debbie, you go home and obey your parents or you're going to Hell!' Well, why was I obeying my parents?

"They didn't say, 'Obey your parents because they love you and they are going to teach you how to live a good life.' They didn't say it that way. They said, 'You will go to Hell if you don't obey them.' Well, so I went home and obeyed my parents because I was scared not to. And that's the wrong reason! They told me the wrong reasons for things and made me feel guilty about everything.

"They said, 'The more you suffer, suffer, suffer in this world, the better place you'll get in Heaven.' See now, I don't believe that anymore. And this is what they taught me! That's why I don't go anymore."

Ms. Williams responded with, "All right, de bible speak about going to Heaven. It's only who come from Heaven who go back to heaven. Heaven is a prepared place for prepared people."

I asked her what she thinks about the idea of reincarnation. "God says, 'Dis body shall decay and you shall get a new body.' You will have a glorious body in de resurrection and you will be a new person!"

"But do you think you come back in the physical world again and again?"

"Well, in dis world, no. He said, 'He who is earthly shall be earthly still. And he dat is heavenly shall be heavenly still.' We will still live on Earth, but dis earth shall be purified for de people who try to do de will of God. So we're all living in hope. We have love, charity. Do good to odders. God knows. So no one knows God's plan. God knows where we will be. But all you have to do is live perfect. And dere is no perfect!"

I thank Ms. Williams at this point and bid her farewell. She's upset that I'm leaving. "Are you going away? I want to talk more!"

I excused myself and went to find Bibsey. She was out in back, laundering a blouse of mine in a big wash tub. What a sweetheart she is! Race Course doesn't have the water problem that Oracabessa has and the Lindsay's kindly told me that I was welcome to use their shower any time I wanted. I was thrilled and took advantage of it right away.

What a luxury! The last shower I had taken was two days ago at Deedra's. Seeing as it is extremely hot and humid in Jamaica, hygiene is a definite problem for me right now. I'm used to being very clean all the time and in this climate it's really tough to go two days without a shower. There is no hot water here, but just having water available is wonderful! Cold showers feel good in this heat anyway.

Since I never know when and where an opportunity for a shower will crop up, I must carry my bag of toiletries with me at all times. I just carry the basics, soap, shampoo, razor, towel and baby oil. This is an inconvenience that I must put up with. But only by experiencing this can I really understand how these people live.

I also must lug around my tapes, camera and books everywhere I go, because I'm constantly writing and recording. I must be prepared at all times, because I never know what's going to happen in the course of the day.

Anyway, Friday is market day, so Bibsey and I headed out after my shower. I love it here because no one ever pushes me to hurry for any reason. We plan our days as we move through them. The general attitude is, "If we get there, then we get there. If we don't, no problem."

We stood under a shade tree and waited for a bus into town. The teacher and some students from a near by Basic School meandered by. Bibsey introduced me and told Ms. Pottinger that I would like to sit in on a day of school if it was possible. Ms. Pottinger was excited and we made plans for me to go next week.

About fifteen minutes later, we caught a taxi to the market. The mile and a half ride cost JA$1.50. The market is an adventure in itself. It is all open air and has an air of a party about it. People bring their goods and find a spot of land to spread them on.

The first place we headed was to the meat section. Big slabs of meat and animal parts hung all over. A butcher is there to chop up your purchase. It surprised me that I didn't see flies and bugs clinging to the meat. I was concerned about food poisoning since there was no refrigeration. It all looked really gross to me. I seriously thought of becoming a vegetarian, but I managed to act calm and just ask what it all was.

Bibsey had the butcher chop a cow's head in half right in front of me. She took the whole skull, insides and all. I almost lost my cookies, but she was delighted at her find. She told me that it's very good meat, very tender, and also good for your nerves. However, I know when she cooks it that I won't have the nerve to try it!

From there we wandered through the market gathering different fruits and vegetables that were on Bibsey's grocery list for the week. That's always a fun experience. Everyone is always happy and in a festive mood, laughing and joking with one another. I met a lot of Bibsey's friends, including her mother, who has a stall at the market. She is a sweet lady who sells little coconut cookies and candies.

Bibsey took me up to her mother's home, about one and a half blocks away. One of her sisters lives there with her five year old son. They live in a very small, poor, modest home. It doesn't have the frills that the other homes up here have. There is a sign typed and taped to the front door with a prayer on it.

Everyone here seems very religious. One can go into almost any home or store or bar and find religious pictures on the walls. Invariably, along side of them will be a picture or a calendar of a sexy lady in a string bikini, often topless. Another thing that I find amusing is the fact that everybody enjoys filling their homes with plastic flowers, even though there are over three thousand kinds of lush flowers and plants on this small island. Plenty of ceramics and little lace doilies complete the decor.

Laughter is heard ringing over the island as often and loudly as is Reggae. Even though most churches preach against having lots of sexual partners and children by them, the people still do it. They don't worry about it. It doesn't seem to be a part of their personal morals even though the churches try to make it so.

The people go to church and pay attention to other values, such as love and charity and caring for your brother. The other stuff they just seem to toss casually out the window.

When we finished shopping at the market, we went to the grocery store to get the rest of the things on the list. Then we went to the post office to see if either of us had received any mail. We hadn't. I had left this address as a place where I could be reached for a month. I had left no forwarding address after that, since I had no idea how long I would be in Jamaica.

While we were standing in line at the post office, I met one of Bibsey's dress makers who has a little shop right down the street. I decided to have a skirt made, but we needed to go to Ocho Rios to purchase material.

Marie and Chris, friends of Bibsey, saw us standing at the bus stop. They had a car and offered to take us to drop off the groceries and then into Ocho Rios. What a treat, as it is difficult to board a crowded bus with packages. It is difficult enough just to board and find something to hang onto so you don't go flying out of the open doorway as the bus lurches off! The local busses are always extremely overcrowded. It's rare to find a seat. When you're ready to get off, you simply yell, "One stop, driver!" and hope that he hears you over everyone's chatter and boom boxes.

Chris's car was old, dilapidated and had all the signs of a typical Jamaican rattletrap, but the car ran and that's all that mattered! He had put little speakers in the back and had the music blaring so loudly that I couldn't understand anything anybody was saying, even though they were shouting at each other in an attempt to be heard.

Bibsey told me that Chris often doesn't show up when they have plans to do something. This behavior is very common in Jamaica and has always frustrated me to no end. Often times it's simply because people have no telephones and therefore have no way to reach each other if plans need to be changed. But sometimes, something else will come up that they would rather do, so they just do it.

The girls scolded Chris now for so often behaving in such an irresponsible manner. All the way to Ochi, they pounded playfully on him to punish him. Everyone laughed joyously as he careened down the road.

When we arrived in Ochi, I stopped to see my friend Jennifer. I discovered that she is pregnant with her fourth child. Her husband, Donovan, is in Puerto Rico, but is expected back soon. These people are very special to me and we had a wonderful reunion.

Donovan and Jennifer own a tour company called Holiday Services. They worked hard for this and have developed several magical day long excursions around the island. I used to sell the tours to my clients and often went on them myself. The experience never got old for me.

Jennifer told me now that their business was hurt quite a bit by Hurricane Gilbert. They had to shut down completely for three months, which really put a strain on them because they have a new home. And, of course, the bills kept coming in. Jamaicans never give up and even though it's a struggle, Holiday Services is getting back on its feet. I will pray for them.

The fabric shop was fun. Most of my skirts are shorter and more fitted than is comfortable for my gypsy lifestyle. I wanted something light weight, mid-calf length and full. For $4.00 US, I got just what I wanted.

From there, we went over to the patty shop. Patties are hot pastries filled with spicy meat or vegetables. I'm quite addicted to these goodies and always amazed at the price. They cost about .25 US.

Back at Bibsey's later, we rested up for another night at Helsinki's. I was too tired to enjoy myself much, but went anyway, as Bibsey and Sunshine were wound up and ready to play. It's 12:30 and I'm ready for sleep. Good-night, Jamaica.

Saturday, January 20

After pleasant dreams I opened my eyes, feeling loved and secure. Bibsey was standing before me, about to tap me on the shoulder. She handed me a plate with scrambled eggs, a hot dog, tomatoes and bread and butter. When I thanked her and commented on how kind she is, she smiled and said, "Debbie, there is nothing I wouldn't do for a good friend!"

The kitchen of the house is started, but as of yet it is only half built. It consists of a small stone frame. Inside is a little pot filled with coal. This is where all the cooking is done. The food is kept in the main room.

I must admit that breakfast tasted fabulous. Bibsey is always taking care of me. She's always worried that I'm not getting enough to eat, but I have far more than enough. One thing I've come to realize is that we normally eat a lot more than we need.

I would really like to eat just fruit for a few days, because I desperately need to lose some weight. Everywhere I go, people are telling me how fat I've gotten. I knew this would happen. Every time I come to Jamaica I hear this. Jamaicans tell it like it is.

I do feel in good health, though. However, my joints are swollen up. I don't know what from, possibly the heat and humidity. I'm sure it's nothing to worry about. Other than that, I've been eating fruit, patties, salt fish, things like that.

It becomes easy for me to understand our Oneness with the Universe when I think about eating. For example, just follow the process through. A seed needs the earth to grow. It becomes a vegetable. We need the vegetable to grow. And so forth.

Sunshine and Bibsey are Seventh Day Adventists and attend services on Saturdays. I decided to go with them today, as church here is always an adventure. I thought my clothes looked fine for church. Wrong. Sunshine insisted that I bring my clothes over to her house and iron them crisply first. Bibsey wanted me to wear a pair of her dress sandals and even went so far as to tie them on my feet for me.

Bibsey wore a beautiful gold brocade dress and fancy stockings. The stockings were once panty hose, but the top of them had been cut off. They had black velvet butterflies on the sides, with rhinestones climbing up her legs in between. Bibsey had to tie the stockings up with shoelaces. As we walked to church, the stockings kept sliding down to her ankles. She was undaunted and would just stop walking, hike up her dress, and re tie the stockings onto her ample thighs.

All the ladies wore high heels. It had recently rained, but they thought nothing of traipsing through the thick mud across the church yard. I find it very strange that earrings are not allowed in this church either. I mean, it would make sense if all the other frills were also banned, but it seems that only earrings are thought of as sinful temptation to men.

Sunshine looked lovely in her pink outfit and hair ribbon. Even though it was a hot day, she wore a white jacket over her blouse. I guess looking proper is more important than being comfortable.

The church has been half finished for years. It's basically a stone shell with no windows in it. At service today, they talked about having a fund raiser so they could put a toilet in there somewhere.

The service usually runs from about 9:15 to 12:15, but it went on until 1:00 PM today because they had a special guest speaker. There were a lot of sermons and singing, but it was a quiet, mild ceremony compared to the one I went to last week in Rose Heights.

Five different people got up and spoke. The overall theme for the day was 'Help us to see ourselves in a new spiritual awareness, as we never have before.' One person spoke about 'Brother Holy' and 'Sister Holy', people who think they are holy simply because they go to church. Another person implored us to "Take time to see yourself as you really are."

There is something that bothers me personally about all the churches I've been to. They seem to separate God from us, giving the impression that God is perhaps beside us. I believe that God is within us. Focusing on this makes me conscious that I have to take responsibility for my thoughts and actions. I wonder how people can grow if they can't perceive the reality of this. These people all seek spiritual truth, but I don't see how they can find it when they separate it from their own soul. People need to feel God within them and listen. Then all truth will be revealed to them.

After church, we stopped at Sunshine's for cake and a wonderful mixture of orange juice and lemonade. Sunshine's boyfriend also works on a cruise ship and sends her money. She is relatively well off for a Jamaican. She has a TV, VCR and electricity. Every Jamaican home that I have been in has been immaculate. It seems they are always cleaning.

It's also rare to be in Jamaica and not hear music coming from somewhere. Every night the tree frogs sing me to sleep and every morning the roosters wake me up. It's so lovely! There's something about the heat and the lushness of the tropical vegetation, the way it sways in the soft, fragrant breezes. It creates a very sensuous mood, relaxing, hypnotizing. I have such a sense of truly belonging here. Could I have lived here in a past life?

This afternoon was so pleasant. We walked over to Bibsey's Dad's house and visited them. They were aware of my need to spend some time alone writing, so they made me some hot soup and gave me a cozy little room to rest in. The rain gods were drumming loudly on the roof, enchanting me with their song. I curled up, feeling totally at peace. I had journeyed far, but found heaven.

Sunday, January 21

Bwoy! I can feel humidity clinging to everything, even the pages of my journal. I'm trying hard to monitor my diet so I can transform my body into the slim, healthy one that I want to have. It's amazing how very little we really need in order to sustain ourselves. Right now I feel in tune with my body and the universe.

I spent the afternoon at the beach, swimming in the soft, warm sea, meditating and reading. Bibsey and I were supposed to go to a Pocomania ceremony tonight, but she said she was too tired. She wouldn't let me go alone, and kept me from trying by refusing to give me directions. I'm extremely disappointed. I'm sensing that most of these people are somewhat frightened when it comes right down to attending a Pocomania ceremony. They offer to take me because they know how important it is to me. But they really don't want to go, so at the last minute they find some excuse not to. I think in their hearts they don't feel comfortable about the kind of spirits being invoked at such ceremonies. Oh well, if I am meant to get to one, I'm sure it will happen.

Only by living day to day can I hope to understand life here. Time doesn't really exist for me now. It doesn't need to. Strange, but it's a good life.

Monday, January 22

What a perfectly wonderful day this has been! It started when Bibsey woke me up waving a plate of dumplings, eggs and coffee under my nose. So much for my fruit fast. But it was worth every calorie. How I love my Bibsey! What makes some people so kind and others so selfish?

Later in the morning, I sat and had an interesting chat with Mr. Lindsay on his front porch. I'm amazed at his yard. There is a beautiful pond on it swimming with lily pads. Roosters and chickens run everywhere. My mouth watered as I learned about the various trees in the yard. There is a naseberry tree, a sweetsop tree, a banana tree, a lime bush and a mango tree.

We wandered around to the back yard where Mr. Lindsay pointed out an ackee tree and an almond tree. Bibsey was sitting on a step, bent over a wash tub vigorously rubbing a shirt clean. Her eyes sparkled and she smiled broadly when she saw us. A kitty and dog were keeping her company. Beside her was a box of "Eezee Detergent."

Mr. Lindsay continued the tour. For some reason, Jamaicans call avocados pears. We walked by a pear tree, a breadfruit tree, a coconut tree, a cocoa tree, and a broad bean tree. It seemed endless. There was also a butter bean tree, a jew plum tree, lots more banana trees and to my surprise, there were green and purple grape vines. I didn't know grapes were grown in Jamaica. I doubt if the Lindsays will ever go hungry.

Mr. Lindsay's house, Bibsey and Dad

I did wake up with a nasty cold today. Everyone here is convinced I got it by going barefoot so much. Mr. Lindsay brought out an old liquor bottle, opened it and told me to take a whiff. I got too close, took too big a whiff and let out a yell. It was ammonia! Mr. Lindsay said that whiffing it is good for my cold and I should let him know when I want another whiff. No thanks! But it did clear my sinuses.

I sat down to visit with Bibsey for awhile and learned some things I had not known about her. She was born in Kingston, but much prefers life in the country. I knew about Bibsey's sons Devon, sixteen and Steve, nineteen. Steve works on a cruise ship. But I didn't realize that Bibsey has a daughter, Yvette, who lives in Kingston. Nor did I know that she had a child who was crippled by the age of three due to German Measles. At the age of four, the child died of brain damage after falling off of some stairs. My heart went out to Bibsey, as I am sure that was a very heartbreaking time in her life.

We turned to the subject of duppies. Bibsey said that she doesn't let them cause fear in her, but she can feel when they are around. Mr. Lindsay said he saw one in a dream once.

I told them about the duppy experience I had when I stayed over night at a local place near Ochi called Hunter's Lodge. Three times I opened my eyes and saw the spirit of a man in the room. At first I thought he was a human and I wondered how he got in.

I overcame my fear and got up to go to the bathroom. To my surprise, he was sitting on the edge of the bed when I came out. I boldly asked him what he wanted and why he was there. He got a sheepish look on his face, seemed to slide down the edge of the bed, and disappeared!

By then I was wide awake and terribly excited. I woke my friend up and told him about it, assuming that he would be just as excited as I was. He didn't question the truth of what I said at all, but told me that this is a common oc-currence here. He smiled sleepily and mumbled something about the duppy being jealous of him because he was with me. Then he was sleeping again and I was left alone to think about it.

Bibsey and Mr. Lindsay laughed and slapped their legs in glee. They didn't doubt my story either, but found my reaction incredibly funny.

When I asked Bibsey why Devon didn't go to school today, she smiled mischievously and said that she didn't have bus fare for him. Possibly, but I knew that she also needed him to carry the dirty laundry to Race Course. It's very common here for kids to go to school only off and on. I think it would make teaching a very difficult thing to do. How could one have any structure?

With joy bubbling in my veins, I realized it was time to go the half block over to Wilbert Woodham Memorial Basic School. I had been looking forward to this for a long time. Ever since I first set foot on the island many years prior, I had a dream of sitting in on a Jamaican school. Now it was happening.

Audria Pottinger is the only teacher there. She studied for a year in Port Maria. That is the only qualification she needed for this position. The children are fortunate, because her love for them is deep and genuine. She is a soft spoken, gentle, beautiful young woman, who always seems to have a smile on her face and in her eyes. The children adore her.

The children and chickens were playing in the school yard when I arrived.

Miss Pottinger gathered them all together so I could photograph them. Uniforms are required in Jamaican schools. The girls all wore navy blue jumpers and white blouses. The boys wore khaki shirts and pants or shorts.

Wilbert Woodham Memorial Basic School, Race Course

As I glanced through my camera lens, I had to smile. Two things in particular stood out. One was the brightly colored tams that the little Rasta children wore and the other was a dark wet spot on the shorts of a child who had just peed his pants. What a priceless shot! It captured the beauty and innocence of the day.

Two lines were formed, boys in one and girls in the other, and they marched into the classroom. After singing a thank you prayer, they all sat down and eyed me curiously. Miss Pottinger said, "I see you all looking around at our visitor. This is Miss Melichar and she will be watching you all afternoon, so be on your best behavior."

The school itself is made of cement blocks and is about the size of a double car garage. It has a zinc roof. Although the school is nothing fancy, it vibrated with love. Big charts hung from a clothesline, charts about the weather, counting, our body parts, colors, shapes and pictures the children drew of home and social situations.

One corner is called the 'home corner.' Here the children learn about housekeeping. Another corner is the 'grocery corner.' It looks like a store and here they learn about nutrition, food and shopping. An alphabet hangs on the back wall above the chalkboard.

There are thirty children enrolled in school this year, ranging in age from three to five years. On an average day, attendance is about twenty-eight. They all sit at little tables, about six children per table.

Throughout the afternoon some of the children sat quietly, while others constantly rattled their chairs. One little guy simply refused to settle down and was made to stand in the corner for being rude. He looked so cute I wanted to giggle, but didn't dare. Miss Pottinger focuses her teaching on becoming aware of all of our senses as we grow. Many of her lessons are taught through songs and poetry, which I found to be very effective.

Miss Pottinger and class

I assumed that I was too old to learn anything at Basic School myself, but the children taught me a good lesson in manners. Because of my cold, I found myself coughing all afternoon. Finally a child piped up and was soon joined by the others with this ditty: "It's very rude to cough or sneeze, so you should say 'Excuse me, please!' "

I apologized, excused myself and thanked them for teaching me that. They glowed.

Miss Pottinger smiled, then spoke earnestly, "I'm going to read you a story, but when I talk you must listen. Can your mouth listen?"

I heard a chorus of "Noooooo!"

"That's right! Now show me your ears and listen."

She proceeded to read them a story about animals who had a lesson to teach. Then she taught them to print the letter 'B' and they all drew a picture of a boy. Next, they put their heads on the table for rest period. She called them back by ringing a little bell.

I was amazed when they sang "Ten Little Indians." I assumed that only Americans knew that one. When I asked if they know what Indians are, Miss Pottinger said no. No one thought to ask either.

Another song I liked was one thanking God for their strong hands, strong legs and strong feet. Once again, I realized that it would seem irrational to Jamaicans to leave God out of their lives, schools included. There are several religions on the island, yet no one ever protests bringing God into the public classroom. School ended at 2:00 PM, but before the children were dismissed, I played back my tape of them singing. They all giggled in pure delight and gathered around me with questions. I thanked Miss Pottinger before I left and signed her guest book.

The children picked up their little backpacks and ran out jumping and laughing and hollering. Right then I was also five years old and I longed to join them in their play. I felt ecstatic, surrounded by all that is good in life.

The neighbors stopped me on the way home to ask if I had enjoyed my afternoon. A lady told me that her daughter is in Secondary School and that I must also go and visit there. Her husband was in the yard chopping open jelly coconuts and he kindly offered me one. We had a good chat. With a sense of wonder, I realized that the whole world feels like home to me, and everyone feels like family. I'm very happy to be a part of the human race.

Bibsey greeted me at the door and handed me a drink made from fresh squeezed lime. I was very thirsty and it was like nectar from heaven. Once again, I marveled at her kindness, and vowed to be a better hostess myself when I return to the States.

The house smelled delightful. Bibsey took me to the kitchen to show me what she was cooking. Three big pots boiled on the stove. In the first was beef, beans, onions, thyme, black pepper, garlic powder, soy sauce and water. She said the beef and beans are important sources of protein. The second pot contained chocho, green bananas, yams, Irish potatoes, pumpkin, dumplings and water. Calalu is good for high blood pressure, and was the main ingredient in the third pot. It was combined with onions, tomatoes, dried salt fish from Canada, black pepper, cooking oil, butter and water. What a feast!

After dinner, we did the dishes and then sat on the porch for a while, reading and visiting. Our walk home later was peaceful and lazy. We stopped here and there to chat with neighbors. What a great feeling not to be rushing all the time.

Later: It's 10:45 PM. What is happening? I feel so transparent. I feel like I'm floating somewhere between the physical world and life after physical 'death.' I'm not fully in either dimension, just floating between. It's sort of eerie, and yet I'm really not frightened. I've given myself to the spirit guides and I trust them. My body is not fully mine now, but just a channel for them to work through. I am listening to them, and to all the forces around me... nature... other people... powerful spirits here in Jamaica.

Tuesday, January 23

Bibsey woke me up at 6:30 this morning. It monsooned as we dressed. I longed to climb back into bed and enjoy the storm from there, but Bibsey kept assuring me that it would soon be over. Sure enough, by the time we were walking down the hill the sky was turning very blue and was lit up by a huge rainbow. What a magical treat!

Amazingly enough, we were able to catch a taxi immediately. It was an old station wagon with ten people already crammed in. The driver was humorous. He told me that he'll always love me even though a lot of people don't like my kind (white).

In Ochi we had to transfer to a minivan for our ride to Duncans. While people were piling in, the early morning vendors came up to the windows selling peanuts, ginger beer, Wriggley gum and banana chips. It turned out to be a luxury trip because there were only seventeen people and their luggage and chickens in this fifteen seater van. I've counted up to twenty-nine people in such a vehicle at one time.

At 8:50 AM we arrived in Duncans. I heard my name being called as I got out of the van. The voice was coming from a Rastaman named Roy who used to sell ganja and wood carvings across the street from Trelawny Beach

Resort. He had with him today, a detailed carving of a Rastaman that he had made. He was here to purchase sandpaper and stain to finish it off.

Bibsey and I are now waiting by the clock tower for my friend Sam, who offered to take us on his route today. He drives a milk truck for Northshore Dairy. It should be fun.

The morning is now bright and sunny, filled with the hustle and bustle of school kids waiting for taxis and people waiting for a lift to nearby towns. Grocery stores are already open, as are fruit and vegetable stands. I can see the little restaurant where Denton took me for dinner the last time I was in Jamaica. Sweet memories. There is a pig marching down the street like he owns it, and goats are all over the roadside. Across the road is a Texaco Station and across from that is "Daily's Tavern and Super-Service Wholesale and Retail Store."

Whoa! Denton just showed up. I spoke briefly with him but he was really nervous because he lives near here and was afraid his woman would show up. She heard I am around and has her fangs out. I said, "For Pete's sake Denton, I'm no threat to her! Why don't you stand up for yourself?"

He said he told her that, but she doesn't listen. She knows I'm here and she's out for the kill. I think it's hysterically funny. I can't help it. I'm astonished that this woman seems to have so much control over Denton. What happened to him? Jamaican men always rule the roost. Yet I can tell that he's actually frightened of her. Maybe she is an obeah woman.

I didn't want to cause trouble for him by being seen with him, so we quickly made plans for him to come to Mo-Bay when I go back. There we can talk freely. Strange, but long ago, when I loved him deepest, I saw all of this happening in a dream or something.

I still feel a pull around him, probably just because of our memories. It always hurts to have to let go of something you cherish. I know without a doubt that Denton really loved me. I don't know how he feels now. I feel that perhaps his mind was poisoned by this woman and after a while he succumbed to it. I don't think he could see long range.

Now I'm trying to face honestly my own feelings. I truly did hold in my heart the ideal that if I made enough money I would've come back to him and tried to set us up in a business. I think he quit believing this. I know he has an unrealistic view of America and the material wealth there. It's not shared equally by all.

Anyway, my dreams dimmed when his letters stopped coming. And when I received a letter from his new woman, (who I didn't even know existed), I knew with certainty that I would never give the relationship another chance. She had found one of my letters under their mattress. When she found out that I had plans to return to Jamaica, she wrote me a rather illiterate, scathing, vile letter calling me, among other things, a white harlot. She told me she would be looking for me and would kick my face when she found me. The hate and anger contained in the letter almost knocked me over. It felt as if she was right in the room with me, not off in another country. Enclosed in her letter was the letter she found that I had written. She had set fire to it and it was mostly in ashes.

I understand now that I knew only one side of Denton. In truth, I know very little of what it takes to survive here, and how that builds the stamina and values and character of the people. I guess I feel like I just need to resolve this. I need to hear directly from Denton what happened, so I can bring it to closure.

More and more I'm thinking that I must have been here in another life. Too much has always seemed too familiar. Yet whenever I climb outside of myself and look down, I see someone who isn't Jamaican and won't be while in this body. So, I am growing, moving on, although I still need to understand that elusive "thing." It is important.

When will it happen? Maybe it's already happening and I just don't know it yet. I do know one thing. I don't want to spend the rest of my life longing for it.

10:20 AM: Sam just pulled up in his milk truck. He told us that the dairy in Kingston is on strike so there is a great milk shortage. Because of that, his route had been cut short and he only had two more stops to make for the day. He felt bad and offered to take us another day. Sweet man.

So Bibsey and I hopped a taxi to Trelawny and are now eating jerk chicken at the Country Club. It's located across the street from Trelawny Beach Resort, where I used to live. The Country Club is one of my old hang outs. I love the name because this Country Club is nothing like the ones in the States. This is open air, no frills, laid back and open to the public. It's a fun place to relax and everyone here is very friendly.

Bibsey told me that everyone in Duncans was staring at me oddly, wondering what I was writing. All of Jamaica will think me odd before I leave. Good thing I've got a sense of humor.

Ahhh, jerk chicken... so yummy, so, so hot and spicy. I ate only a few bites. I must be careful, as I haven't eaten much in these past few days. But jerk food is so tasty that the flavor of one bite can linger deliciously for a long time and be very satisfying. Yes, it's good to be home.

This quest of mine is a combination of great spiritual revelations and also a taste of heaven on earth. It's like being in the Garden of Eden before the downfall of Adam and Eve.

I noticed several improvements had taken place at the Country Club. George, the owner, told me that Gilbert had done a lot of damage, but due to the radio, they had been forewarned and were able to remove all the food, liquor, etc. ahead of time.

George has a typical Jamaican attitude. Instead of crying about his loss, he saw this as an opportunity to make the place even better than it was before. The old thatched roof had leaked for a long time. I noticed it has been replaced with a solid wooden roof. The attitude of Jamaican people has always been a source of inspiration to me, especially when I face a big challenge. I see that attitude as a gift to all of humanity.

We finish eating and head down the road. The parish of Trelawny is one of the poorest in Jamaica, yet one of my favorites because of its primitiveness. It feels like a jungle to me. There's a lot of dense brush everywhere and the trees are totally covered with vines and flowers. I don't know why, but something about it is very erotic to me. It's so wild, so natural and beautiful, causing my body to pulsate and dance in a rhythm all its own. It takes me back to the source of myself, to my very essence. Aha, so that's why I'm so drawn to this place! The pieces of the puzzle are starting to fit together.

We walk a bit further, amid huge magenta colored flowering bushes. The colors are so intense that I can actually see them vibrating. Oh! We just turned onto the little road which leads to Burwood Beach and the sight took my breath away. The contrast is dramatic. There are dark stormy skies moving above bright aqua seas, which are shimmering in sunlight. This evokes intense emotion within me. I see several brilliant colors in the sea.

We just passed through a field of grazing cows, and then by a little pond with birds bobbing on the water. Some men are jerking pork over a pit. I know that if we turn right and walk a little ways, we will find some very primitive huts where the local fishermen live. I feel like I'm dreaming, and I don't want to wake up.

Sometimes I wonder. Is this Earth life merely a dream? We so often only see what we want to see. There is so much more. Sometimes we wake up and understand that. And sometimes when we do wake up, then we think we're dreaming. It seems strange to me when people speak of reality. To me, everything is reality. How could it be otherwise?

Later: I'm doing a little experiment here. I've had a few Dragon Stouts (dark Jamaican beer), and I want to see how it affects my perceptions. Actually, I want to stop being so serious for a while. I've become too wrapped up in trying to discover the meaning of our existence. It has almost become an obsession, and I need to find some balance and ground a little.

I always feel like I could live my life on this beach. Why? I can be perfectly content just BE-ing here. It's a state of peace, bliss. I can't imagine wanting anything more from life than I have here. I took a long swim in the warm, soft, clear sea. Then, I just sat and visited with old friends.

Life here is elusive in a way that it isn't in most places. It takes me to a part of myself that I know exists, yet I am unable, at this point, to grasp exactly what is happening. Again, I ask why? Is a certain reservoir of spirit released here? Is it a doorway to the beyond? I don't ask these questions in jest.

Sonny is wearing a ripped T-shirt that says, 'Lifeguard' on it. He has an orange whistle around his neck. Anyone walking down the beach would live in the illusion that he actually is a lifeguard. And he wants them to. But those of us who know him, know that he can't even swim. I ask myself what lesson I can learn from this.

My lesson is that things are often not what they appear to be when we view them from the physical eye. That is why it is so important to develop our intuition and learn to trust it. When we look through the eye of our spirit, we have a much clearer perception of what is really going on. It makes sense that it is to our advantage to do so.

Later still: I had to go to the bathroom, so I headed down the beach to Trelawny Resort, an all-inclusive. I knew that if I acted like I knew what I was doing no one would question my being there, because I am white and looked like a registered guest. It was easy, since I had lived there for eight months when I was a tour Rep and I was familiar with the property.

It started pouring as I headed up the walkway. I didn't want my notebook and tape recorder to get wet, so I started running. What happened next was a nightmare! I slipped and fell flat on the hard pavement. I had a bottle of Red Stripe beer in my left hand and it smattered under me, cutting my third finger deeply. I was terribly embarrassed and scrambled madly to pick up the debris.

Suddenly I heard, "Debbie, are you okay, dear? Oh, you must go to the nurse!"

To my horror, it was Ms. White and Mr. Fairweather, two prominent people on the resort staff. They made a huge fuss over me, but what really shocked me is that they acted like they thought I still lived there! I had been gone for close to two years.

Well, I was in a pickle. I thought that if I went to the nurse it would be discovered that I'm not staying there, and really, I had no right to even be on the property. I wrapped my finger in a napkin and insisted I was fine. But when I got into the bathroom, I admitted to myself that I wasn't.

The gash in my ring finger was about three fourths of an inch long and very deep. It was bleeding profusely. I swallowed my pride and went to the nurse, knowing full well that if I didn't I may end up in the hospital. I've been to Jamaican hospitals, and I'm not exaggerating when I say they can be terrifying. The hospital in Falmouth often has no doctor there, and no bedding is provided so you must bring your own.

While working as a tour Rep, I developed conjunctivitis. I had never had anything like it and I was miserable. My sinuses were swollen. I coughed constantly and I couldn't see because my eyes were swollen almost shut. Everyone laughed and assured me it was just pink eye and would soon go away. But it didn't. I was advised to do things like rub my face in the morning dew, and stare directly at the sunrise. I finally got some medication, which didn't help either.

After three weeks of this, I was so afraid of going blind that I was willing to risk losing my job. I called up the big boss in Chicago and didn't ask for a flight home, but told her that no matter what she said, I was going home to have it taken care of. She allowed it. I walked into the office of an eye doctor in Janesville, Wisconsin and within thirty seconds he had diagnosed me correctly and given me proper medication. I was so very grateful.

That experience came to mind now and I felt sick with fear. I was honest with the nurse about my situation. She was very kind and assured me that I wouldn't get into trouble.

As she cleaned my finger with hydrogen peroxide and bandaged it up, I chided myself for drinking that much beer. That'll teach me! The nurse was insistent that I go see a doctor and get a tetanus shot. She also advised X-rays and sutures. She said the little tendons and muscles might be cut and that my finger could be paralyzed for life if I didn't have it properly attended to.

As I headed back down the beach, I passed Denton and another long time friend of mine, Freddy. I did a double take. Freddy had always had dreadlocks down to his waist. He was now a baldhead! When I asked him about it, he said that it's easier to deal with society without the locks. He has come to believe that his true power comes from within, not from his locks.

I have such fond memories of these people. Denton, Freddy, another friend named Chubby Checker, and I used to take bamboo rafts down the Martha Brae River at night. We'd carry drinks and fish and stop along the shore to cook and dance. One of my favorite photos is of Chubby dancing with my boom box balanced on his head.

My finger is numb and hanging like a dead organ on my body. How interesting that I hurt my left hand, because I am left handed. Did I do this subconsciously so that I would have an excuse to give up on this project?

Well, I won't give up. I'm grateful to have my tape recorder. I'll rely almost totally on that for a while. I think I had better rest and read for a few days, so that I can allow my finger to heal.

3

DREAMS AND PROPHESIES

"She was going to make dis big fire and was going to boil up and use de blood. Dey was going to give me a bath to take off dose evil tings."

—*Sunshine*

Wednesday, January 24

I had made up my mind to not go to a doctor, but Bibsey talked me into it. I think I went more to ease her mind than my own. As I was taking a sponge bath this morning before we left, I pulled my back out. Now I'm really a mess physically!

As I hobbled down the road, I noticed that Bibsey seemed very worried. When I asked why, she said, "Well, I just hope the doctor is in today!" I discovered that he doesn't keep regular hours at all. Besides practicing in other villages, he runs a coffee shop near Tower Isle and is also a farmer. So it's hit and miss as to when one will be able to see him.

Luckily for me, the doctor arrived at 10:45 this morning, the same time we did. There were six people waiting ahead of me, so I took a number and sat down. The medical clinic is in Race Course and consists of a waiting room, two dressing rooms and two doctor's rooms. The waiting room was very clean and had a fan, which helped a lot in the intense heat.

An hour later I was called into Dr. McGill's office. When I told him what had happened, he was adamant about giving me a tetanus shot. I resisted at first, not wanting to spend the money. I asked him to explain what tetanus is. When he did, I embarrassed myself by crying like a big baby. The thought of getting lockjaw frightened me so much that I felt like I was going to faint. I realized that when the body weakens, everything else does too. I was no longer the fearless rebel I had been when I boarded the plane two weeks ago.

Part of what had held me back from getting the shot was my fear of Jamaican medicine, but once I learned how prevalent tetanus is in the tropics, I agreed immediately to have the shot. Dr. McGill was so very kind, so fatherly. He said gently, "Oh, my dear, don't cry. Don't cry! It's okay."

I felt humiliated and stupid behaving like a two year old, but the child in me had emerged, and I meekly turned over my trust to the doctor. He checked my finger and said he didn't think the tendon was cut. On one of my other fingers he showed me where the tendons are. He thinks the numbness is caused by the trauma it went through. He told me that if it doesn't heal right, then I can have surgery on it when I return to the States. I knew that wasn't a possibility, as I, like so many, can't afford health insurance.

He implored me to not worry about it all. He saw no need for sutures, but cleaned and covered the wound, advising me to keep the finger elevated for three days and not change the dressing until then.

The whole visit cost me $120 JA, which is about $19 US. I was in his office for over an hour. You can't even look at a doctor for $19 in the States!

As I was walking down the street this afternoon, a young man came up and joined me. He was from Boscobel and had been working as a wine steward at the Sheraton until recently when he was in an auto accident. He is still off recouping. I lived at the Sheraton in Ochi for a long time while repping and I had worked at Boscobel Beach, so we had a lot in common. He seemed anxious to return to his job and told me he really loves to work.

I found Terrance amusing. He told me he loves white people. "I likes white people for many reasons. White people, dey communicate togedder. And white people, one third of white people, dey are intelligent, and next ting, dey keep up enough to stand dere own responsibility. You know? Jamaican watch each odder. Jamaican don't give you a chance to make a dollar. White people don't do dat!

100

"Yeah, white people, dey are unique person and tell it genuine, genuine, genuine! And a white mon have a car and he pass you on de street, he would give you a ride very easily. And black mon pass you, you know. He don't see you until he is in danger. Yeah, dat's why I like white people. I work in many hotel and it's white people who get me de job."

We walk on and he says, "You is a fine lookin' lady. Can I ask you, is you married?"

"No. I'm a gypsy. I don't stay in one place long enough to get married."

"Oooooh! Well, I tink it's full time for you to find someone to tink about. You know how many Jamaicans like white? In Jamaica you can really check a lady just like dat, cuz dere's a lot of respect for her. All right, in Jamaica a job is very hard to get. And if you get a job, you get $150 JA a week. If you buy a shirt, dat's gone!

"Yeah, and food is expensive! Jamaican woman don't work as nice. Dat's two hands dat work light. If I worth $50 and my girlfriend worth $10, dat's $60, so I don't keep a Jamaican girl. Yeah, I love white people cuz white people let my country run."

I cringed with shame, although he didn't know it. These white people that he thinks so highly of expect him to work forty to sixty hours a week for $25 US. And women, simply because they are women, earn almost nothing. It makes me furious! I feel like Jamaicans are sorely taken advantage of by many of the American and Canadian resort owners The resorts couldn't function without Jamaicans. Oh well, in time the tables will turn and all the greedy people will have to answer for their behavior.

Terrance and I talked a bit more about our lives. After a while, I bid him farewell and went home to rest.

The remainder of the day was spent resting and doing an emotional cleansing. I faced the fact that I had not really let Denton go the way I told myself that I had. I confronted the pain and sense of loss today, allowing myself to cry it all out. I honestly didn't expect seeing him to be so painful after all this time.

I allowed myself to think back. Even then, I knew that I could not spend the rest of my life on that little beach with him. I needed to develop my talents and contribute something back to life. The hard fact is that opportunities simply are not here. I would've had no job, no money for anything. Love wasn't enough. I had to say good-bye. By this time, Denton had decided that

I had betrayed him. He'll never know how close I came to marrying him and staying on that little beach.

I don't know what I'm doing here now. Maybe I just came to let go. In a way it seems like we have thrown away something of great value. I need to work through this.

On reflection: Am I being hypocritical? I keep stressing how I hate the way people in the States put the pursuit of money above the pursuit of happiness. It appears to me now that that is what I have done with Denton. I just couldn't accept the total poverty. Even now, I feel confused about this, somewhat ashamed. It hurt me not to be able to help him. I'm struggling financially myself all the time just to make ends meet. But the hard reality is that we in America do have vast opportunities compared to most Jamaicans. I know I let him down, but I would've gone crazy in the long run. I'm so sorry, Denton.

I had a wonderful surprise Tuesday night. A friend named Milton, who I hadn't seen in years, showed up for a visit. I dated Milton when I lived in Ochi. He was a waiter at Plantation Inn, a very posh resort. The job required charm and good manners, and these he also carried with him into his personal life.

Milton worked hard for several years and eventually built a beautiful little home way up in the mountains. It's an extremely tranquil place. To get there, one could only drive so far, then had to park and walk across a swinging rope bridge which hung over a river. From there, it was a short hike to his home. I can't imagine how he transported supplies when he was building! Persistence had to play a major role.

Whenever I think of Milton, one thing immediately pops into my mind. He used to constantly shake his head, click his tongue on the top of his mouth and say, "Debbie, whatever you do, expect the unexpected!"

I enjoyed our visit and went to bed feeling really tired. I must be adapting to my environment because I finally got over my shyness and used the bed pan last night. I had to go so bad I didn't care who was there!

I have one more reflection now, before I go to bed tonight. People here are so kind. I know I've said it before, but it truly is a way of life for them. I don't know why I fight so hard to cling to my independence and my belief that I don't need anybody, that I don't need anything. That's not true. I'm seeing that sometimes I have trouble being honest with myself. When all this kindness spills over on me, it's a very emotional thing.

Thursday, January 25

Well, I didn't go to bed after writing last night, like I thought I was going to. Instead, Bibsey and I went across the street to Sunshine's house. While they watched "The Karate Kid," I sat on the porch and read.

Suddenly I felt totally lost and I started crying again. I saw my body from above and I wondered sadly what that poor little girl is so frantically searching for. I felt confused about what I was seeking. All I knew was that I grieved for that little girl and wanted to comfort her.

I was still crying when Milton appeared. We sat on the porch and talked quietly for hours. Our conversation was very serious and it was comforting to be able to share my fears and confusion. Milton is very spiritual and I felt tremendous love and compassion pouring from his soul. Although he couldn't fully understand what I was talking about, he did try. Just having him listen was a blessing. Thank you, Milton, for being there for me.

I woke up today feeling so frustrated, that the big old tears made an appearance yet again. Will they ever stop? Not only my finger, but my back also hurts so much. I guess I'm tasting real life Jamaica. It isn't always paradise. My spirits are sort of sagging. I'm already tired of the simple, everyday problems, mainly the lack of opportunity for personal hygiene. And right now, it's worse than ever because I can't get my finger wet. Therefore, I can't do laundry, wash my hair, or swim. I told Bibsey that I'm just going to hibernate and try to heal.

I feel so shocked, not just physically, but emotionally, mentally and spiritually. What am I doing here? Whatever drove me to this wild land where toilets and showers are a luxury? I've only been here a few weeks and I'm already so tired of feeling grimy all the time, and of living with mice and roaches. I know that I am part of all of nature, and an energy force just like everything else, so I'm trying not to feel bothered by the rodents. But they don't feel good around me.

I still can't bend my finger, although it doesn't hurt so much now. My back makes me feel crippled when I move. I'm dizzy and my stomach is upset.

And I feel so all alone. I'm sitting in the open doorway to Bibsey's room, looking out on the side of a hill. Among other plants and trees here are breadfruit and coconut.

Every time I try to speak I burst into tears. What is happening to me?

I'm beginning to think this book will be simply a transcription of tapes, "Conversations with Joe Jamaica." Right now, everything is so vague.

Why do I always have to challenge myself to the limit? Does my life really have any direction besides the pursuit of spiritual awareness and advancement? Right now I can only describe myself as in limbo. I'm floating, not really of this world, yet not totally beyond it either. I'm lingering in the doorway, trying to find a balance.

I cannot be content to do something simple. First and foremost, I want to help mankind, but I don't know if I can put my program together. I always seem to get just so far and then dead end.

It turned out that my day wasn't going to be spent alone after all. A beam of Sunshine filtered over to me and lifted my spirits. This is the day I really got to know Joan. Her pet name, Sunshine, fits her like a glove. I had to laugh at how eager she was to tell me about herself. Her enthusiasm was contagious and refreshing. Yes, just what the doctor ordered. Sunshine helped me get up off the pity pot.

A dynamic woman who always seems to be smiling, Sunshine is of medium build and height and has straight black hair and somewhat oriental features. When I turned on my tape and asked her about her childhood I thought she would never come up for air. She jumped from one thing to the next almost faster than I can think.

"I was born in de parish of St. Mary. My parents are from St. Ann. We were living in Port Maria. My father was an overseer for an estate. When we were small, we used to have lots and lots of fun because we had this big place all to ourselves. There were lots of fruit trees and stuff and we would climb them, especially me. I was a tomboy!

"And we would go swimming in de river. After school, we would hide and go down to de river and take off our clothes and swim and have lots of fun. And I would go fishing. I been swimmin' since I was three. I remember I saved five person's lives. Yeah! I was quite young den, maybe twelve, thirteen.

"Den after I leave Port Maria, I went to Kingston to school, to Norman Manley School. I do athletics, five gold medalists. I was a sprinter. I run mainly short distance, a hundred meters, and I throw de shot put and do de discus and I do karate. I still go to de gym and practice occasionally.

"I'm a very fun lovin' person. I love outdoors. My hobbies are reading, swimming, and I like dancing and going to movies. I like to meet interesting people, people who talk about reality, inspiring tings, right? Dat's de type of company I really like to keep. But matter of fact, I'm just a social person who like everybody and love kids. I have a daughter. She's very beautiful. I'm sorry you didn't get to meet her. She was here Friday. She goes to school in Kingston.

"And well, I like men, but nice ones. I like men who is straight forward, men who speak de truth. I love de truth! As soon as I find out you're a liar, I hate you! You have to speak truth no matter what.

"If dere's a problem and you come and say, 'Joan, well I did someting wrong and I'm sorry about it," I forgive you same time. But if you let me find out about it widout you telling me, I'd be so angry. I'd hardly find it in my heart to forgive you. It would be a very long time before I'd forgive you. I'd be soooo mad! In fact, I don't like people use me and I don't use people, okay?

"Next ting about it is dat I'm a very religious person. I like de Adventist Faith and I go to all de churches. It's very inspiring. I believe in God and I believe in love, because dey say de word is love, and love is God. Widout both of dem I tink you are nutting.

"I'd say my life ambition is to be a writer. I even started a novel. I reach about four to five scripts and den because I was involved in sports and it take up a lot of time and exercise, and den, being so young now and so pretty, so giddy, and I like flirting a little, well I just say I can't bodder wid dat. Dat is for when I get old. You sit down and write at your typewriter, start writing about your past life. But I still have it in mind, you know. If I should migrate, I tink I'm going into writing.

"I read a lot. I used to write a lot of poems. I would go outside and I would look at de grass and de trees and I would just put dem togedder and come in wid a poem."

Sunshine told me that she thinks her mother accidentally threw out all of her writing. She said that she loves to help children learn. She helps them with homework, reads to them and helps them understand a thought. She had a dream of pursuing a medical career, but didn't have the money to do it.

Nutrition also interests her. She said that she would be a vegetarian if Jamaica had as many fruits and vegetables as the States does. Jamaica does. I began to see a pattern here. Sunshine has lots of dreams, and equally many excuses why she can't make them come true. I began to think she is doing exactly what she wants to be doing. Maybe she can't even see that. She also used her age as an excuse for not being able to pursue her dreams. She's only thirty.

I had to smile. Sunshine has already provided me with many reflections. I think we can do anything we want in life. We allow our fears and laziness to become limitations. What we think, we become. If we put out an idea and then cancel it out with a negative belief about that idea, then of course we'll never achieve it. We're back at square one. We drive ourselves crazy doing this and eventually label ourselves as failures. Our self esteem goes right down the tubes.

Since everything is first a thought, we must take responsibility for our thinking. We must hold the belief that we can achieve our dreams. Our subconscious accepts, literally, everything we tell it. Why not feed it and nourish it with what we want. It won't happen for us if we keep changing tunes on the radios of our minds. And we wonder why we have so much inner chaos.

Back to Sunshine. "I'd like to travel de whole fifty-two of de United States. Yeah, and maybe go down to Jerusalem and dose places, to see all de history I read about in de bible. And I'd like to go back to school for medicine, writing or drama.

"I'm a clown. I act in a lot of plays and I could make anyone laugh. I still have it in me, you know. Whenever my girlfriends are wid me I would go to a bar or restaurant and I give so much jokes dat everyone say, 'We want to stay wid dis clown! She's such a nice clown.' Yes, dat's de type of person I am really.

"I have a serious side, you know. People like my modder would say, 'Joan, you never get high blood pressure or nervous breakdown because you always clowning around.' Sometimes I like people to tink dat I'm always clowning around, but I do have a serious side, especially when it comes to love or relationship.

"Or, if I like somebody den I like to see dem going in de right direction. I like to see dem doing de right ting. I don't want to know dat you are my friend and you are doing de wrong tings. I like to know dat you are on de right track. And I don't like to see people use odder people or get hurt by odder people. So, well, dat's my views on life. And I'm here, just takin' it easy right now."

I mentioned to Sunshine that I had a really painful backache. She laughed heartily and said, "Maybe you need to have more sex! That's what a Chinese doctor said. He said that people who have backaches need more exercise. Well, I don't know if it's true, because I'm having a backache, too. Maybe we are having de same problem!"

I replied, "Maybe it is true because I can't even remember the last time I had sex! Okay, let's get serious. I want to know how you feel about dreams. Do you remember your dreams?"

"Well, you know someting? I forgot to tell you about dat. Dat's a secret part of my life dat I never told you about. I would say I'm a dreamer. I almost had a dream every night dat I go to bed. And I could say I'm almost like, like I could go out and prophesize.

"Dose people like what are really about in de book, dose Indian people, sorcerers, I knew quite a few of dose people in Jamaica. And especially a very sweet old lady named Kuz. She is de grandmodder of my old boyfriend. Yes, she's a healer. She could tell you anyting. I want to go see her, but it's very far up in de country. I'd have to get a car to go up dere.

"Even last night I had a dream. I dream I saw my modder and she was in de kitchen making dokunue. Do you know what dat is?"

"No, I never heard of it."

"We have a pet name for it. We call it Blue Drawers. You make it wid cornmeal and wrap it in a banana leaf. You mix cornmeal wid milk and you add raisins and currents to it. Den you tie it in banana leaf and boil it. It come out like a little cake. It is very nice when it is cooked.

"I was even planning to make some, and den I dream I saw mummy make some. In dream, I was in de yard and dere was dis mango tree. I pick up a stone and throw it at de mango tree and hit off a mango. Three mangos, as a matter of fact. My brodder pick up two and dey is green. I say to him, 'You go into de house and put dem up to ripe.'

"I have one hidden behind me and he never knew, so I take it to de kitchen now and say, 'Mummy, I have a mango for you.' And she say to me, 'Your mango is green.' I say, 'No, look at it.' And when I look at it, it's all soooo ripe! And she take it and she cut it up in de dokunue dat she made, and she drop all de seed in it. De raisins just come right up and I just take out de raisins and seeds and just start eating de mango seed and I wake up out of my sleep.

"And I remember de dream book told me dat whenever you dream and see your modder, dat's a very good omen in life. It means prosperity and lots of good tings. And ripe food means money, and Tony just called and told me dat he post me $1000! So, I know dat someting good was going to happen.

"I would dream tings. I would go to my bed and I would dream of green lizards and tings. I would wake up and say, 'Yes, I've got an enemy.' I know dat's an enemy when you dream of green lizards.

"And de odder night I dreamt dat I plant de whole house full of roses, and on de street and everywhere. As soon as I plant dem dey start growing up and I wake up and say, 'Yeah, somebody is going to die.' And my Aunt died Thursday.

"Yeah, I have lots of dreams. Sometimes I would dream I see Tony wid girls, and I would listen to everyting dat dey talking. And den I would call him and describe de girls and tell him dere very names. You know, at first he wouldn't admit it, and say I must have heard de news from some people talking. But I dreamed it! And an old lady tell me dat any time dat I put my head on de bed and I see someting before me, dat is exactly what is happening! Yeah, so I believe in dreams and dey are real!

"Sometime I don't remember my dream. Den it happen and I do remember. And sometimes I would be so sad and I would say, 'Oh no! I dreamed dat ting about a month ago or two weeks ago.'

"Almost every night I dream someting. And I get up and sometimes I use dose dreams to guide me. I use dose dreams to guide Tony, too, because most time I dream dat he's in some problem. I'm always de one who is fishing him out.

"Kuz tell Tony, 'Let me tell you someting. All you future lies in dis girl. Anytime if you ever slip, you is going to lose a good ting, because she is always bailing you out.'

"Like de odder night, I dreamt I saw Tony. I was sitting down by dis tree, and dis huge green lizard was dere to take off his arm and I was just in time to grab him and throw him out on de street. Just heave him! And my next door neighbor said, 'Dat's terrible enemy and witchcraft! So you have to tell him to be very careful!'

"Yeah, dreams is real and dey are reality. And de bible said in de last days young ones shall see dreams and old ones shall see visions. Dat's me, I'm a dreamer. I always does dream big, very, very big, you know.

"De big dreams come especially in de morning. And when you open your eyes, it's daylight. One morning I was in bed sleeping, and den I saw dis truck driving, and I saw dis van coming by and it was laden wid people. I was at my modder's house in Port Maria, but it wasn't in Port Maria. De place was like, down in de country.

"And den all of a sudden I feel like some grease was on de road, and de bus just run right up into de truck! And I could hear de scream of de people! And a bright light from de truck shine right into my eyes you know, and I screamed and jumped out of my sleep and woke up and saw dat it was broad daylight and de sun was shining.

"And Tony said, 'What de matter wid you? Why dat screamin' in your sleep?' And I said, 'Someting terrible is going to happen! An accident. I see a lot of people going dead in it and it's down in de country. Turn on de radio! Turn on de radio!

"And him turn on de radio, you know, and I said believe you me, it was about ten to seven, and by seven o'clock de news flash dat a minivan going to Kingston run underneath a truck, killing seven! I say I will never forget it!

"And in de same week, I dream again. Dis time I was at a small island across de sea. I've never been to dis place and I saw dis huge building like a hotel going up. A lot of men working on it and dey was passing buckets to each odder like cement. Dem was on a ladder and I stand up and watch dem. All of a sudden I saw de ladder cut off, you know. And about five or six of de men just come down head way and plunge to de earth!

"And when dey plunge to de earth now, I walk over to dem same time, and dey get up and sit down, shaking dere heads like dis. And I say, 'Modder! Fall like dat and you don't dead?'

"And I wake up and tell Tony about de dream, and I say, 'You know Tony, dose people died. Dose men died.' Because whenever you had a dream dat somebody, like say a car run over somebody and dat person get up and sit down and talking again, dat person died. But if you dream dat dat person died, den dat person don't die! No, no matter when dey meet in an accident, dey surviving if you dream dat dey died on de spot.

"I tink it was about two o'clock news dat day, dis news bulletin came across from some small island, dat dey were working in dis hotel, and de same ladder too, dat I say cut off, yes, half of de building just lopsided wid de men on dem, killing seven of de men on de spot! And I sat dere and I listened to dat. It was small island like Barbados or one of dose.

"After dat, Tony afraid of me, say I'm a witch. Him afraid I put a curse on him. So, I mean I don't like to put a curse on anybody, don't like to tell him anyting I know, because I'm scared it will happen! Cuz almost anyting I talk, it happen!"

A lizard suddenly appears near us and fear is obvious in Sunshine's eyes. She tells me that she has been afraid of them since birth, but doesn't understand why. She said she is not afraid of anything else, such as snakes, rats, scorpions or frogs. She said that many Jamaicans, including Tony, are very frightened of frogs. Then she laughed hard as she told me how she used to chase Tony around the house with a frog and he would go running and scream for her to stop. He would retaliate by chasing her with a little lizard.

I commented that we all have our fears and I wondered what causes them. Sunshine said, "I don't know, because I'm a Gemini, right? I was born de fifteenth of June, in de middle of de year, in de middle of de month. So I don't know why I'm afraid of lizards. Sometimes I will tell myself, 'Joan, you're not afraid of lizards because look how small dem are, and you are big, so why don't you hold dem?' And I would put my hand close to dem and say, 'I am going to touch dis lizard to show dis lizard dat I'm not afraid.' And as soon as dat lizard turn around his head I would go screaming and go like hell!"

We both laugh. "I don't know why I am afraid of de lizard. I don't know if it is a birth sign, if it depends on de time you are born and everyting. I notice most Geminis are afraid of lizards. De fear is terrible!"

"Sunshine, this is such an interesting conversation, because just this morning I was thinking about my own fears. We're all part of this big energy force of nature. I've learned so much from nature, from the trees, flowers, animals and all, and I don't want to be afraid of anything.

"I was feeling bad about myself because I saw a cockroach last night and it bothered me. I wondered why I had this feeling, because if I think logically, I know that these things aren't harmful to me. I am not afraid of lizards though, and you are."

"Yeah, lizards on a whole are harmless, right? But de green lizard and one odder in Jamaica are dangerous. Dey will bite you, especially in dry time. Dey have a saw, de green one, and dey will saw you wid it. So must be careful."

"But you said the green one is also the symbol of an enemy, so are you perhaps seeing beyond just the physical presence of the lizard?"

"Yeah! One night I dreamt I was under dis big tree. When I look up, I see on every leaf of de tree dere was a green lizard, terrible enemies! But den I always conquer my enemies you know. Because every time I look up and my eyes see a lizard it's like dey were hiding from me. And as soon as my eye look at one of dem dey would fell from de tree and drop at my feet and die. About a million lizard drop at my feet and die!

"Dey say when you dream about anyting black, especially black cow, dat's always enemy as well. And I remember a dream about a black cow. I went into dis cow pasture and dis huge, black cow came running, rushing at me! I just jump in de air and start flying!

"Kuz tell me dat when I dream dat I'm flying, it mean a great upliftment in life, prosperity. So, it cool when you dream dat you flyin' mon! Just like when you dream of your modder or of ripe fruit, it's riches and prosperity.

"And I was dreaming like you're going to an orchard where you see a lot of little trees growing up. It means prosperity, too. And what is a very good dream again is if you dream you see a lot of young children, like babies. And I'm always dreaming of dat, you know.

"And last time I dreamed dat I had a baby it was a son. I pick him up and say, 'What a pretty little baby!' And I dream dat my baby was - dat dey had my baby in a bag - like de minute he was born, he swim down in de bag wid de plastic all over it.

"And I said, 'You crazy people! You killin' my baby!' And dey said dat he's already dead. I said, 'No!' And I just grab de bag and burst it in two, and de baby just get right up and sit down in a little red shirt and start playing wid me.

"And I said, 'Look at him who is so sweet and look like him fodder. You wicked set of people! You do not scrape up my baby!' I always dreaming tings like dose.

"But I know dere is some evil force in my life. I can feel it. I know somebody's putting it dere, because as soon as I reach out to grasp and my hand is almost on it, dere would be a problem right dere. I know it, and Kuz tell me de same ting. Dat evil people is always trying to do tings to me, terrible tings, like trying to work in witchcraft and science on me.

"And she said dat I have no luck, especially when it come to young people, especially women and tings like dat. Dey are always envious of me, especially wid my men dat I have and tings like dat.

"Dey always so cruel, and I am so kind. I would give away everyting, even de last piece of clothing on my back. You know, dat's how I'm feeling. But it seems like it doesn't help. So I sort of have to take precaution now. I say I really want to know more about dat kind of ting.

"I want to know what dey are doing and who is doing it. And if dere is a way to stop it, I would like to stop it. But den again, I believe in God so much. And he said dat wid him all tings are possible. Psalm 37 just turn up before my face now. It says, 'Fret not thyself because of evil doers. Neither be thou envious of the work of iniquity because dey shall soon be cut off.' And now is de last days. If you have enough faith and trust in God, no matter what people say dey are doing wid dere witchcraft and iniquities, it won't overcome you.

"If you allow it to overcome you, den it will overcome you! I tink you have to have a lot of willpower and a lot of faith in yourself and de Most High One. Right? Because I know Satan is very, very terrible person! And especially when him have de help from de sorcerers who doing terrible tings like dat.

"So I'm not going to really dwell on dem, because if you really dwell on dem den you're going to be a part of dem. And dey are going to get say, a bypass, so dey can get to you. Because if you dwell on dem you open yourself right up. Dat's de way dey is able to take over you! You understand?

"I believe dat Satan can never overpower de Lord. You can use your bible and de Lord to fight back people who believe in witchcraft and dose spells and tings.

"I don't tink it a very nice ting to do unless it is beneficial to your health. Like den, you are sick and de doctor can't cure you, and maybe someting from a medicine mon could cure you, den I tink it a good ting. It's good if dey can cure you from a sickness dat de doctor cannot cure.

"But if you have a sickness dat de doctor can cure, den I tink it's best to go to de doctor. De lady I was telling you about, Kuz, she don't do anyting evil. She only helps people who needs help. Like if somebody stole someting from you, she could tell you where to find it and who stole it. She said she stop telling dem de name because people would go out chopping off odder people's

112

heads to get dem tings back. Well, I do find dat very fascinating.

"And she said dat I have powers, yeah. She said dat if I just do a little study, like maybe read de books and meditate, den I could do exactly what she's doing. Cuz I have a very strong force field inside. Dat's why it's pulling out all dose dreams and tings. Say if I spend one more day in my modder's tummy I could do de same tings like she's doing.

"She said her powers are a gift. She feel dat her gifts are special and come from God. She deal wid angels. She wouldn't ask you nutting. She would open de bible and she would takes de whistle and blow three times, and den she would just start telling you everyting. She just look in de bible like she reading from it and she would just tell you your whole life story.

"One time Kuz say I need a bath to get dis evil spirit off me. I laugh, but she serious. She say dat everywhere I go dere is huge black mon dat follow me around. She say, 'Someone put spirit on you. It was set. You need a blood bath.'

"I even bought some pigeons cuz she say it's a pigeon I'm supposed to use. She was going to make dis big fire and was going to boil up and use de blood. Dey was going to give me a bath to take off dose evil tings. Although I don't get it as yet, and it's been years, I tink I need it.

"And de pigeons are starting having odder pigeons. I would say dere are about twenty-five birds now! My brodder have dem. And everyday I tell myself, 'You know, I'm going to get dat bath.' And den I don't get it.

"I don't know what to say, but I know she's not telling no lie. She tell me many tings from my childhood, and I wonder how come she so smart. How she know?

"De first time I met Kuz, I was nineteen. Dat is de first time Winston and I were talking and de first time he take me to his home and introduce me to his parents. And he take me over to his grandmodder. And I thought, 'Dis is an old lady you know. It's so amazing!' Winston said, 'Dis is my girlfriend, Sunshine.' Kuz said, 'Hello. How are you doing and how is your little daughter?'

"And I want to tell you, nobody in de family had known dat I had a daughter! Winston's brodder was saying, 'You crazy? She don't have no pickney.' I say, 'No, she not crazy. I have a three year old daughter.' It's only Winston alone had known. And him say, 'How she know? Who tell her?' I say, "I don't know! It is de first time in my life I see her!' And yet she knew. "

113

We talked about trying to find a way to go see Kuz. We would definitely need a car because Kuz lives way up in the mountains, about thirty miles from where we were. Sunshine said that Kuz must be close to one hundred years old by now and may not still be doing readings, but she was feeling an urgent need to go see her. I certainly wanted to meet this incredible woman!

"She don't work on de Sabboth and she don't do dis for a living. She's a genius, you know. She's God-gifted. She doesn't deal wid de devil."

I said, "Her psychic powers are highly developed. My whole family has had psychic experiences. I remember one time when I was little and my brother ran away. My mother was frantic and had no idea where to find him. She got in the car and just started driving. Without knowing why, she went up to a strange house and knocked on the door. And my brother was in there! My mother had no conscious idea what led her there. You can imagine how shocked both she and my brother must've been to see each other! I believe that we all can develop our psychic powers."

"Yeah mon! I want to know what is going on in my life. But de problem is, I know people tends, if dey know dat you go to dose places in Jamaica, dey will tends to say dat you is going to obeah people and so on. So I really don't talk about it. I want to see Kuz now cuz I want to hear someting about a dream I had de odder night.

"I dreamed dat I saw dis girl in my sleep. She was about thirteen. And she come and put her hand on my side, and I opened my eyes and it come real! It wasn't like a dream, right? And she was so pretty. She was like my daughter, Erica, but she was two years older. And she call me Mummy.

"I said to her, 'Who are you?' and she said, 'I am your unborn child.' And I said, 'What???' and she said, 'Yes.' And den I don't remember de conversation we kept up, right? But we were talking for a very long time. De only part dat I remember is dat I said to her, 'So tell me, am I going to have any more children in my life?' And she said, 'Yes, you are going to have a son for Tony.'

"And I said, 'How do you know about Tony?' And she said, 'Yes, I know about Tony.' And I said, 'How soon dat?' And she said, 'As soon as you two tie de knots!'

"Den de night after dat I had a dream dat I was telling Tony about dat dream. But I never really tell Tony about it. I tell Fatty (Bibsey) too, and she say, 'Shine, you must watch dat dream, you know.' "

One time Kuz knew psychically of another dream that Sunshine had had. She repeated it to Sunshine when she saw her, then chided her for telling so many people about it. Part of the dream had been in a language that Sunshine didn't understand. Kuz told her that the man that had appeared to her in the dream was one of the former owners of the house she was then living in.

Kuz said that he loves Sunshine very much because she is never rude to her parents. The spirit follows her everywhere to protect her. Kuz said that the spirit is very vexed because Sunshine talked so much about the dream. He had wanted to give her a hidden treasure, but she should've kept the dream to herself. According to Kuz, the message of the strange language was, when interpreted, 'You should put a flask of rum, a piece of tobacco and a box of matches by the paw-paw tree in your backyard at midnight. And you will get a pint jar full of gold.' Three months later, Sunshine and her family moved away.

"Yeah, so we move out and I saw him, you know. One night I went around de backyard about eleven o'clock. I would always go up dere and sit in de backyard cuz it was near de sea. And you could feel de sea breeze. I would go dere and meditate on dose tings.

"And I was coming back. I alone was sleeping in my room. I never have no boyfriend. Each one of us girls have our own room because it was a five bedroom house. And I go back into my room and sort of doze off a little, and den I feel de presence of somebody come into de room. So I open my eyes and I saw dis little guy. He was so cute, but so short, about three feet short. And he had on dis blue tennis cap wid de initials in de front right here.

"And him come right around de bedside, you know. And I turn my face to de corner, and him bend over like dis and look right up into my face like dat! And I jump up like dis! I sit on de bed and look. And den I don't see him again.

"And I fly out of de room and into my modder's room. And I say, 'Wake up, Mummy! Wake up! I'm not sleeping back in my room alone!' And Modder say, 'Are you stupid? Nobody is dere. You was dreaming.' I say, 'I wasn't dreaming, Mummy! I feel him! I know him dere! And I not going back in dere. You have to send my sister to come and sleep wid me.'

"Everyone was laughing. My fodder had just recently died. 'It's your fod-

115

der you have on your mind. Now go back to bed.' But I wouldn't go unless she send my sister wid me.

"So I get up de next morning and go visit my neighbor, Miss Rosa, who lived here a long time. She know de owners dat used to live here and say dey was very nice people. Dey never have any children. Dey was foreigners from some small island.

"So I describe dis mon and say him wear dis blue tennis cap wid dis white peak and he say he call his name Mr. Frazer. 'Ohhh! Mr. Frazer! Him was de owner for dis place, you know.' So I said, 'Ohhhhhh!!!'

"Kuz tell me it de same mon. She said him always follow me around. Now, if I didn't have dis good spirit wid me all de time, probably I would've come to my death already. Because of bad spirits coming from odder people, just grungeful, suicide..."

I asked, "So Mr. Frazer is dead?"

"Yeah, he dead for years. He was de first set of people to own dis place. Kuz say he love me and dat he was de one who wanted to give me all dat gold. He had it buried in de backyard.

"But I have no luck because I talk about it. Kuz say if I want someting I must not talk about it. I must just get up and do it. But once I talk about it, it hardly ever going to come true because of dis bad spirit dat is here, holding down my ting like dat.

"And den she tell me dat my faith is going to make me whole cuz I have dis great belief in God. She said dat is going to give me a breakthrough when I am older. She said I was going to be rich. And she said dat now I use my money to help people, squander it not, and people trick me in witchcraft. She tell me I'm going to live to be very old and get very wealthy. And anodder gentlemon told me I'm going to get married twice."

"So when can we go see Kuz?" I ask anxiously.

"Anytime, but not when rain is falling. She don't work when rain is falling or on de Sabboth. I guess de rain prevent her from doing what she do. She tell me dat her powers come from de heavens, and when she blow her whistle de angels would come and talk to her. And she would always look through de window at de sun, talking to somebody outside up dere.

"And den I remember dis lady in Port Maria called Miss Essie. Everybody said dat she's a most evilest womon. She deals in De Laurence. I remember one day we had stopped dere cuz we did hear somting was going —"

Here I cut in, because I was so shocked to hear the name De Laurence again. This man was obviously well known on the island! "De Laurence? What's that?"

"Back in de States dere is dis witchcraft ting where dey use fallen angels. You never hear dem talk about De Laurence? Dat from Chicago. Real magic dat catch de — if you owe dem money, de angels would catch your house on fire! And your cups, everyting would fly up in de air and walk out of your house. De furniture would walk out and everyting!

"Dose are type of science. Yeah, de odder day it was happening in Port Maria. Everyting was flying out of de house! Dat table just get up and fly out! De telephone, de chairs fly out! But de husband was de one who set it on de wife. He was dealing wid De Laurence. And he want de wife to get out of de house.

"Dey say if you go dere, stones throwing and you don't know who throwing de stones. And if you say anyting, you just get a slap in your face. Yeah mon! Terrible tings! I don't know you didn't know of dat."

I say, "So that's what that man near Montego Bay was talking about! I was confused about what Daniel God was trying to tell me."

"Of course! Dat's terrible magic! Witchcraft, mon! Dey say dat dose people who deal wid dose tings a lot, part wid God. Dey are de evilest! Dey get all dere riches through dat, anyting dey want, as long as dey deal wid him. But if dey stop paying him money, him would take it all back and would burn dere house wid fire! And if you go deep down, den you would have to start going to de blood sacrifice. Every year you have to sacrifice somebody in your family. Dey would kill dere brodder, dere children, dere niece, dere nephew."

What Sunshine was saying certainly coincided with what Daniel had told me about Mother Heart. I must say that I was surprised to be hearing the same things so far across the island. It seemed all of Jamaica was aware of this De Laurence creature.

"Yeah, most Jamaican people deal wid him. Dey get rings from him, for guard and dose tings."

"So basically, it's an evil spirit that they're dealing with?"

"Yeah! Dey say it's fallen angels. And den, remember dat ship dat sank, de one where dey were singing 'Nearer my God to Thee'?"

117

"You mean the Titanic?"

"Yeah! Well, dey said, all de ghosts of de Titanic, dat's what he deals wid. People who visit his place in Chicago say dat he has an underworld tomb, right? He has a ministry, a dealer as a minister.

"His fodder die and give it to his son, and downstairs dey have de coffins. Everybody dat died for dem, dey are still in dere coffins. And den he would go down and just call dem, and de coffin would just open and he would talk to dem. Dey would tell him what to do and den dey would just go back in dere coffin and lay down and sleep."

"So there's a certain person that is running this whole thing?"

"Yeah, de son. De fodder had died and de son take it over. Once I went up to Miss Essie's and she said four evil spirits is on me, travels around wid me. And what dey are trying to do to me, she said she couldn't help me to get dem off.

"She gave me an address and said I could only write to De Laurence and ask him to get dem off. I didn't write him cuz I know is a fool to start involve wid dose people. Is terrible. So I tell her I leave dem all to God. You know if dey want to destroy my life and don't let me come out to anyting, dat's fine. But when de day of judgement comes, dey have dat on dere shoulders, not my shoulders!

"Yeah, and I have de address all along. Maybe I still have it. If I find it, I'll give it to you. Kuz said myself should write to him and ask him for a ring and a guard. I said, 'No way, baby!' "

"But why would Kuz tell you to go to an evil man?"

"De ting about it is dat his power is a lot higher dan her powers, for de guard dat I need to keep dose evil spirits off. He do good tings too, you know. But mostly tings dat are evil. Him call it science. But de guard is from evil spirit. So it is de way in which he goes about it. You know, once you start, you always has to keep paying him. Any day you would stop paying him he will turn evil on you instead."

I mused, "So he's got these high powers, but he's abusing them tremendously. That's really scary!"

"Right! Den again, anybody who have anyting to do wid him, I feel de Lord will never forgive you for dose tings! Because he is very evilous, you know. He's like a witch! Dey have real witches in de United States, you know.

De Laurence worse dan a real witch, mon! Him bad, bad, bad!"

"Down in Stewart Town, about three or four years ago, dere house down dere catch a fire, too. And everyting was walking out and stones was throwing. De Laurence, dat's who him.

"And some little girls were coming from school and dey get dere fodder, right? Only dere fodder must can deal wid it. And de fodder take out de science and put it on one of de little girls. De little girl just catch a fire! And before dey couldn't do nuttin' to hold it, she died! She burned to death! And I hear dat de fodder take out de De Laurence spirit and put it on her!

"A lot of evilest tings going on in dis world, you know. Yeah mon! Especially in Jamaica, cuz it's all over here. My friends would come from de States and say, 'Dey don't work sciences abroad.' But in Haiti dey use dis ting called sosumba to work science. And in Jamaica we eat sosumba! Dey call it gully beans. It grows out on a tree, looks like some little green peas. So dat's why Haitians afraid for us. We eat dere science, ha-ha! Dey can't catch us! Yeah mon!"

The subject then shifted to how Sunshine is feeling. She knows that she has a lot of ability and talent, but she is frustrated and bored. While Tony is off working on a cruise ship, she just takes care of the home. It's clearly not enough to fulfill this vibrant woman.

"You know, I should have a special goal. I should be doing someting dat's important. I shouldn't be stuck here like I don't know my head from my tail. I know someting is totally wrong, and I have to get out of dis shell!

"You have a visa and you can travel. If I had a visa, tings would be a lot different for me. I would go out and seek my goals."

"I understand your frustration, Sunshine. I also feel that shell and long to break out of it. I know I'm seeking something, but I can't seem to clarify just what it is."

"Right! Because dere is two different countries. But I'm going through de same tings dat you are, even though we are in two different countries. We both need to break through our shell.

"Sometimes I put on my clothes and I would like to go somewhere. Den I just take it back off, like I give up. And I get dis determination in me, say soon you have to get tings right. I still have it in me!

"I'm going to stop putting tings aside and I'm going to pull my reins up.

Bwoy I tell you! I'm really going to have a goal out dere and I'm not going to let nobody stop me from dat goal. I'm serious. Even if I have to step in somebody's head, because dem always stepping in my head.

"I say now, 'Lord, I love you and need you, but if I have to step on somebody's head, I'm going to do it!' Dere. Dat is my determination for dis nineteen year, ninety year. I'm serious honey, serious.

"I'm not supposed to be doing dis. I'm supposed to be going up, you know. Not in a shell. Not going in a circle, either. No baby! I'm going to bust out of dis cocoon and I'm going to fly! It's driving me crazy inside!

"I've tried to make myself happy. Sometimes I even drink whisky in de night. I don't say anyting. I'll drink some whisky and den I'll lay down on de bed and say, 'Whoa!'

"But it doesn't make sense. As soon as de whisky wears off, it's still dere. So I would rather face it alone. De whisky won't help, so I have to get out of dis my own self mon. I don't want it to be too late, cuz den dey will get you so far under dat you feel helpless. I'm not going to perish. No way!"

I said, "I wonder why some people are so content. They don't seem to have this drive that we have, to keep pushing ourselves and bettering ourselves."

"Yeah, I'm always wid friends say, 'Cho! Don't make it so important!' When dey are really important. Dat's not really my will. It's like somebody else is doing it, not me. So I know it is someting implanted, some powers higher dan my powers.

"Let's make a deal! We have determination and we going to get out of our shell! Dere come a stumbling block, we just fall right across it!"

Thus ended our conversation. We were both feeling uplifted. It's hard to believe that I was so depressed this morning when I woke up. What a totally fascinating day this turned out to be. That's what makes life so magic. We just never know what we're in for each day. As Milton said, "Always expect the unexpected!"

Friday, January 26

There is a relatively new kind of music that is very popular in Jamaica now called Rap. I hate it. It's loud, monotonous and often vulgar in its message. I can listen to Reggae twenty-four hours a day, but not Rap.

Last night I went to bed early. I must've been very tired because I fell asleep quickly in spite of the thunderous rap coming out of the neighbor's boom box. It had been pounding in my head all evening and I longed for relief. I found it in sleep. I tried to remember my dreams, but I lost them upon awakening.

My back was vastly improved today. This may be due to some tea that Sunshine brewed up for me yesterday. A few months ago Sunshine was having back trouble also. Someone, she thinks maybe her father, came to her in a dream and advised her to boil five leaves from a custard apple tree and drink the tea.

Since she has such a tree in her yard, she tried it, figuring she had nothing to lose. It cured her problem, so yesterday she made some for me. It was dark green in color. I was curious about it since I prefer natural cures over medical doctors. The concoction was delicious, light and fruity, and it really seems to have helped. Help can come to us in many different ways if we are willing to be open to it when it presents itself.

There is another drink that Sunshine likes to make. It's one of my favorites and definitely a thirst quencher. She blends water, fresh ginger, fresh squeezed limes and a little sugar. This one is strong and sort of burns as it goes down, but I derive great strength from it. Of course it can be diluted, but I prefer it strong.

I feel like going on a liquid diet for awhile. I want to lighten my being to pure inspiration. For sure, I am slowly transforming my physical being. It is the natural order of things then, that the transformation will also affect me on an emotional, mental and spiritual level. This is good.

Saturday, January 27

Bibsey and I spent yesterday in Ochi. It rained a lot and we were tired by the time we got home, so we decided to call it an early night. We lit the kerosene lamp, did some reading and both fell asleep by 7:00 PM.

I had a very vivid, intense dream last night. I've had it before and recognized everything in it. Since it came back to me, I knew that I needed to analyze it. I learned some interesting techniques for doing so when I lived in Madison, Wisconsin many years ago.

I believe that it helps tremendously to first write down the dream in detail. By writing it in present tense, as though it is now occurring, recall is intensified. Then, I describe in detail everything in the dream. I can look at this from the perspective that, since it is my dream, I am really describing myself and situations in my life. Much insight occurs on how I'm seeing and feeling on a subconscious level. It's often a surprise to my conscious self, but very therapeutic.

Another thing I do is to go into a meditative state and then talk directly to the people and objects in my dream. I ask them who they are and why they came to me. Sometimes the messages of my dreams are very clear immediately. But when they're not, then I find these techniques immensely helpful.

I think of going to sleep as going to school. My dreams are excellent teachers. I often jokingly tell people that I can't wait to get up in the morning so I can get some rest.

I meditated on last night's dream and came up with the following:

Me: "Oh no! We're here again! I didn't want to come back here! It's dangerous. There's something over there that I have to see. I'm walking up a rocky hill. Crystal clear water is running over it. What is on the other side? It seems like it's some kind of amusement park or something.

"Oh no! I'm on the crest now. Why did I do this? I can't get safely to the other side. I knew this even before I started. But I so want to go there..."

Back to the beginning of the climb:

I am the rocks: I am solid, strong, clean, smooth. I have soft, green moss clinging to me.

I am the moss: I am velvety, full of life giving energies. My purpose is to add beauty and enchantment to life. I am a positive element, always radiating joy. I am soft to the touch but can be slippery, so tread on me with care and caution.

I am the water on these lower rocks: I am clear and cool and I flow gently with nature. I am peaceful and non-threatening. My music delights all and has a calming effect.

Me: "I am at the crest now, which is a rocky, narrow ledge, so very, very high up. I am terribly concerned about my plight. I feel frightened, frustrated and trapped. I look very brown from the sun and I am wearing a pretty yellow shirt."

I am the shirt: feminine, lacy, soft...

Me: "The sun feels so warm on my skin and the water feels so refreshing. I am afraid to look at the thundering falls because I know how easily I can be swept over the crest. To me the falls are deceiving. They are beautiful to look at, yet I know they are much stronger than I and if I fall they will crush me."

I am the sun: I am so bright, warm, sparkling and joyous. I am a friend to all and a source of light and comfort. My beams shimmer with energy and lift things into pure energy form.

I am the sky: I am rich blue and soothing, deep, endless, peaceful, free...

I am the thundering waterfall: I am clean, pure, cool, soft and yet powerful. I mean no harm to anyone, but my power must be respected. Debbie's body is human and cannot withstand my strength. I want her to enjoy my beauty from afar. I do not want to hurt her, but if she falls I will not be able to help her. I am living according to the laws of the universe.

Why did Debbie come up here? Debbie, you are curiously drawn to my great power and want to learn more about it. I will help you, as I love you, but you must listen carefully to me! You are brave. Most would not venture so far and so high.

Behind my cascade is hidden the great danger, the sharp, rugged rocks that tear through flesh and kill. There are some places that one should travel to in spirit only, not in flesh, or you will sever your ties as a channel in this dimension.

Debbie, feel my breath, my mist, my energy rising to help you to safety. You will reach safety. Be strong like I am. You are trying to reach the other side, beyond these mighty falls. You are curious as to what is there.

It is lovely and fun, but beware. There is also deceit and phoniness. Move into the light and you will then recognize when you are trying to be led astray. Rise above it. Always look beyond the surface of things and then you will know which forces will help you progress, and which ones are merely disguises leading you to regress. You are frightened up here, but we are your friends. You can always come back here for advice.

If you follow this path, you will lose your fear and understand that you can return to this special field of energy anytime. The more time you spend here, the less hazardous it will seem. You will no longer cling and fear for your life, but you will realize that you can balance easily here. This is a place for you to meditate.

Me: "Waterfall, I thought you were my enemy, but now that you have *spoken to me I see that you are my friend, my source of inner strength. I need not be afraid of my own power and passion. You are ever here for me. You have shown me that how I direct my power and passion will either destroy me or enhance me. Thank you for your gifts.*

"I see in the sun and sky my friends also, my spirit friends who twinkle lovingly and wait for me to simply accept them and call on them for guidance and protection. I have grown today, removed a huge negative force. I lovingly open my spirit and accept your help. Guide me. I listen. I feel so much peace."

This is the end of my meditation. The dream taught me much. I reflected on it this evening as I walked along the sea. I communed with the rocks, the crashing waves and the glowing sunset. As I gazed around me, I realized that my strange 'yearning' is gone.

I think I've figured it out. The dream helped me. What is happening is that every time I feel that yearning I am actually in an energy field where I have easy access to other dimensions. I now understand that I am meant to live in many realms, not just that of the earth plane. And I can now travel to the crest of my waterfall any time I want, merely by closing my eyes and willing myself there. It is a place of answers to my questions. Yes, life is magic and we are all magicians.

Sunday, January 28

It's 3:00 PM now. I've been whiling away the afternoon at a little fisherman's beach. Just soaking up the scenery is a real treat. I see old canoes dug out of cottonwood trees, hand made lobster pots and clear, warm seas sending spray up the rocks. Looking inland, I see myriads of flowering trees, mountains, palms, vines climbing up old stone walls, the remains of two ancient buildings and a tiny wooden bar which has Reggae constantly blaring out.

There is a nice breeze blowing, yet I am parched. I just gave a cute, young boy $5 JA to run and fetch us something cold to drink. He and his buddy have been fishing from shore, using only a fish line and some bait. They hold the end of the line and dangle it in.

Ahhh...my drink tastes great! I silently propose a toast to my friend Monique who used to live in Jamaica with me, but who is now in Denver, Colorado, in grad school. She loves Jamaica as much as I. Wish you were here, Monique.

Well, I've lived local -local long enough now to start losing my sanity. So many of the things that I used to find endearing and amusing are now a source of irritation, ha-ha! I'm starting to think and behave like a Jamaican. For instance, I just realized that I've been sitting by the sea all day, almost passing out from the heat. The water is only inches away, calling me, teasing me, and yet I chose to think that I couldn't swim because I don't have a place to shower off the salt water later. The heat is clearly frying my brain piece.

Later: It's now night time. I'm again walking by the sea, where I feel most at home. The moon is but a big smile lighting up the sky. Whose smile? Mine?

Monday, January 29

Mr. Lindsay, bless his heart, wants me to be able to stay in Jamaica. He knows someone in real estate and offered to help me try to get a job there, or at least a loan so I can purchase property here. He suggested that I buy a home and get an agent to rent it out and take care of it when I'm not here. I'm touched by his concern for me. Maybe someday I will do that. I do consider Jamaica my second home.

This evening when I was sitting by the sea meditating, Sunshine silently appeared behind me and handed me something she had written down for me. It speaks of her philosophies. I feel honored to receive this gift.

Here is what she gave me:

"Live each day to the fullest. Get the most from each hour each day and each age of your life. Then you can look forward with confidence and back without regrets. Be yourself, but be your best self.

"Dare to be different and follow your own star. And don't be afraid to be happy. Enjoy what is beautiful. Love with all your heart and soul. Believe that those you love, love you.

"When you are faced with a decision, make the decision as wise as possible. Then forget it. The moment of absolute certainty never arrives.

"Above all, remember that God helps those who help themselves. Act as if everything depends on you, and pray as if everything depends on God."

Tuesday, January 30

Well, I feel like a new person this morning. My finger and back are both much better. I've hardly eaten in four days and I feel very in tune with my body. I feel renewed energy and purpose once again.

For the last few days I've felt lost and couldn't even relate to my purpose for being here. But now I am once again ready for action. I'm going to make something happen.

Last week Milton promised that we would go to places and have a great time on his days off this week, which are today and tomorrow. It's now 10:40 AM and I haven't seen him. I'll be disappointed if he doesn't show up. But I won't be surprised. It's so typical in Jamaica to have a change of plans and not be able to get a message to someone. Very few people have phones and even fewer have vehicles.

Well, I'm just going to go about making plans to accomplish my goals alone yet again. I'm determined to find a way to get where I want to go. I must finish making my tapes and get on with my life.

4

THE OTHER SIDE OF PARADISE

*"We are not drug addicts. We are trying to support
our communities. This is our livelihood."*
— Decton H.

Wednesday, January 31

Milton never showed up yesterday. I didn't want to admit to myself the extent
of the disappointment I felt. I guess I had been looking forward to a day of
play more than I realized. Patience isn't one of my greatest virtues.

While out walking this afternoon, I ran into a group of Rastafarians. I
stopped to chat, knowing they would have an interesting story. When they
asked me who I was and what I was up to, I told them I'm trying to write a
book and let the voice of the real Jamaica be heard. Because I wanted to be
taken seriously, I told them I've been writing for thirty years. Actually, I have.
I've kept a daily journal that long.

One of them shouted, "She is a famous journalist! She can help us!" The
next thing I knew, they were fawning all over me and invited me into their
chambers. I was given the only bench in the place to sit on. The building was just
a small room with zinc covered walls and was surrounded by a zinc fence.

They all squatted beside me, eager to talk. One of them was drunk and
said that he would be glad to be interviewed for the small price of a drink.

The others told me that they love me and pray for people like me to come by because they want to be heard. I was touched by their faith in me and suddenly felt like Barbara Walters.

Regardless of what happens, this experience is invaluable to me because it provided me with these reflections: They think I'm famous. How does one become famous? Or attain one's dreams? I came down here under the pretext of being an author, and I find that I'm accepted at face value, accepted as already being what I want to become! Is it really that easy?

This group of men varied greatly in age, being born anywhere from the 1930's to the 1960's. I spoke mostly with a tall, gentle, serious man named Decton. He was very handsome, polite and well educated. His dreadlocks were pushed up under a tam and he's one of the few Rastafarians I have ever met who doesn't smoke ganja. Decton is very into helping people learn to help themselves. I think that this is the greatest service that any of us can provide.

He introduced me to his older brother, King Jet Swang. The name King was given to him when he was a little boy because people saw him as a leader. While talking and smoking a spliff, King suddenly yanked off his black cap in a dramatic sweep and shook free his eighteen inch long locks. This was done in an effort to show me his power and strength.

Decton told me about an organization that he is involved with called CNRID, short for Caribbean Network for Rural Integrated Development. He said, "So all dese bredern here, dey are doing dere little tings. Some are farmers, some are food workers, fishermen, some work in arts and crafts, furniture making, peanut and vegetable production and so on. And dis is de organization dat was formed to do dat.

"We started two years ago at de micro level. It is a marginal enterprise, often with no fixed location and virtually no access to any banking and advisory services.

"We are not drug addicts. We are trying to support our communities. This is our livelihood.

"We have a contractual agreement between a Canadian organization similar to the Peace Corps of the United States. We support Race Course Youth Club, and we have a poach project, dealing with broilers for meat. We also deal with small enterprise training at the University."

Decton pulled out some papers and proudly showed me his University exam grades, which were all very good. He is obviously sincere in his work. "Our organization is a Third World Grass Roots organization. Yeah, and we help disabled persons. And women. We have a woman and developmental idea. We're trying to create projects for women because we know about feminism and what abuses women go through. You understand?

"We are really aware. We have workshops on sexual abuse and all dose tings. We love women and we know dat de world depends on women. And I have my kids and I know de importance of women. And we work wid unemployed youths, try to get dem off de streets.

"What we really want is more assistance. We need people to come down and help wid dere specialties. Like you. You is a writer and can come and put tings on paper for us. We don't just want help from odder countries. We want to help also."

At this point the drunken fellow, Peter Rastafari, stumbled up and tried to kiss me. The others found him humorous and just took him with a grain of salt. They did, however, keep him in line around me.

He is known as Father because he is the oldest of the brethren. I could tell they all love him in spite of the fact that he had had too much white rum today and was behaving so cocky. He was a sight to behold: freckles, two teeth, long locks, wore a blue, yellow and pink tam and pink pants with one leg rolled up.

Father kept punching me on the arm and sticking his face in mine with his silly grin. This was very distracting, so I finally demanded an apology for his behavior. The others giggled at my boldness. I kept my sense of humor about it, but I wasn't about to keep putting up with it.

I said, "You sure your name is Peter Rastafari? I think it's Peter Bullshit!" I asked him where he was born and he replied, "I was reincarnated in Kingston. I don't born."

"When?"

"In 1933, twenty-fifth of September."

Decton and I spoke for a long time and he went into great detail about the projects that are going on. His work is voluntary. The only time he gets paid is if the projects make a profit. He is so dedicated. I really would like to help.

We finally moved on to other subjects. I am curious about Rastafarianism, so I asked Decton, "When you get up in the morning, how does this religion affect your life? Do you think about it first thing?"

"Well, him give us food to eat, clothes to wear and good people like you to talk to. I personally don't smoke marijuana, but that is a part of our religion. Yeah, we use it as a sacrament and give tanks to Jah and we play drums."

I was amused to discover that Decton had converted from Catholicism to Rastafarianism Most people that I know would say that Rastas use their religion as an excuse to smoke pot. And granted, some do. But I believe it is sacred to those who are sincere. Like other things, it can be used as a tool for growth and a ritual for ceremony.

Who am I to pass judgement? In general, I find most people extremely opinionated. They don't realize how foolish, narrow minded and pompous they appear when they condemn ways other than their own. Most often, they are showing ignorance of something they don't understand.

Decton claimed he saw people suck other's blood in the Catholic Church. I finally realized that he was speaking of bloody wars in the name of religion. He was also referring to con artists and mentioned "De guy who wear de Rolex watch, Swaggert, who suck de blood of his congregation. We no into dat kind of religion!"

I asked, "What does Rastafari religion mean to you personally?"

"It mean food, clothing and shelter, lightning, thunder, fire, earthquake. God create, you know. If you have a weak heart you can't survive dese tings."

"What do you think of the concept of duppies?"

"Satanic mon! I've seen dem! My higher mind can control dat, rise above dat and obeah workings. Meditate, you know."

Decton told me there was an obeah woman right down the street. When I expressed an interest in seeing her, he told me to be careful because obeah is against the law in Jamaica and they don't promote it. He said they have Satanic power from the De Laurence books in Chicago. He believes they work off myths and superstition.

Next I spoke with King, who asked me to do a small booklet on their projects so they could use it as a fund raiser. He believes that opportunity lies in Ethiopia for them and told me to ignore what the Western media says about Ethiopia. King believes that the Jamaican government will never acknowledge or recognize Rastafarians or give them the opportunity to be productive. This is frustrating and sad for him, because he knows what they can and want to contribute. Ultimately, what it boils down to is the power struggles that governments get so caught up in. And what an illusion that is. How sad.

We spent the next hour discussing politics. The guys claimed that it was the Black man's sweat and blood that built the world through slavery. They've got a point. I wonder how I would feel if I was black.

Someone said of dreadlocks, "De bible say in chapter six dat locks is holiness, fullness of mon. It's my heart. Long ago there was no comb. Hair shows power. It is a symbol of power, although our powers come from within."

On dreams, I heard, "Old mon gets dreams. Young mon gets visions."

"Do you have them when you're awake and meditating, or when you're asleep?"

"Both! Meditation shows dat I am not here. I am wid modder and fodder and odders."

It's clear to me that most Jamaicans have a strong connection to other realms of reality. Like me, they seem to flow in and out of them as naturally as they breathe. I enjoyed my visit today and hope to see those characters again.

Thursday, February 1

6:10 PM   I'm sitting by the sea now. Milton showed up last night and was very apologetic. His car had just been painted, and because of the rain it wasn't dry and he couldn't drive it. I could tell he was genuinely disappointed about wasting his two days off. He promised to take me to Kingston next week.

Bibsey and I went to Ochi this morning and hiked up to Carinosa Gardens to try to find Jimmy. It was a glorious hike, but we discovered that Jimmy had moved back to the States a year ago after his uncle was defeated in the elections. Jimmy is the nephew of Edward Seaga, the former Prime Minister of Jamaica. I was hoping to be able to interview Jimmy, as he certainly had a better idea than most people of what was really happening with Jamaican politics. He was very close to his "Uncle Eddie."

I was disappointed at not getting the interview and also sorry that I wasn't able to visit my old friend. I had met Jimmy a few years prior on my way to a party one night. We took the same little boat down the White River and ended up dancing the night away under the stars. That was quite a party. Keith Richards of the Rolling Stones also happened to be there that night. Jimmy was a very sweet guy and I saw him several times afterwards. When I returned to the States, we exchanged a few letters, but I had since lost contact with him.

Phone calls are so difficult to make in Jamaica, as one has to go through an operator and often the operator must ring you back. It can take forever if the line is busy to start with, because often the operators just don't bother calling you back. And if you keep calling them in regards to the same call, they get perturbed and then they purposely ignore you. So you just play the game and try to make your phone calls when you have nothing else to do that day.

I was so grateful that Jennifer King let me use her phone this afternoon to contact Sara in Mo-Bay. I made plans to meet her in Trelawny tomorrow. I realize that I'm copping out, but I just got my period and it's a nightmare to have it in the land of no toilets. So I'm going to pamper myself and go stay with the Reps for a few days.

Friday, February 2

Eight people were squashed into an area made for three on my minibus this morning on the ride to Ochi. I was literally pushed against the door and prayed it wouldn't open while moving!

Then while riding another bus to Trelawny, I glanced out the window and saw Keith Aztan on the roadside. Keith does flower arrangements at the resorts and used to bring me exotic bouquets all the time when I was a Rep. He saw me at the same time I saw him and did a double take. Diving into his truck, he frantically flagged down the bus until the driver stopped. I was embarrassed, but also flattered. He hollered into the window and asked me to join him for the day so we could catch up on old times. I thanked him, but told him that I couldn't because I already had other plans. Only in Jamaica could someone get away with almost running a bus off the road just to chat with a passenger!

It was great to see Sara again and seemed odd to be talking with an American. Later I met up with Deedra, who gave me the keys to her little apartment. What a treat! I had the entire afternoon alone to relax and take a leisurely shower.

I weighed myself on Deedra's scale two weeks ago and again today. I've lost fifteen pounds since then! Great! All I've eaten this week is some fruit.

Who wants to eat when you live with no toilet or even an outhouse? Maybe I'll write a new diet book called "Life Without John."

I feel dynamic. I also feel like being silly and celebrating tonight. I've been subdued for so long.

Saturday, February 3

I was out with a bunch of Reps last night until 2:00 AM and really had fun. It seemed we never ran out of fascinating subject matter to discuss. I couldn't help but be aware of the contrast of life in Mo-Bay as opposed to Oracabessa. I love Bibsey dearly, but her whole world has been so limited that she never has much to say. All of her concerns are about survival in her immediate surroundings.

Deedra is working at Seawind today. I rode out there with her so I could enjoy the beach and visit old friends. The reefs and marine life in this area are especially colorful. It feels good to put everything aside for awhile and do nothing but daydream.

I wonder if Daniel God or someone put a spell on me. To my amazement, my entire outlook on life seems different. I still love Jamaica, but I don't need it anymore. I'm realizing that right now I have no ties anywhere. Therefore, I can explore endless places and work possibilities. Life is so exciting! I want to stay young, vibrant and healthy.

Sunday, February 4

Whew! I'm really living in luxury now, staying at the Rep house tonight. The girls are sneaking me in and I really appreciate it. Rules are that only company employees can stay here. It's a gorgeous home and even has a swimming pool. I lived in hotel rooms the entire time I worked for the company.

Sara and I had a long, intense talk last night about life. Then we loosened up and went to a disco. We found ourselves surrounded by men who treated us like queens, so we ate up the attention. I was a dancing fool and I laughed so much that my whole body hurts today. I needed that.

Monday, February 5

Another good day. I'm taking a break from my writing this week. This morning I went to Immigration, which was quite an ordeal, but to my relief, I was able to extend my stay in Jamaica all the way through April.

Later I hopped a bus back to Oracabessa and actually got a seat, so I kicked back to enjoy the scenery. For some reason, I found myself surrounded by little children all day. I'm so drawn to their innocence and really enjoyed talking with them.

As I passed McKay's Floral Shop, I decided to stop in just to see what kind of floral arrangements they had. To my total shock, I discovered that they were all made of cheap plastic flowers and feathers. There wasn't a real flower in the place! The island has over three thousand varieties of plants and flowers, yet people fill their homes with plastic ones.

When I stopped at the Post Office, I was delighted to find a letter from home. I was sitting by the sea, writing a response, when I realized that I was no longer alone. Glancing up, I saw a young boy clad in his beige school uniform. He looked lonely and lost and was clearly in a world all his own. When he reached my side, he stopped and stared intently into my face. I started talking to him, and after a few moments he broke out of his reverie and answered me.

"Your skin is a different color dan mine," he said. I could tell that this fascinated him immensely. Seating himself on a rock next to me, he introduced himself as Curtis, said that he is twelve years old and that he used to live in Oracabessa. He still goes to school there, but now busses back and forth from Ochi.

As he pointed up the hill to where he used to live, Curtis told me that he likes living in Ochi better because people in his neighborhood in Oracabessa said mean things about his family. His mother used to work at a guest house, but a madman came there and murdered her a few years ago. My heart went out to this gentle child as I realized what he had been through. No wonder he was so timid.

Curtis asked me where I live and if my mother and father are still alive. When I told him that I live with my brother, he asked if my brother has black or white skin. As he stared dreamily out to sea, questions just poured out of him. "How did you get to Jamaica? Did you come all de way across de sea? What is across de sea? Or did you come in a big plane?"

When I told him I came in a big plane, he looked up and asked me how airplanes find their way around. "Are dere highways in de sky dat dey follow?"

We sat in silence for awhile like comfortable old friends, I writing my letter and Curtis just lost in his dreams. Then he stood up, shook my hand, said good-by and that he must catch his bus as it was getting late.

What will happen to this sweet boy? He is so curious about the big, magical world around him. I pray that his dreams will lead him down a happy road in life.

I finished my letter and sat there thinking about my friend Bibsey. She's such a precious human being! Her life isn't easy, but she loves it anyway because she chooses to be happy everyday. I still think it's funny that she and Max are gradually purchasing all the material luxuries of life before they even purchase the bare necessities. Personally, I'd rather have a toilet, a shower, and electricity.

Devon cooking in Bibsey's kitchen

I thought again of Bibsey's little kitchen. It's just the frame of a room and she does all of her cooking in a wok over a fire. Since she has no refrigeration, it's hard to keep food around. The rodents always get into whatever is there. It doesn't seem to bother Bibsey or Devon, but I just can't eat something that roaches or mice have chewed through. I can't brush hundreds of ants off of

135

food and eat it, either. The mere idea makes me feel sick inside.

Devon is a sweet boy, always kind and makes me feel welcome. He's tall and skinny, but very cute. Bibsey thinks he's lazy because he never picks up his clothes. At night he just wanders around, hanging out on corners with his friends, and lately he has been getting drunk. As all teenagers do, I'm sure he's going through some major changes right now. What will he do with his life? He's probably asking himself the same question. Devon goes to school in Ochi because he won a football (soccer) scholarship. It costs about $75 JA a week for bus and lunch.

Bibsey moans about the cost of children, but like most Jamaicans, she will have all the babies she wants. The general attitude is that "Somehow everyting will work out." Then when things get tough, the government is often blamed.

I believe that a lot of complaints are valid though. Blacks are still legally paid slave wages in most places, so I can emphasize with the ones who flat out refuse to work for those wages.

This is Jamaica, 1990. Prices everywhere are skyrocketing. What is to become of this country, this incredible, mystical island? What is to become of its people? They have so much to offer the world. If we can't band together and help provide the opportunities, then ultimately it will be our loss.

Everyone here has great respect for the fishermen who go out in little wooden boats and risk their lives night after night. Many people here are afraid of the sea. It is too powerful and mysterious to them. I can't imagine having something this wonderful in my backyard and not merging with it.

Many people are afraid of obeah and Pocomania, too. I've discovered that obeah is a lot more predominant here and now than is commonly believed by people who are not islanders. By really asking around, I've found it to be almost everywhere that I've been. It is kept hush hush though, as it is illegal. I haven't as yet been able to speak directly to an obeah practitioner. I've been warned by many people not to start messing with it because it is too powerful.

That feeling, that yearning, that sense of great mystery that I've always felt in Jamaica, is starting to really make sense now. Almost everyone is deeply involved with their spirits. I've discovered that there are many different religions and practices, but everything is ultimately linked to the souls of these people.

Most believe in the basic values of just treating your fellow man as you want to be treated. The morality over all, behind all the dogmas and rituals, is a strong sense of obligation to care for one another, share whatever you have and help in any way you can. That's really the big draw for me, because isn't that what really matters in life?

It always makes me chuckle to accompany people to their churches, hear the hell-fire sermons, and see the people leave - knowing they feel better for having gone - and then watch how they set up their own rules and standards anyway. They live with a clean conscience in a way that is common sense to them. No matter what is preached, many of them really don't see having multiple sexual partners or babies from several partners as a moral issue. Many don't even see marriage as a sexual commitment. All they see is what is practical to them. They seem to reach beyond the man made rules and somehow grasp the spiritual values that are important.

For most Jamaicans, daily life is filled with the simple matter of survival, such as getting and preparing food, doing laundry, personal hygiene and simply getting from one destination to the next. All of these things take so much energy here, whereas in the States all of this is at our fingertips so we are able to concentrate more on mental activities such as furthering our education.

Living here has shown me what it is like to live in spirit. Most people in the States don't seem to truly perceive their spirit as a real part of themselves. I want to discover why. Many people that I know act embarrassed and uncomfortable about even discussing spirituality. The general consensus seems to be that it's "a very personal thing," not something to discuss, share and make real in our everyday dealings with life.

Are people afraid of themselves? So many people have had religions crammed down their throats, but I see in their eyes and sense that they are not able from all of that, to come in touch with their own spirit. Life holds too much fear and not enough understanding. I get a feeling that most people think that everyone else connects more with their souls than they do, so they go about pretending to connect. But I know they're not connecting.

I think what I'm really trying to do here is to find a way to help people connect. That is my overall objective in trying to write a book. Hmmmm.... I would also like to write something short, but creative, some kind of ode to my island people, something light hearted and joyous. Regardless, I will somehow find a way to repay these people for what they have done for me.

Tuesday, February 6

Milton was supposed to take me to Kingston today, but when he didn't show up by 11:00 AM, I decided to go to Port Maria with Bibsey and Sunshine. Bibsey had to go to the dentist because a tooth fell out of her partial. I had never been to a Jamaican dentist and found this to be quite a frightening experience. I was glad my teeth didn't need to be worked on.

The dentist himself was immaculate, donned in dress pants, a white shirt and a necktie. He looked extremely professional and very out of place in his office. The office consisted of one small room with dirty green walls and a broken tiled floor. Bare light bulbs and wires hung from the ceiling. An ancient dental chair sat in the middle of the room, underneath some hoses and tools which also hung down from the ceiling. A picture of the Sacred Heart hung on one wall.

Dentist office in Port Maria

Two men sat at a desk working on plates. They would dip their instruments in fire from an oil lamp, then mold and scrape the teeth and plates with the hot tools. The bathroom had a sign on it, "Out of Use." The only other things in the office were a small burner and pot in one corner, a row of liquor bottles on the floor against one wall, and of course, a boom box. I presumed the liquor was used to numb the patient's mouth when the dentist worked.

I was the only one who appeared to be intimidated by this office. Everyone else was jovial and relaxed. The dentist is a friend of Sunshine's. When she told him that Bibsey is having financial difficulties, he fixed her teeth for free. Think it would happen in America?

Later we stopped for lunch at a restaurant owned by Sunshine's sister and then we window shopped. It was fun for me to check the prices of things. Here are a few examples: a beautifully carved wooden dining table with six chairs sold for $14,206 JA ($2237 US); a double bed with a simple wooden headboard was $3980 JA ($627 US); a thirteen inch TV went for $3150 JA ($496 US); and a small refrigerator cost $4830 JA ($761 US). I was surprised to see a store like this in Port Maria, as I didn't think anyone who lived near here had that kind of money. How do people manage to buy anything, considering the average paycheck for so many is about $159 JA per week, or $25 US?

I want to mention some of the signs I've seen around Jamaica because signs are such a part of the culture. Many signs are hand painted and very misspelled, but they always provide food for thought.

This afternoon at Patsy's Cool Shade restaurant, I saw a sign that read: "Peace for all mankind. Let peace encircle all the world. Let men walk hand in hand. A living bond of brotherhood. A voice from land to land."

Also in Port Maria: "Welcome customers. We welcome you every time. Without you there would be no need for us to be here. We are here to serve you, so we thank you for having us here. May the Lord have His richest Blessing on you and May You Come Again. From all of us at Highgate Electrical Supplies Company, LTD"

Sign in a bar in Port Maria: "Lord help me this day to keep my big mouth shut."

Painted on a wall: "Word is Love" "House of Joy"

Newspaper art hanging on a wall: "Serve people, don't rule them"

Sign in a local patty shop: "The worst time to find your tongue is when you have lost your head."

Headline in newspaper: "Hotel Maids Fired for Refusing to Wash Dogs Clothes"

Painted outside a Mo-Bay disco: "Please do not piss in this corner."

Sign in a field in Port Antonio: "Beware of sudden death" This sign had a painting of a skull on it. A small wooden coffin dangled underneath it. Also dangling was a vial with some kind of liquid in it. My guess is that it was some kind of obeah, performed to keep people away from the farmer's crops.

Jamaicans always name their taxis and minivans. Public transportation can only be described as 'an experience.' You can ride in any of these vehicles: "Soul Power," "Puss Rice," "Superdad," "Irie One," "Pressa Foot," "Orion," "Faith," "Sir T, de don mon," or the "God Bless Cab."

Mr. C's car has a sign in it: "No smoking please. Take your soul comb, knife, ice pick, and all sharp objects from pocket please. Thank you."

I saw this sign hanging upside down in the doorway of a bus: "Passengers leaving moving vehicle do so at their own risk." Other bus signs: "Notice - Shocking -Do not touch if you are wet." "Let's not meet by accident."

Painted on a mud flap of a truck: "God is alive. I must survive."

At a gas station: "Caution, High Sleeping Policeman"

Stores, bars and restaurants also provide cultural insight. In the States we have "K-Mart." Kingston has "A-Mart" and "King Burger," as opposed to our "Burger King." And the craft markets all have "Blue Light Specials."

This is but a sampling of the signs of Jamaica, but one gets a feel of what it is like to roam around here. Spirit is prevalent even while doing simple everyday things like shopping, eating or having a toddy at the local pub. There is no escaping it on this magical island.

Everything in life is a teacher if we but allow it to be. The signs of Jamaica taught me daily.

We reached back home around 3:00 PM and I was told that Milton had been looking for me. It seems he had car trouble again. Always something. Guess it wasn't meant to be.

Since we were having so much fun today, Bibsey, Sunshine and I decided to play all through the evening. We went down to the sea and swam all through the sunset. We took photos of each other for our boyfriends, attempting to look sexy, but laughing all the while. I love my friends. It's so important to lighten up and play. Play adds so much quality to life. I think I've finally relaxed and accepted Jamaican pace. And I love it, too much maybe.

5

REFLECTIONS

"Sometimes messages spring out of seemingly nowhere. And certainly my dreams have been powerfully affected."
—*Debbie*

Wednesday, February 7

Sunshine had parent teacher conferences in Kingston today and invited Bibsey and I to join her. We hopped onto a minibus and what a ride it turned out to be! The beauty of the mountains was hypnotizing. As I sat back to enjoy the view, I felt certain that I was glimpsing heaven itself.

The bus was packed as usual, but I was lucky enough to get a single seat by an open window. I drifted off, allowing myself to be completely mesmerized by the magic. Suddenly I felt a hand on the back of my head. It very gently and slowly started caressing my neck and hair. The hand gradually moved to my shoulders and started massaging them.

The entire situation was hysterically funny to me. I knew I was being seduced, but I pretended not to notice because it felt so totally wonderful and I didn't want it to stop. No one else noticed what was going on because the bus was so crowded. This kept up for over an hour, until we arrived at our destination in Kingston.

When the bus stopped and I moved, I felt a tap on the shoulder and finally turned around to see who had been seducing me. To my surprise, it was a nice looking guy in jeans and a white shirt. He asked my name, told me his was Dave and said that I am "very nice and feel good." I thanked him, bid him farewell and hopped off the bus. I certainly got more than I bargained for on that ride!

We found our way to Kingston Technical School and into a huge room where all the teachers were gathered. They sat at desks and parents were lined up to speak with them. Sunshine insisted that I interview her daughter's teachers for my book. I did want to, but felt a bit uncomfortable as I knew it would delay visits for people who were supposed to be there.

Sunshine took me around with her, and after talking with each teacher about Erica, she introduced me and asked if I could record them. Everyone was polite and more than happy to oblige. One thing I noticed as I spoke with the teachers was that they all seemed to be extremely dedicated and love their work. This impressed me very much, as I feel it definitely has an effect on the children. I also noticed that they spoke very proper English.

I asked Miss Douglas, a Home Economics teacher, what she finds most interesting about her students. She replied, "I find that they are very friendly. Quite a number of them are very interested in learning. Some couldn't care less, all right? And I think that maybe that stems from the home environment. You'll find that the students who have parents who push them and encourage them to work will work. But others whose parents don't make an effort or show interest in their learning, well, you find those students don't care.

"But, like for example, Erica, you can see that she wants to learn. She is interested in her learning and although I have commended her on her work, she is telling me, 'Miss, I am not satisfied.' I find that very commendable, because very few students will care where they're at at the moment. I am pleased when I meet a student like that! It encourages me to put out my best at all times.

"But, if I meet a student who couldn't care less, well, it demotivates me a lot. And then I may not be motivated to make much of an effort. But overall, I try my very best. And if I find that I can motivate a student, I will go all out to motivate that student in any way possible!"

When I asked her if she likes Kingston, she told me that it has the advantages of educational opportunities, easier transportation, hospitals, etc. But if she had it her way, she would live in the rural areas because the life style is much simpler. Also, it's quiet and the air is much cleaner. This seemed to be the general opinion of most of the teachers. Kingston is very different from most of Jamaica, much more modernized. Most Jamaicans cherish the country and the old ways.

Kingston Technical School, teacher, Erica, Sunshine

Miss Douglas explained to me that there are two kinds of high schools that Jamaicans can attend. One is a traditional high school, where more emphasis is placed on grammar, fine arts and classical subjects. The other is a technical school, where one also receives some kind of vocational training. Vocational schools have more to offer. They also pay close attention to the ability of the children, and guide them into an area where they will be able to do well. The goal is for each student to become a productive member of society.

I was amazed to discover that Erica's math teacher didn't have a teaching degree. After tutoring students while he was in high school, he came here directly to teach. He has a scholarship to a university and plans on attending full time next year, majoring in engineering. He has however, discovered that he really enjoys teaching and feels it's one of the best contributions he can make to society. Eventually, he plans on finding a way to combine his engineering career with time left to do some teaching.

In his own words, "I find teaching to be somewhat of a very challenging job. And being the type of person that I am, I like a challenge. I mean it's really something to try and nurture students who start out with limited ability, and see them work on it, and see them develop, see their achievements."

Mrs. Clarkreid, Erica's sewing teacher, said that sewing is a mandatory subject. "They all have to take it. But I think it's very important! Whatever job you might acquire, whatever profession, being able to sew your own garments is important. One should know the right colors to wear as an individual, because we have different complexions. We should know the different colors that suit us for different occasions and places we are going. So it's not just to sew something. It's a wide, wide area.

"You also learn household, how to make drapes and curtains and all the interior decorations. All of that, so I think it's very good."

Marion Vernon, another home economics teacher, agreed on how vital this subject is, and said that the students often fail to see this until later in life. "You have those who will hate needlework in school, and they will end up sewing their own clothes later on because of the economic situation. You are forced to help yourself. And these things that we teach in the class, like how to decorate a home, how to renovate certain things... well, they don't appreciate it until they get out of there in the hard situation, into harsh reality! And then they just have to fall in line and help themselves.

"We have some who graduate here and they just pass through and don't achieve much, and then they come back and join the evening classes. But they have to pay now! They have to pay to come back and get the same thing that they could've got for free for four years! So they don't realize that they will need it.

"I find that it is important to encourage the students. They just love it when you praise them! There is a girl in my class now, a first year, who is making a simple, gathered waist skirt, and we don't have a machine. They have to sew it by hand, so it's tedious! I'm sorry she has left, because she brought it here today. And she made these big stitches here with her hands, and I said, ' Oh my gosh, that's terrible! I'm sure you have the ability to do better.'

"And this morning, she brought that thing in and showed me. And you wouldn't be able to notice whether it was a machine that did it or a hand. It was so neat! And we blew it up in the class. It was like a concert! We kissed her and we cheered her! And then she feel so encouraged that every little stitch she makes now she brings and shows me. So I have clearly caught her interest. So it's good.

"I love that, because even if I get just one student out of the entire class, I feel good. So I'll continue to stay. Yeah, I will, I will! And basically, I just enjoy my area. I love to sew and make all of my own clothes. I am lost when I'm at the machine. You don't even ask me to go to the bathroom, cuz I'm lost at the machine! You know what I mean?"

I know that I would love to have her for a teacher. And all of the others. Their enthusiasm was contagious!

I didn't want to leave without also talking with Erica. She is a serious, shy thirteen year old beauty. I could see why Sunshine is so proud of her.

Erica starts her day at 4:00 AM and doesn't get home from school until about 6:00 PM. She then has chores and homework to do, so she really doesn't have a chance for the social life that most of her friends enjoy. Sunshine sends her to Kingston because she believes the quality of education is so much better there.

I realized just how ambitious Erica is when she revealed to me that she hopes to become a surgeon one day. She certainly has the brains and dedication for it. And she's so well mannered and charming. I hope you follow your dreams, honey! I'm rooting for you.

Thursday, February 8

I feel kind of depressed today, because my time in Oracabessa is nearing an end. I refuse to think about how difficult it will be to say good-by to everyone. It tears me apart.

I'm disappointed that Milton wasn't able to come through for me. I'm also disappointed that I wasn't able to go see Kuz, the old psychic. I hate to miss a chance to meet her, but I simply wasn't able to arrange transportation to go up there.

I'm going to move most of my things back to Mo-Bay because one of the Reps has moved and Sara asked me to come. Toilets and showers are hard to pass up. At this point, I don't have the willpower to refuse.

I'm also frustrated because the moon is full again. I've been repressing my sexual needs and this hits me really hard when the moon is so big and bright.

It's so romantic and wild. Sometimes I wonder why I am so passionate.

Friday, February 9

Well, here I am back at Trelawny Beach. I'm going to interview some of the people down here. Donna is a local girl who is often seen strolling up and down the sand. I asked her to tell me about Falmouth, where she was born. "I would like to be in Falmouth anyway. Falmouth is very poor. A lot of poor people live in Falmouth. We need some more money and help to set up our business."

"What do you do for a living?"

"Well, I do craft work, sell like little baskets, and do braids for the guests here. I like that job very much. I used to do waitress before, but they don't pay any money, so I have to leave it and go on my own now.

"I go to Church of God. They try to help poor people. It's a nice church. Who don't have it, dey give us what dey can. It's like Christianity, you know?"

"Do you believe in duppies?"

"No sir! Me no believe in a duppy! Ha-ha-ha! Dead mon have no power!"

"What do you think is going to happen when you die?"

"Well, we going to rest til de Fodder come. Everyone know what would go wrong, but when you die, you just die. You cannot move til de spirit, Jah, he's de only creator. He know everyting, yeah mon!"

"Do you think there is a heaven and a hell?"

"Yeah, I know dere is. But when de Creator come, you choose to which spot you should go. You should know de right place when it comes."

So you don't believe that dead spirits can rise up and come back here like duppies?"

"No mon! If you believe in dat, dat is just like imagination. Somebody imagine ting. But if for I don't see you personal, you cannot say dat my spirit is dere. You don't know because de body's life you leave it where it lies. Some people see like somebody dead, and den dey going around say, 'Oh, I see Donna on de beach!' Lie. Some people go around make mischief. Ha-ha! No duppy business."

"If you could have any dream come true, what would yours be?"

"Go to de States."

"Where in the States?"

"Canada."

"That's not in the States."

"Oh, well den England."

I turned my tape next to someone who had been watching Donna and I. He wouldn't tell me his name. "My life is kind of personal, you know."

"Oh, so you don't want to do a tape?"

"Maybe. It depends upon what you really want to know."

"I just want to ask a few questions. For instance, do you think duppies exist?"

"No, I don't believe in a duppy world."

"Isn't this interesting? No one along here seems to believe in duppies, and everywhere else I go people have seen them."

"People have seen dem? Well, actually, one time I see tings like dem spirits. But it not really jive me out, like being afraid of dem. My belief towards dem is like it's just de Devil himself in all form. If I see a duppy, it was just de Devil himself. And him appears to dose who is afraid. But I'm not really frightened, so dem not really try me."

"What do you think is going to happen when you die?"

"Here comes de end of your life mon! After you're dead, you're just dead. I don't believe in all dem tings like evil, heaven, hell, all dem tings."

"Haven't you ever felt a sense of your soul?"

"Soul? No. Me felt meself is alive in all forms. But dis soul business to me is like somebody just try to do some bit to protect. Do you understand?"

"Hmmmm... very interesting. Where were you born and how big of a family do you come from?"

"I was born in Manchester. My Mom has six boys and two girls. I don't have any children. Well you see how I would like to see my children grow. Well, I just can't afford it, so I put it aside. I suffered a lot in my life you know. So I can't afford to suffer a child like myself.

"Most people don't really tink dat way. I mean, enjoy yourself, yes, and what comes after nobody cares. But, I mean, somebody has to cares!

Somewhere along de way you has to cares. What I feel mon, I'm telling you lots of people kill demselves for certain little tings. Dey don't feel eighteen percent of what me feel."

"If any dream in the world could come true for you, what would it be?"

"Dream? I'd like to be hoppy, mon! You see, material tings can just fade away. Today you can be a millionaire and tomorrow you is a poor guy. Yeah! But be hoppy mon! It take you a longtime to lose all your hoppiness, cuz de tings dat make you hoppy, right, you might lose a little piece and you poor for dat, but dat doesn't say you not hoppy still. Well, like being a millionaire really make you feel like a mon, and tomorrow you lose it, you no more a mon. Hoppiness come first mon! You know, long life."

He told me he had never been out of Jamaica, so I asked him what he thought it would be like to suddenly land in Chicago. He had a pretty good idea. "I'm sure I would be looking at a whole lot of white people, right? And I imagine dere would be a lot of tall buildings, a lot of motor cars and tings like dat. Pretty fast paced living up dere."

When he found out that I live near Chicago, he said, "I've got a good friend in Chicago. He's living by North Wabash Avenue. Do you know where dat is?"

"I sure do. I love Chicago to play in, but it's too hectic for me to live in."

"Do you want to know de name of my friend?"

"What is it?"

"De Laurence. Ha-ha-ha!"

"Are you serious? How do you know about him?"

Here Mr. X lights up a spliff. "You don't mind me smoking? It's famous world wide, de ganja."

"But what do you know about De Laurence?"

"I know everyting about him."

Mr. X has a little stand on the beach where he sells things. We are interrupted now by a customer. I wait patiently, eager to resume the conversation. Finally, "I know de type of person dat he is and what he can do, cuz um, I was in touch wid him once, you know."

"You actually met him?"

"No, we communicate. I write him. He's a magician, right? Like I told you earlier, I do stage magic. And after I finished quite a few shows, de people would come to me and ask me like for helping dem wid some problems dat dey might have along de way. Cuz in Jamaica, being a magician, a lot of people, most Jamaican would tink dat you working wid de duppy. Dat's what dey tink.

"So dese guys saw dis show, and after de show dey come by and ask me, 'Hey, I lose my girlfriend. You could a help me to get her back.' I say, 'Come on mon! I'm not dat type of person.' "

"What type of magic do you do in your shows?"

"Well, like ropes, cards, balls. Like make you tie a rope around my neck and get some people to pull it. Like wid four hands dat, and four on de odder end, and dey would pull it, and standing just like dat, I would be free. Change tings, like I would take a ball and squeeze it into a lime. I'd roll a kerchief into my hand until it disappeared. Tings like dat."

"That's wonderful! You should be working in hotels."

"Well, I tried it, but as I tell you, I'm not one of de fortunate guys. I don't take much pushing around. I wouldn't mind having a job dere, but de obligation dat you really have to go through to get a job over dere is too heavy for me. You know?"

He was referring to Trelawny Beach Resort. I had heard many complaints from talented artists who were treated poorly and expected to work for almost nothing.

"I did about four or five shows dere. Never got any money more dan say a bit, like a hundred Jamaican for a show. So it wasn't encouraging."

"I agree. I know that they really take advantage of entertainers."

"Jamaica is like dat you know. Dat's why you hear a lot of Jamaicans say dey don't want to work. De whole island say, 'You guys is lazy.' But it's not we lazy. Anybody would want to have a good job! I don't know who wouldn't want to."

That's right. I understand that you don't want to work for almost no wages."

"You live out your end, but dey don't really pay you for it."

"Well, back to this De Laurence guy. I never heard of him before I came here, but I heard he's really a bad guy."

"I don't know if he's a real bad guy. But I know dat he can do tings dat freak people out."

"Do you think he's into obeah?"

"Yeah mon!"

"What do you think of obeah?"

"I don't believe in it you know."

"You don't believe in it, but yet you think he can do it? So you acknowledge that it exists?"

"Actually, he has his own world dat he's into, right? I am in mine. Do you understand?"

"So you just keep your mind away from that stuff. Is that what you're saying?"

"Yeah, I don't really, like, I wouldn't spend my money towards it. I wouldn't spend a dime towards it."

"So why did you write to him?"

"Oh yeah, I was telling you dat dese guys was asking me about helping dem to regain dere girlfriends. I say, 'Alright, I can't. But I know somebody who might can help you.' And so dey check me out. I say, 'Well, first you got to write dat person.' Cuz where I bunks around in Trelawny I went to an obeah mon's home. Dat's where me a living now. He died, and all of his obeah stuff and tings..."

I cut in, "And it's still there?"

"Yeah, him still have an office. Dere are all kinds of tings. So me come across de book wid de address. His kids are afraid to go into de house even in de daytime."

"Oh! I'd like to see that stuff though. Is it still there?"

"Ahhhh, quite a few tings still about de place. His office still dere. Dis guy was a real obeah mon. I went into his house about seven years ago. All his letters, like people from all over de world write to him. And all his letters, he didn't destroy dem.

"But well, I burned up a bunch of dem you know. But him still have all kinds of letters in his office."

He said the house was about a mile out of Falmouth and agreed to take me there if I would pay him the wages he would miss for lost work time. No problem! Next we had to figure out when I could go. Unfortunately, I was about to leave Trelawny for awhile.

When I told him I would have a friend drive me back and take us, he eyed me somewhat suspiciously and said, "I can ummm, I can feel people's vibes you know, Debbie. I'm kind of, I'm trying to look upon somebody dat come up on dis, and I try to glimpse certain tings about himself. You know?"

"So what are you saying? Are you saying you'd rather I went alone to see it? Well then, I'm going to make a point of coming back here. And if I come back, will we be able to go?"

"Dat's what I'm saying. We going to have to make up arrangements towards dat, right? Dat will be de first ting I will check out. Tomorrow you going to be at de hotel?"

My heart sank. Tomorrow I'm going to Negril, which is at the other end of the island. I have to go, because my friend Birgitta is soon being transferred to Mexico. I must see her first. We ended up making tentative arrangements for a week from now. I sure hope it works out.

I wandered down to Burwood Beach. My friend Sonny was there, so I asked him to comment on duppies. "Duppy? Me a tell you about duppy, cuz me no afraid of duppy. Me see duppy already mon! Down at de house at me yard. He was big!

Sonny at Burwood Beach

"I was in me yard and looking through de window. Looking, and at de same time dis ting go 'poom, poom, poom, poom!' Me hear a noise downstairs and de mon walk wid a piece of stick.

"Me jack up in bed, couldn't sleep you know, cuz me get so afraid! Yeah, and dere was de kids. Dem asleep. Yeah mon! Is true mon. Duppy!"

I asked another guy who was listening to us if he had ever seen a duppy. "Never experience, never see it. Not me, but my sister."

"What did she see?"

"A little baby boy dat was supposed to be drowned in de pool behind de house. But she was pregnant at dat time, so she was up at de house, my two sisters and me. She have her own room. And me hear her scream out in her room. So me went and opened her door, She said, 'Devon! Devon! Me seen him! Me seen a little boy! Did you see him?' Me a go and move de curtain and she say, 'Devon, him a right over you!'"

"And she could see him, but you couldn't?"

"Yeah! Me no see him. After dat, she afraid. She no go back in her room. Yeah mon!"

When I asked him what he thought about death, he said he doesn't think much about it because there is nothing we can do about it anyway. True. Let's put our energy into living.

I asked the group that was sitting around if anyone knew where I could find an obeah practitioner. A new voice spoke up, "I'm a obeah mon."

"Will you talk to me about it?"

"Well, I can't just..."

At this point, everyone started talking at once. They were amazed that I didn't understand why he wouldn't talk about it. Actually, I did understand. For one thing, he didn't know me, and obeah is illegal here. I could be someone trying to cause him trouble. For another thing, it took many years of study to learn the rituals and ceremonies. Plus, if he really believed in their power, why would he relinquish that power to me? I could then use it against him and steal his clients.

Oh well, I had to try. I'll never get anywhere if I don't.

Saturday, February 10

One month ago today I arrived in Jamaica. So much has happened in that short time. It's going to take awhile for it all to sink in. How amazing my life is.

Mo-Bay has a fantastic beach party every Friday night. It's geared for tourists, but I know all the Jamaicans who work at it, including the entertainers. Normally it costs $35 US to get in, but Reps always get in free. Deedra and I went last night and once again, even though I am no longer a Rep, I was welcomed at no charge. I felt honored.

I love that party and used to sell it to all my clients. When I lived in Mo-Bay, I used to go every Friday night. It was so easy to sell. All I had to do was tell people that I always go. They figured it must be fun or I would get tired of it.

Beach party night is a night to dance barefoot in the sand, wade in the sea, watch an incredible outdoor show, and feast on pumpkin soup and jerk food. I was thrilled to be able to visit with so many friends last night. Everyone welcomed me with open arms. Jamaicans never forget you.

One guy, who I don't even remember, said, "Debbie, dere is no one in de world like you. You are so special. You're like a mother duck. You just want everyone to always be happy." I was touched. All Jamaicans seem like family to me.

I'm really run down and have a nuisance of a cold, so I let myself sleep most of this day away. I'm also spotting blood and trying to convince myself that nothing is wrong. But I'm stuffing a lot of fear. I haven't been eating, going to the bathroom, or taking care of myself very well, so I guess it's normal for my body to react like that.

Sunday, February 11

I'm taking it easy again today. Everyone is at work and it's heavenly to have this time to myself. I got up and made some coffee, a luxury for me since I so often go without it here. Then I showered, did dishes and did laundry. It took a long time since I had to do it by hand, but I feel like I'm back in civilization again. My, I've been spoiled in this life!

I love the wilderness, but I also love my creature comforts. This is a difficult thing for me to admit because I have this fantasy image of myself as a nature sprite. I love the outdoors so intensely that I feel like I should be totally self-sufficient out there at all times. I long to be as free as the birds, not needing clothes, money, cars, appliances or toilets.

I'm going to daydream today, as dreaming gets me in touch with my true essence. Our minds are so wonderful because they allow us to perceive things any way we want. I find all of life to be romantic.

Monday, February 12

I woke up at 4:00 AM and heard strange animal sounds calling to each other. It sounded like it was right in my bedroom, but I could see nothing when I turned on the light. Hmmm... I wonder what it was.

Last night I called Mom in Wisconsin. It was so wonderful to hear her voice again and know that everyone at home is well. I really miss my family and the friends I left back there. It seems like another world and another life. Sometimes I feel like I'm about six different people. I have lives going on in so many places at all times.

I feel different when I come into tourist cities after spending time in the country. I sense the material world more here. I can't help but notice that I am so affected and influenced by my environment that I even see personality changes within myself.

When I stay in the country or small villages, I find myself alone a lot. And I am generally very serious and quiet. I withdraw strongly into my spirit just to be able to cope with the daily hardships. I seldom eat and actually lose any desire to do so after a short time.

Often I am so deeply into my spirit that if someone comes along and says something, I'm startled into an awareness of my physical being. I'm shocked to realize they can actually see me and that I'm really there on that remote spot of earth. I've always been able to talk to anyone, but at times such as these, I find myself unable to say much more than a kind word in passing.

What happens to me when I'm so deeply in my spirit? I communicate strongly with nature, for I learn by listening and observing. Sometimes messages spring out of seemingly nowhere. And certainly my dreams have been powerfully affected.

My writing weighs heavily on me at all times. Sometimes I feel like such a fool in the material world. Big shot Debbie is off to Jamaica to write a book. But she gets here and feels like she doesn't know what she's doing. Her confidence falters and she wonders how she thought she could ever do this. Humbly, she realizes how much she has to learn yet. Her love of this mysterious island and its people are her driving force.

It's uncomfortable too, because so many other people believe in my dream and are counting on me to produce something of value. That is quite an awesome awareness I have. I feel very pressured to produce. I must find a way to finish what I've started, whatever that is.

Sometimes I hear myself talking and I wonder where the words come from. I want to tell myself to shut up, but I just keep on talking.

I know that the most important thing of all is to keep placing my faith in my spirit guides. I truly still believe that I was led to do this by listening to my spirit. And this is the kind of work I eventually want to do, to teach people how to go within and listen to what is there. Be guided by your inner self, your soul, not your material self. Most people that I know say they don't know how to do this.

I was led to this place now so that I could fully grasp this. I needed to be able to get fully into my spirit for an extended period of time in order to have this revealed to me. I comprehend the difference between a path that I consciously choose in the physical and one that is revealed to me through my spirit.

Grand Lido Negril, Joey Issa, author, reps

Tuesday, February 13
Last night the Reps and I drove to Negril, which is on the west coast. Birgitta

had arranged for us to spend the evening at Grand Lido. It's a new, very exclusive, all inclusive resort which costs about $300 US a night for a room. It was such fun. We all dressed up. I had to borrow one of Birgitta's dresses, since my backpack attire wasn't suitable.

What a contrast from the way I've been living! All of this was free to us. (Why did I ever quit being a Rep? Temporary insanity?) We started out with a tour of the grounds, complete with the scent of exotic flowers and the music of tree frogs. From there we went into the formal dining room and indulged in an elegant five course dinner. The main course was lobster thermador and the champagne was endless.

Now this next part is really funny. Joey Issa,the resident manager of Grand Lido, sat next to me at dinner. When Birgitta told him about my book, he said that he remembered reading about me in some newspaper. We realized that this couldn't possibly be true, that maybe he was mistaking me for someone else, but all the Reps had the foresight to keep quiet. In any case, he was very interested in my project. He very seriously asked me to let him know when it gets published because he wants to throw a party at Grand Lido to promote it! I won't forget this, Joey! Thanks, my friend.

I found out that Dennis Malcom, a well known singer in Jamaica, was performing last night at Grand Lido. Wouldn't you know it! For once I had decided to leave my tape recorder behind. I did manage to meet up with him and arrange to interview him at Seawind.

I met Dennis when I lived in Trelawny where he used to do shows. He had asked me out for dinner one night, but for some reason I couldn't make it. It had been at least two years since I had seen him, and I was really surprised and pleased that he remembered me. He's adorable and has a dynamic voice. I'm looking forward to the interview.

After dinner we went into the discotheque and danced. It felt so good to play and get silly as we moved to the rhythm. I'm not really a disco person, but once in awhile it's a great release.

Well, it's not last night anymore. It's afternoon and I'm sitting on a beach thinking. I feel like writing is the baby I never had. It's like, sometimes I can't stop my hand from writing and I can never stop myself from dreaming. I dream big. I always have. I simply couldn't concentrate all of my energies into changing diapers. I realize that Mom did that for me, and I am eternally grateful, but I just can't. I need to touch all of humanity. I see all people of all races as my babies. Is this crazy? I'm sure most people would think so, but it's something I feel from my heart and soul.

I just took another swim. I am really enjoying this day. My friends have wandered off to do their own thing. It gives me time to simply stop and be, just be. This is the scene in front of me now: clear sea, then light sea, then dark turquoise sea. Right above my head I see puffy grey, white rimmed clouds. The sun is peeking through, yet is covered enough by the clouds to look like the moon. Out at sea I see brightly colored sunfish sailboats, windsurfers, jet skiers, the horizon. God's touch. It looks like showers pouring in the distance. I hear the waves crashing and I feel the gentle, warm breeze on my back.

Soft, white sand caresses my feet. Bronzed and burned bodies lie all around in brightly colored, often iridescent swimwear. Everyone is relaxed. Directly behind me is a tree with a grey trunk. Its bright green, fat leaves have a deep red vein running through them. Also on this tree are light green stems of sea grapes. They hang and swing in the breeze like the hammocks underneath them. My deepest awareness of today is of color. It is so vibrant and contrasting everywhere. Color is magic.

6

BIBLES AND DUPPIES

*"I know about dem tings, too. I know a local
duppy conqueror. From early childhood I heard
about it."*
—*Gregory Isaacs*

Wednesday, February 14
Oh no! I'm spotting again, have been for two weeks now. God, please don't let
me be sick. I need to live. I have so much to do before I leave this planet! One
thing I dislike so much about the media in America is the fear they instill in
people. It has gotten ridiculous. They send a message to the public that unless
you run to the doctor all the time you can't possibly stay healthy. According
to them the majority of us will fall prey to cancer of some kind or AIDS or
heart problems. I believe that this is very destructive, because if people listen
to this and believe it, then they will create it within themselves.

It takes constant consciousness, but we must draw from our inner strength.
We must call health to ourselves and do what we can to stay healthy. We need
to examine our fears and toss most of them out the window, because what we
think about most we actually draw right to us. If we believe that we will get
sick, then we will get sick! I wonder what would happen if the media was
full of all the good news and joyful things that are constantly happening in

159

the world, instead of the doom and gloom. And what if they spoke of vibrant health for all of us? The shift in attitudes, beliefs, emotions, etc. would change everything!

We humans are pretty funny. We have a tendency to look externally for answers and accept things at face value, rather than going within for our own truth. We use so very little of our potential! Each of us is a wonderland in itself, a storehouse of magic and creativity. Why don't we see it? Maybe it's because if we really and truly acknowledge it, then we will have to accept responsibility for it.

I'm going within, and it's taking me on the ride of my life! I can't turn back anymore. I must accept responsibility for myself and for my contribution to society. It takes courage to do this. I stumble and falter a lot, but it's also exhilarating. I'm not waiting for life to happen. I am life. Magic is everywhere and we can see and experience it if we choose to, if we have the ability to believe. Yes, we have the power.

Today while I relaxed on the beach, speakers were piping out the music of Gregory Isaacs. Known as 'The Cool Ruler,' he is my all time favorite Reggae singer next to Bob Marley. So my head and heart were full of his music and rhythm.

I stayed at T-Water Hotel with Birgitta last night. Little did I know what an amazing evening it would turn out to be! Late in the evening when Deedra dropped us off, we heard music coming from De Buss next door, so we went over to investigate. I couldn't believe my eyes! The Cool Ruler himself was on the beach singing! He is internationally known and gets big bucks for his concerts around the world, and here he was, singing for the locals on the beach for free!

I was so excited I could hardly contain myself. A dreadlock on crutches asked me to dance so I did. No one can sit still to that music! Even crutches cease being an obstacle. The sea, the sand, the stars and moon all danced and celebrated with us.

After the show, I suddenly got the wild idea to interview this superstar. Birgitta told me that I would never find him, but I said, "Watch me!" I was on a mission and nothing was going to stop me. Opportunities like this don't come along everyday. (Or do they and we just don't see them?)

It was meant to be because the most incredible thing happened. Mr. Isaacs had disappeared, but the very first person that I walked up to and inquired of his whereabouts knew him and where he was staying! What are the odds?

As I walked boldly up to his door and knocked, I suddenly felt nervous and almost ran in the other direction. To my surprise, Gregory himself opened the door. He invited me in and we chatted. My first impression of him was that he is a very warm and friendly man. I told him that I really enjoyed his show and asked him if he possibly had a little time because I would like to interview him for a book I'm writing. He said he'd be happy to if I could wait until he showered. Then he laughed, asked me what sign I am, and told me he's a Cancer.

Gregory Isaacs and author, Negril

I sat outside and visited with a band member named Karl while I waited. Gregory came out a bit later and sat next to me on the couch while we talked. He's a tall, slender man with a moustache, beard, smooth brown skin and kind brown eyes. His dreadlocks were tucked up under a white baseball cap with an emblem of Africa on it. He was clad in blue pants and a maroon silk shirt, and wore a necklace with a gold medallion on it. I noticed the hair by his left temple looked reddish up close.

I asked if he minded if Birgitta took a photo of us together. No problem.

I knew this photo would mean a lot to me. It would be a reminder to have the guts to pursue my dreams. I got my interview and it was easier than I thought it would be.

Mr. Isaacs told me he was born in Kingston on July 15, 1950. He has lived there most of his life, but has also done a lot of traveling. I asked where his favorite place is.

"Well, I love all over de world, you know? Cuz God created de world. So anywhere in de world I go, I love it still."

"I know that you've traveled extensively with your tours. Can you tell me where you've been?"

"Yeah. I've been to Africa, Germany, Paris, France, all over America, London, England, all over Canada, all over de Caribbean, many places. So far so good."

"But you always come home to Jamaica."

"Yeah, dat's where my family is."

"Are you married?"

"I tried it, right?" He smiles.

"What happened?"

"It didn't really work."

"Do you have any children?"

Proudly he says, "Yeah, eleven children, six boys and five girls."

"Wow! Are they musically inclined like you?"

"Yeah, well I don't force dem to do it, but dey love it."

"If I ask you something that you don't want to answer, just say so, okay?"

"Sure! Go ahead, go ahead."

"I find Jamaica to be very spiritually oriented and I love that. People here really connect to their souls and I'm trying to find out why."

"Yeah, it's true. It's an inborn concept, right? It's born into de people, and I just so still."

"Do you practice any particular religion?"

"Well, I live up to de basic principles of more law of Rastafari."

"So basically, what do you believe?"

"I believe in de Rastas. I actually live up to de basic principle of de law."

"What does that mean to you?"

"De kingly world of de Almighty all over de world is round, seen? Cuz in de earth dere are many gods. Some worship like dat. Some worship wild tings. Some worship wid stones. Some people worship... You understand what I'm talking about?"

"Yeah. What do you think of duppies?"

"Duppies?" he looks surprised. "Well, I never see dem, but I hear about dem." Here he gives a long, low laugh.

Then everyone erupts into loud laughter. I ask why and Karl says, "It's all rubbish! But you have some widout faces. Like say I see you walking up de road and I call to you. And you turn and I don't see no face, but I see a body. Might be as like dat, you know? So I call it a spirit, a ghost."

Gregory says, "I know about dem tings, too. I know a local duppy conqueror. From early childhood I heard about it."

I loved his answer to my next question. "What is your big dream in life?"

"To uplift all dose who need to be uplifted and to assist dose who need assistance, you know? Both mentally, physically, financially, in all forms. True, yeah."

Here is a man who has worked hard and done well for himself, yet he's not focused on greed. His biggest dream in life is to be of service to others. He didn't even pause to think when I asked him that question. He knew what he wanted. I felt touched and inspired.

We chatted a bit longer about music, school and his childhood, but it was very late and I didn't want to take up any more of his time, so I thanked him and said good-by. He asked if we had a place to stay tonight and told me I was sweet. Then he looked at Birgitta and I and said, "You both are wonderful. Take de best care of yourselves. And enjoy yourselves."

I said, "I wish you all the blessings in the world, Gregory. Keep giving your music to the world because it's a great gift."

"Same unto you. You're a darling!"

I went back to our hotel with a big smile on my face. I was wishing I had been more prepared for this particular interview, but I hadn't foreseen it coming.

Adventures of Coconut Woman

Thursday, February 15

This morning I rode out to Wyndham Rose Hall with Sara. I went down to the beach to meditate. This is one of my favorite beaches because it's always very windy here and the seas are wild. The dark clouds today added even more mystique. My emotions felt like the sea, churned up and intense.

I cheered up when Sara and I arrived at the Country Club for lunch. We enjoyed a live Reggae band as we chowed down on jerk chicken and rice and peas.

After lunch I went across the street to Trelawny Beach Hotel. I found my old friend Mooney over by the water sports department and we had a great reunion. Looking out to sea, I saw his big smile bobbing on the waves. He has a tremendous love of the sea, so it didn't surprise me to find him there.

Mooney was born in Rock District near Falmouth, and has lived there all his twenty-six years. He told me he has never seen duppies, but believes in them. "Yeah, I have a fear feeling, because of how I heard people talk about it and what dey are doing."

He practices no particular religion, but thinks about death sometimes. "I tink about what would happen, say if I go to Heaven or Hell. I would like to go to Heaven someday." He thinks we only have one chance in life. I asked where his beliefs came from.

"You hear people preach and tell you dat if you're ungodly den you're going to Hell. If you're a true person and a Christian, den you go to Heaven. I tink it's best to go to Heaven, you know? Cuz you might want to go see God."

"So what do you think God is? Do you think God is a person sitting up on a throne?"

"Yeah, dat's what I tink."

"What do you think Heaven will be like?"

"It's when you have no fear, and everyting is nice and you're real comfortable. Nutting bad. Everyting is good."

"What do you think we'll do up there?"

"We'll have fun, a lot of fun."

"Do you think we'll eat, drink and have sex, everything like we do here?"

"Yeah, probably." He laughs. "We can eat, drink, make love, everyting, you know, as long as it is good wid God."

"Do you think we'll look the same?"

"Probably. I don't know."

"How do you think you're going to get up there?"

"Be a Christian."

"When I was a little girl, I used to think we would take an elevator up there."

"Well, God will be coming for his chosen people. The sky will be open, and you know I don't know how we will ever go up dere, by a train or a plane or whatever."

"What do you think Hell is like?"

"It's real hot. Exhausted. Fire and stuff like dat. I heard dat if you're thirsty down dere and you ask for water dey give you someting like hot lead to drink."

I asked Mooney what he thought he could do in this life that would be so bad it would possibly send him to hell forever. He thinks he'll go to Hell if he doesn't turn Christian, yet admits he's not particularly worried about it at the moment. He said he needs to start settling down and going to church.

Mooney told me he has seven brothers and two sisters, by different Mom's and Dad's. He also has a four year old daughter named Jodianne.

"Where did you go to school?"

"All age school in Falmouth. Den I go to de Cedric Ditus Secondary School. Dat's where I was graduated."

"When you were a little boy, what kind of things did you get punished for doing?"

"Uh, going to de sea, to de ocean. You know at dat time, a lot of people's kids drown and stuff like dat, so my parents always worried about me going swimming. I get punished for dat."

"How did they punish you?"

"Sometimes I get flogging and sometimes I couldn't play or nutting."

When Mooney finished school, he worked as a general mechanic in a garage for awhile. He had a falling out with his boss and decided to become a waiter. "I was trained as a professional waiter in Fisherman's Inn, the Chinese restaurant, where we did practical and theory for de test, because dey dedicated to first class service.

"Some people came from all over and we get eight weeks training. We get a lot of training on how to set de table, how to serve wine, how to carry de tray, how to even meet people and see people, and do a lot of stuff, you know? Dere was twenty-eight of us in training, and den dey did need about twelve of us starting and I was in de first twelve. I end up getting like ninety-six percent. I got someting like a certificate at home dat I received. Only ting I used to be really neat in white shirt, bow tie, black pants, black shoes, blue socks.

"I was doing quite well, but tings start to get slow and I don't get too many hours of work, so I leave and start working at de marina at Glistening Waters. I work on de sport fishing boat and on de cruise, which I really did enjoy."

I met Mooney while he worked on this cruise. The people who stayed at Trelawny Beach Resort could take this cruise for free. It was in the evening and included all the rum punch one could drink in an hour. Mooney was the tour guide and would provide a history of the area. I asked him to tell me again about the magical water there.

"It's called de glistening water. Dere are some microscopic organisms living inside dere, which are called dinoflagellates. Whenever dey are irritated, dey light up a lot like fireflies.

"Well, scientists discovered de main ting dey lives among is a layer of brackish water, wid de red mangrove and de oysters. And what dey call de brackish waters is a mixture between salt and fresh. Inside de bay is de ending of de Martha Brae River and de beginning of de ocean, which is salt water. So it is a mixture of salt and fresh.

"And de trees dat are inside of de bay are called red mangrove. Dey have a lot of oysters beside de red mangrove, and inside de mud, sort of silt. So dose are de main tings de scientists discovered dem lives off of.

"So if you take up a bucket of some water and irritate it at night, de water will glow like electricity. And if someone goes swimming, you can see everywhere dey go. And when it's perfect, if de rain begins to fall you can see all de rain drops on de surface, but only at night. De darker it is, de brighter you see.

"When it do get affected is like too much rain falls. Dat brings too much fresh water to de surface, so dey pretend to go much deeper. Or if dere is too much moonlight you do not see very bright. But whenever de night is dark and having good weather, it is amazing. You wouldn't believe it! I used to jump off de boat during de cruise and swim around. You know you can see all trail, all movement. Dat mean if somebody can't swim, fall off de boat, it's no problem finding dem!"

I know that I never tired of seeing this phenomenon. I used to take my clients out on the charter fishing boat also. I remember one time when we hooked two six foot long blue marlin within thirty seconds of each other. Mooney and the other guy running the boat both jumped down to help reel them in. I was ordered to head up into the top of the boat and drive it. I was terrified as I had no idea what to do and the swells were about twelve feet high out there. "Just turn de wheel so dat de compass keeps pointing east, so we don't capsize." I prayed hard and allowed instinct to guide me. What an adventure! We made it, marlin and all. That evening, the captain cooked one of the marlin for us and we feasted.

Mooney said that several different kinds of fish are caught on the charters. "We get blue marlin, white marlin, sailfish, kingfish, tuna, albacore, dorado dolphin. When we say dolphin, some people tink we is talking about Flipper, but is different. We also get salmon, and sharks like mahoes and tiger, but no great whites."

I asked who Mooney is working for now. "I'm working out from de Fisherman's Inn Dive Resort, next door to Glistening Waters."

The owners of Glistening Waters Yacht Club were called Mr. Pat and Mrs. Pat. I knew they had been trying to sell the place so I asked Mooney if they were still there. "Yeah, dey still have it. De guy dat was going to buy it is in prison right now in Kingston. He is a Canadian. Dey caught him wid seven hundred pounds of marijuana and four hundred pounds of hash oil. Him try to bring it in on a sailboat."

I asked Mooney what he liked about his childhood. "Ahhh... favorite childhood memories...playing dolly house! I always like to be de fodder or de doctor. We send de kids off to school so I could take good care of de modder." Mooney emits a dirty laugh.

"Now that you're an adult, what do you like to do for entertainment?"

"Not much now. Right now de cruise started so I is out fishing. When I don't have a charter I assist by de hotel at Trelawny. De company I work for owns de water sports department here. I go scuba diving, snorkeling, do everyting."

I know in the States one must have at least the certification level of Dive

Master in order to be able to take a group of people out diving. I'm a Dive Master and had to go through several levels of rigorous training, including Rescue Diving. So I was absolutely shocked when I found out that Mooney isn't even a certified diver at all. Yet he is allowed to assist with groups as long as a certified diver is along. I'm sure he's a good diver, but I wonder what he would do in an emergency underwater. I found my training invaluable.

We spoke a bit about the house he is building. He had a dream of building a home and he focused on it and now it's happening. Mooney used to make excellent rum punch, so I asked for his recipe.

"Well, to be frank wid you, dere's a lot of different tings kept in de rum punch for flavor. When making a real Jamaican rum punch, you say, 'one sour, two sweet, three strong, four weak.' Do you know what dose are is? You know you have to go by measurements, right? To use a measuring cup you say like one sour is de lime juice. Two sweet is de syrup. Three strong is de rum. Four weak is de water. Or widout using de water you can use ginger ale, or fruit punch, or you can put in a couple of Red Stripe beer or some fermented liquor."

Mooney told me that he was supposed to go out fishing this afternoon, but the waves are too rough today for any kind of boating. I laughed and said, "What a great job! If the weather is rough you get the afternoon off!"

"Yeah. All we do is make sure everyting is in good condition, take care of de equipment. Cuz when everyting is okay, you have no problems, you know?"

"You're absolutely right, my friend!"

I caught a ride back to Mo-bay with Sara and spent the rest of the afternoon talking with local characters downtown. A man carrying a portfolio approached me, so I decided to listen to his sales pitch. He was an artist named Paul Thomas, and his watercolors were so lovely that they sold themselves. I bought one of a Jamaican lady carrying a fruit basket on her head and had him sign it.

He told me he's from the parish of St. Ann and has been painting for seven years. Paul was wearing a black and white felt hat that had a butterfly pin and some kind of military pin on it. His T-shirt had a palm tree on it with the word Reggae on it. He said a lot of people like his hat.

When I asked Paul how he got interested in painting, he said, "Well I guess I was just being inspired by an artist when I went to an exhibition and saw some of his works."

I told him that I had studied art in high school and college and that I think water colors are one of the most difficult medias to work in because once you put the brush to paper you can't change it. You really need to know what you're doing before you do it or it will end up all muddy and messy. Oils and acrylics can be scraped off and reworked.

Paul said he thinks he definitely has some degree of natural talent, but that he also had a bit of schooling for it. His teacher liked his work and that inspired him to continue. I asked where he sells his paintings.

"Well, actually dere are a couple of galleries around town and dey buy quite a lot from me sometimes. But I sell dem to de tourists dat come here, especially during tourist season."

Like most Jamaicans, Paul is from a large family. He has four brothers and three sisters, but no children of his own yet. I asked him what he does for fun.

"Well, my fun just compromise of my own art, as I said before. It was my best hobby and I just kept doing it and dat's all right. I just love it, eh?"

I know a lot of people who just can't figure out why they came to Earth. They don't know how to find their purpose or feel fulfilled. Paul realized early in his life that our talents were given to us in the hope that we would develop and use them. The things we love most and the talents we have are keys to our purpose. If we love what we're doing and we're good at it, then we're on the right track. If we hate what we're doing and it drains us, the universe is sending us a strong message to change it.

A lot of people feel trapped and insist they are powerless to change their situation. With that kind of an attitude, they are powerless. It takes courage to make changes and accept our choices in life, but blaming the world for our circumstances creates a state of hell. No one can change us but ourselves. It all starts with what we believe, and we choose what we believe.

As a child, Paul enjoyed soccer, tennis, and, of course, art. His passion for it has grown over the years as he continues to develop his talent. He has brought beauty into our world. I found it interesting that whenever Paul spoke of art, he pronounced it 'hart.' His art and his heart are truly one and the same.

Paul spent a lot of time with his grandmother when he was growing up, and he is still living with her now. I asked how he was disciplined when he was young. "Well, flogging wid a belt, naturally! But it's all right. If it wasn't for de flogging, maybe I would be an outlaw person right now. But de flogging taught me a lot, you know? Yeah, discipline and a lot of tings dat is good."

I asked if he goes to church. "Well, I'm a Christian, but I don't go to church. Maybe I go once or two times a year. I go to Salvation Army sometimes. I used to visit it more often when my grandmother was more active. And because she's older, she doesn't have enough energy to go to church now, so I just kick it out a little. But I go dere now and den."

"Do you ever think about what's going to happen when you die?"

"Well naturally I have thought about dat on several occasions by myself."

"Are you afraid to die?"

"Gosh, I don't know. I shouldn't be, because I mean I'm not doing anyting wrong, and I'm doing my job and everyting. I tink what I'm doing is right, so I shouldn't be. But I'm not sure at de moment. It's like in between."

"What do you think happens to us when we die?"

"Well, from what I have read in de bible, I tink dere is Heaven and Hell. And I tink dere is a supreme being somewhere. Yeah, I know dat. I feel it sometimes, you know. But I'm not sure what's going to happen when I die. I should be sure. Maybe I need some knowledge about dat."

"None of us knows for sure, Paul. But I think you have the absolute, total, right idea. You said you're living the best way that you can, and that's really all any of us can do."

Talk turned to music and I asked him who his favorite Jamaican entertainer is. "It's Jimmy Cliff. I'm sure you've heard of him. He sings a lot of inspiring songs. 'Many Rivers to Cross' is my favorite song. If you're working and you want to keep—I mean, when you do your work and you feel bored or someting, when you hear dat song it inspires you to work."

"What other forms of art do you like?"

"I like art in de form of dancing, yeah. And I like to look at odder artist's work. And I love criticism. I like it when someone criticize my work, so dat I can know what's wrong from what's right, especially if de person is a professional artist."

"That shows me how very serious you are about your work. A lot of people are afraid of criticism, but you have a very healthy attitude about it. You use it as a tool for learning, as a part of your education.

"I always ask people about duppies. Do you believe in them?"

"Well I have heard a lot of tales dat sometimes it lead my heart go funny, but I mean it doesn't worry me you know. But right now I'm listening to a cassette of a type of story called 'De Jaculette.' It's nice to listen to, a lot of joy and fun.

"I never see a duppy, but maybe dey exist. I have looked into what people say, and maybe dey do exist."

"What was that story you were listening to? The Jackel?"

"Jacula."

"What is that?"

"Well, dat's de story about a mon who owns a castle, and well, he is a vampire. And dere's dis mon who comes from England for dis Jacula to sign some documents for his estate in England. I haven't listened to all of it, so I don't know much more about it as yet."

Here I finally figured out that Jacula is really Count Dracula. I found it interesting that he described the tape as full of joy and fun. I always found Dracula movies frightening and somber.

We were interrupted here by a street vendor. "My name is Cheap Susan, odderwise known as Joan. Lady, you should get your hair braided. You will be local girl if you get your hair braided."

I told Cheap Susan that I wasn't a tourist and didn't have much money. We got to talking and when she found out that I like Gregory Isaacs, she had her boyfriend make me a tape of some of Gregory's best songs. I was delighted, as she gave me a good deal. But when I played it later, I discovered that he had dubbed 'Night Nurse' on the tape over and over because I had mentioned that it was my favorite song.

I thanked Paul for talking with me and headed down to Union Street to see if Harris was around. He wasn't, but I visited a bit with Pearl Harbor.

Later, I headed over to Seawind Resort, where I had an interview scheduled with Dennis Malcom. Something had unexpectedly come up and he had to cancel, but we rescheduled for tomorrow morning. I decided to hang around and catch his show as long as I had gone all the way over there.

I never seem to be at a loss for people to talk to. As I sat back and waited for the show to begin, a nice looking gentleman asked if he could join me. He had on a white shirt and jeans and he smelled great. I was surprised to learn that he was a poultry salesman from Kingston. Robert looked more like an entertainer than a poultry salesman. As we talked, I was impressed by his manners and kindness.

I opened with my favorite subject, duppies, of course. Robert laughed real hard, then said, "Well, from what I have gathered about duppies or ghosts, as you might hear de term, it's really superstitious to me. My grandparents, one of my parent's parent, in dose early days dey tink dat duppies was really someting dat walk down de street and would torment or more less haunt someone. But if you believe in de bible so to speak, you got to realize dat when a person die, dey just die. And dere's nutting dat goes around physically."

"Do you think that the bible really says that?"

"Yes it does. When you die, you die. You go to de earth and you become a part of de earth and you are no more. People say dey see duppy, but what really happen is dat de Devil is forming de image of de person dat you might know before, and come to you and put it in a physical form. And you say, 'Oh, I saw Mr. So and So, who died many years ago.' But basically, it wasn't really him! Dat's really what is duppy. Dat's a fact."

"Do you believe in the Devil?"

"No. Yes, yes! I believe in de Devil! Yes, dey do it. Yes, Devil exists."

"What is the Devil?"

"Well, de Devil is really Satan who has been turned out of Heaven by God. And he's a spirit form. In early biblical days, de Devil usually be on Earth physically. He disguise himself as a human being and mix himself among people and do a lot of terrible tings to people. De Devil has been, so to speak, put into control by God. And he's here, not so much in a physical form, but in a spiritual form. You know?"

"Do you think you have a spirit?"

"Of course you have a spirit! What you call your spirit is really your soul or whatever. And when you die, your body disintegrates into de earth and rots away."

"But your soul goes on. So then I assume you believe in the concept of Heaven, too."

"Well, Heaven is right here on Earth. Okay, Armageddon, which is when God comes back to Earth to decide, or to get people to repent of dere sins and reconcile dere lives, is approximately anodder thousand years. And during dat thousand years, de Devil will never roam on Earth. And you're left to God to really prove dat you are sincere, and try to live an upright life. Now, during dis time, if you decide you're going to take de course of devil like behavior, den you will die a second death and you will be no more. You will never be resurrected."

"Do you believe in Hell?"

"No, dere's nutting like Hell. Hell is a grave! In de bible, Hell, termed Hades, is really de grave. Dat's right."

"So where is the Devil? Is he just floating through eternity being miserable?"

"De Devil was once an angel who betrayed God and he turned him out. Him floating around. Today, de Devil does so many works. Okay, de whole scenario of mankind, and dere laws to govern de land, and de whole question of merchandising, is all de Devil's work. When I say Devil's work, don't get me wrong, right? In odder words, dere are so many tings happen not because God plan it dat way, but because mankind, wid de work of de Devil behind him, dis is what happened. And de day of revelation, dat's when mankind will be put to de test of what he should or shouldn't do, again.

"It's not a sudden (snaps fingers) snap in de pan action. It's a gradual process. It's not everybody just come up out of de grave and come alive. It's a state in reverse. In odder words, your grandparents, your parents knew you, and your parents were known by dere grandparents. Dat's how recognition comes along, in reverse. Dat's how we come to know each odder."

I had no idea what he was talking about here, so I let it go. As we spoke more, he made it clear that he believes that the people who reconcile with God will live forever, but those who don't will simply cease to exist.

"So basically your concept of Heaven would be like Earth as Paradise?"

"It is! It will be Paradise in de days when evil is no longer on Earth. Dat is how it's going to be."

"What religion are you?"

"Ah, dat's a good question! I study Jehovah's Witness. And you know, dey really go in depth into de bible. Dey go far wid it."

"Can I ask you about your dreams?"

"I do dream. Of course I do dream! And what is a dream? Well, what causes a dream really, is unfinished thought dat you have earlier in de day or maybe a week ago. But it was not in your subconscious mind. It was not completed. So it's like a recorder. It goes over de process and brings you back into de same situation. And den it's just finished.

"Sometimes you're sleeping and you wake up from your sleep and you say, "Oh! You know, I was dreaming about so and so,' and you've got to finish de dream, so to speak. How's it going to end? Ha-ha! But it's really unfinished thoughts in de subconscious mind dat is finishing de process.

"Mark you, on de odder hand, some people have a gift of dreaming tings dat's going to happen for de future, and dey foresee it! And say, 'Look, I dreamed you had an accident and you were killed or dead.'

"You know, people have special gifts. All people have different gifts. Some people have gifts to tell about de future long years before, long ago, for de future. And it do happens. It do come to pass."

"What is your waking dream in life? In other words, what do you really want?"

"As I see it now, all I need is comfort. If you're comfortable, whatever, financially or spiritually, or have your kids, your loved ones, whatever, dat's de greatest ting dat you could ever want in life right now."

I commented that I was surprised to learn that Robert has only one child. It didn't seem very Jamaican.

"I don't believe in having a lot of kids and den not being able to take care of dem properly. You know what causes de problem. You must remember, in poor societies, in Third World, a ghetto is de same. People behave like de same in any part of de world. A ghetto is a ghetto when poverty exists in a society.

"It's just dere way of enjoying life! Dey just relax. Dey don't have no money to spend. Dey don't have no where to go. So dey do what God made dem to do. Dey relax and have sex. Dey don't believe in birth control. Whatever happens, happens!

"Dey don't understand it. And dey're not prepared to accept de knowledge if you give dem de knowledge, whether dey should or shouldn't. And so dey just end up having a lot of unwanted kids dat dey can't take care of properly. And dat puts a strain on de government. And on everybody who works. So it's a complex world we live in."

"Yeah, and they're all so cute and so precious!"

"And at de same time, each and every one of dem has a purpose in life.

174

Dat's de truth, so you can't just condemn dem! It's just dat if dose poor persons were able to guide dem in de right channel, de right way of life, den dose kids can come up to be very great persons and make very great contributions to society. Isn't it true?"

I agreed that it is. We quit talking for awhile because the show was starting. I really enjoyed it. It had been a long time since I had seen Dennis perform. I had forgotten how really good he is. What a voice! It re-energized me, so Robert and I went dancing at the Cave Disco after the show. It was time to laugh and play. I felt I had done a good day's work.

Friday, February 16

This morning I met Dennis on the terrace at Seawind for our interview. He apologized for having to cancel last night, then took both my hands gently in his, looked me in the eye and thanked me for my patience. I found him to be very sincere, kind, and down to earth. He had a real sense of purpose and a strong belief in himself. His voice was deep and sexy and he spoke slowly, sounding quite British and educated, but when he got excited or thought about his childhood, he would lapse back into Patois. It was charming.

He began by telling me that he was born in the heart of Kingston on July 25, 1954. He was the fourth child born out of six, and has three brothers and two sisters. Most of his life has been spent in Kingston. I asked Dennis to tell me about his childhood.

"It was a typical childhood for any Kingstonian. I was kind of lucky in that every holiday I got to go to de country wid my aunts and uncles and all dat, so I grew up in two sides of Jamaica. I grew up knowing what de Kingston life was about, and I grew up learning how to swim in de rivers, and catching crayfish, and cooking out under de trees, and (laughs) as we call it, running a boat. Everybody pool togedder and put in a ten cent or a five cent or a dollar and dey would cook wid it, buy flour and make dumpling and rice. So I grew up learning how to do dese tings. I grew up learning how to shoot bird, and knowing de different plants and such."

I asked if he ever still does those things just for fun. He said his brother bought a home in St. Mary. To get to it, one must walk through a river, so they often just sit right down in the river and play and have a good time.

For fun as a child, Dennis and his friends would play war by picking limes

175

and throwing them at each other. He remembered one time when a lime hit him in the nose and gave him a nose bleed. Another thing he found fun was having someone climb up into the star apple tree and throw apples down. The guys on the ground had to catch them. They also enjoyed playing cricket and just running free.

Dennis Malcom

"I remember when I was in Kingston and my family used to play little tings like, in de season when de corn came in we'd get corn and roast it on de fire. And each mon would have his corn on de cob, eating roast corn. You would get a certain amount of grains in your hand and would say to your brodder, 'Ship sail.' And he would say, 'Sail fast.' And you would say, 'How much mon on board?' Dat meaning, how many corn grains you have? And if he guesses like six and you have ten, you'd say, 'No. Give me six.' Den he owes you six. Dere were simple games dat kept us occupied. Dere weren't any backgammon and dese kind of games."

"When did you become interested in girls?"

He laughs heartily. "Girls... Oh wow, unfortunately, very tender age. I got interested in girls from my relationships wid guys in de country, because guys in de country are more promiscuous dan in Kingston. Dere's a little guy, we

176

call him Copey. Copey used to hold down little girls and do all kinds of tings to dem, and he would tell dem—"

I interrupted here, "How little were these girls?"

"Well, we were about seven years old. But I used to just sit and learn and listen. He was one of de bad boys in de village you know. But him turn good because he was growing wid his grandmodder."

"Did you grow up with any superstitions? For instance, someone told me that he will not eat a woman's cooking if she cooks while she has her period, because he's afraid that she's going to catch him and put this little spell on him."

"Tie up dem heart. I've heard about it. Dat is common in Jamaica. I've never been afraid of dat. I don't know if I believe it. Probably half of Jamaica do." He laughs. "I don't tink I've had a relationship wid a woman who would want to do dat. How I heard it is dat if she's seeing her period and she wants to hold you, she wants to make you hers for life, den she cooks like, stewed peas and rice. It's red wid de peas and all dose tings, and she puts some of her menstrual ting in it and dat holds you."

He looks thoughtful for a moment and then says, "I don't know if I've ever spoken wid a woman who would want to do dat. So I never worry about it."

"Do you know of any other superstitions?"

"Well, dere are so many! My God, it's so different. You know like when you have de little children in school, don't make anybody touch dem on dere head."

"Why is that?"

He laughs. "I don't know. Like for example, I have an aunt who was a brilliant teacher. And she was hardly liked by de rest of de staff. One day one of dem staff gave her one boiled egg for lunch. She ate it and dat was de end of her career. She just become deaf instantly!"

"What???"

"Yeah. It's called obeah, Debbie, and it's alive and well. It has to do wid dat you know. If you believe in God, den dere is good and evil. And if you believe in God, den dere must be a Satan. And what dese people do, dey call upon de powers of evil, just like witchcraft or black magic. And it does work, just like how a Ouija board does work. I don't know if you've been told to stay clear of Ouija boards. De same powers dat cause a Ouija board to work is de same powers dat de local obeah mon from Haiti or Africa, our ancestors, draw upon to call evil spirits.

"De bible records a war in Heaven. Lucifer was a guardian of de throne of God, and is now Satan. He was de most beautiful of all de angels ever created. You can find dis in de bible. And he got very jealous of God and said, 'I will rise above de throne of God. I will be as God.' And so he started a revolt in Heaven, and all his angels wid him. Michael de Archangel fight against him. Lucifer fell like a shooting star, got kicked literally out of Heaven, and a whole host of angels wid him.

"Dese are now called de Fallen Angels and dese are de angels dat de obeah mon and de witchcraft persons draw upon. In odder words, dey are demons. Dese are part of de demonic hosts dat dwell in Heaven, because de bible speaks of de God of dis world, which is Satan himself, so he and his demons control dis side of de world you know. So it is very, very real! Dis no joke. It's no fantasy. It's no myth. It is a serious ting, mon.

"My modder told me so many stories of people coming in de Revival Church. A lady came in wid like a swelling on de leg. De minister call down and pray and do certain tings, and dey cut de leg open and a whole bunch of hair come out. Dis is tings my modder has seen.

"She has even seen a woman who have been pregnant, a woman dat have been pregnant for literally almost two years, can't have a child, dis big, big belly. And when dey give her certain tings to drink, well den she start vomit and tings start come out of her, like she give birth to a lizard. You know?"

Jamaicans honor and almost worship their mothers. I knew that Dennis would never say this if it wasn't true. "And you think this stuff happened because somebody put an obeah spell on them?"

"Yeah! Can go to a Revival or Pocomania Church. Dis is a very serious ting. It's not a joke ting. Some people take it lightly, say, 'Oh, I don't believe in it.' Dey are wrong! For example, if I come now to a place like dis, and I'm doing well in my career, I never turn my back on my drink. People can drop one ting in your drink and dat's it! So I have an engineer and he's de only person dat can give me a drink of water or anyting. I don't accept anyting from anybody else."

"Did something happen to you or are you just being careful?"

"No. I have been careful everyday and every night. I am not paranoid. I'm just being wise, because de bible tells you dat you must be wise as serpents and harmless as doves. Harm no mon, but let no mon harm you. So you just protect yourselves you know. And you cannot be naive. Dere's evil all around you, you know.

"Dere's a passage to de bible dat gives credence to dis also. It says, 'For we wrestle not against flesh and blood, but against principalities and powers, spiritual wickedness in high places.' We wrestle against tings unseen dat are constantly bombarding us, and people can turn dem to us. But den again, de power of God is stronger dan evil. So one needs not to fear. I don't walk in fear, you know. But it's real.

"My uncle-in-law had a brodder who had a normal baby. I remember one night dey left him out on a porch veranda for a few minutes. When dey came back, dey saw him foaming. From dat time on, de child is an invalid. Dey say a duppy hit him!

"Duppies are not really duppies. Duppies are really demons, Fallen Angels. Dis is how Satan keep people trapped, because you know, people pray to Lucifer in de States, and maybe even in Jamaica, too. Dese people take on de spirit, de guise of dead people, and dey appear to people as a way to keep people trapped in a satanic realm.

"To say dat dese tings don't exist is to be so naive and stupid because we live in more dan a physical world. It's a spiritual world dat hardly any of us know anyting about.

"My grandparents were Revivalists. Dat is different from Pocomania. Pocomania are people who deal more wid de evil side of tings, dat church. Den you have de Revivalists now, who is more de people who protects you. Like if someting was wrong wid you, you would go to a Revivalist person and dey would make tings right for you. Dat's more like it. Our former Prime Minister himself, Seaga, was a Revivalist. A lot of people don't know, but he's deep into dis. He's deep in for years."

"What do you think is going to happen after we die?"

"I grew up in a Christian home. As far back as I can remember, we always went to church, like Sunday School in Angelican, and den we graduated into what is known as Full Gospel, which is like Baptists and your heavier stuff, more spiritual. So my belief is very deep rooted.

"I was a very serious, one hundred percent dedicated Christian. I still consider myself a Christian, but like, an operational Christian, like I go to church every Sunday. I used to go seven days a week. Dere was Sunday morning and Sunday night at church. Monday you would have a bible study. Tuesday you would have some odder church activity. Wednesday you would have choir practice. Thursday you would have young people's meeting. Friday you would have- so you know, you would have had happened to go to church every single night!

"Dat was my way of life and we enjoyed it. It was great. When we sat down, instead of talking about girls, we would talk about de tings of God. It was a very good life and sometimes I miss it. We still lived a normal life and did normal tings, but we took our God and our religion very seriously."

"So how did you get interested in entertainment?"

"I was married in de church. Tings went wrong in de marriage and I started drifting. I came to Brownstown to live and I was kind of a luke warm Christian. And de marriage eventually broke up.

"I drifted and it was like a new life for me. You cannot embrace de two realms. You cannot be a Christian and sleep around, so I went de odder way. It's de first time dat I'm saying dis, but, you know, it happened dat way. I decided to pursue a musical career. One night I saw a guy singing at de Ocho Rios Sheraton and I said, 'Shit, I can do dis.' Dis was eight years ago."

"What were you doing for a living before that?"

"I was selling insurance. Den a friend say his business in trouble and he need someone who can run tings. It was in export of yams. I felt prestige wearing a suit and tie as an insurance mon, and my wife say, 'Bwoy! Are you sure you want to do dis yam ting?' But dey offered me lots more money, so I took de job.

"Dat's when we started drifting more apart because I was in de country all de time. I made an attempt to save de marriage, but it broke apart. At night I used to have problems. When I finished working, my mind would be in Kingston. I needed something to get my mind off of her and my little son. And so I started singing, and bop, my career began!"

I told Dennis that he is an inspiration. He found something that he wanted to do, and rather than questioning his ability to do it, he just went full speed ahead and did it.

"I went to Rum Keg Disco at Trelawny Beach and told Dalton James dat I wanted to do a show. Him look at me good and say, 'Are you sure you can do it?' I say, 'Yes, mon!' Him say, 'I give you one chance, for $350 for de night. Don't let me down!' I say, 'I would never do dat to you. Tank you sir!' "

Dalton was obviously nervous about it and even came to the rehearsal. Dennis put the whole show together, then called all of his friends from Kingston and asked them to show up and help him look good. His very first night he got a standing ovation. The following year he was nominated Best Cabaret Performer for Jamaica by Rockers Magazine. And his career hasn't stopped. He moved into recordings, and in 1988 he had a number one song in England on the Reggae charts.

When I told him his attitude is wonderful, he said, "My attitude is inborn, given from my modder. People wonder how I do tings and why, what keeps me going. Like Saturday I'm going to do four shows. People wonder, 'How can he do four shows and do dem as hard as he does?'

"But it's a sense of purpose, a sense of direction. It's what I want out of life. I want to be the best I can possibly be! I want to be a millionaire. I want to be rich. And I make no apologies about dis. I want to be because we in Jamaica, all of us dat you can look around, we didn't come from rich parentage. Dey're all humble and poor Jamaicans.

"I have sisters and brodders and I have a family. I have a modder and a fodder. My fodder is sixty odd. My modder is going close to sixty and dey are still working." He sighs. "Dat has to stop! And if it is me dat is going to put a stop to it, den I'll work like a son of a bitch to put a stop to it!

"My brodder is in Miami. He was struggling so long. He now has opened a place called 'De Jerk Machine.' Tank God for dat! It serve jerk pork, jerk chicken, jerk fish, jerk conch, jerk shrimp, jerk chop suey. It is doing well and he has just started.

"So in odder words I would love, for my family's sake, to be rich. And like I said, I don't make any apologies for dat. Some people say, 'Oh, you love money too much.' I say, 'Dat's your ting. You can always say dat.' I know why I want it. I want it for nutting wrong wid it, because de bible says, 'Riches has always been a blessing.'

"Whenever anyone was ever blessed in de bible, like Soloman, it was a blessing from God. Cuz when he prayed to God and asked for wisdom, de Lord said, 'Not only will I give you wisdom, but I'll make you de richest mon dat ever lived.' And Soloman's riches was equal to four times dat of de entire United States. No mon has ever been rich like him since and no mon ever will be. You know Job, his blessing from God was riches, so dere's nutting wrong wid riches. Some people don't want to be rich."

"That's right! It's not the money itself, it's the motive."

"Dat is number one! Dat is right, and I've always said dat hard work is de only ting dat's going to give me mine. And if it comes by hard work, I'm going to get it. If it comes by drugs, all dem kinds of tings, I'm not interested. I'll never sell dem and I'll never use dem. I don't and I won't use dem either! Dat's not for me. I've chartered my course and I know exactly where I want to go and what I want to do. I'm on dat course and nutting is going to steer me from it. Some people don't know where de hell dey are going!

"I started de house where I want to live. It's a seven bedroom mansion wid a swimming pool and Jacuzzi and a game room and library and studio. It's halfway done. It's in Brownstown, in de cool hills. So it's no longer a dream, but a reality.

"People tink, 'Bwoy! Dis guy is crazy.' People have looked at me and said, 'More guys wid bigger money dan yourself would never attempt anyting like dat.' I said, 'Well, you know, de same energy it takes to wish for a loaf of bread is de same it takes to wish for a supermarket. So I'm going for de supermarket!' "

"Good for you! Attitude is everything! People think too small."

"Too small mon! When dey tink big it confuses dem. Because de same people who are looking at me saying dat it can't be done are interrupted by me doing it! I'm glad I'm doing it. I've worked so hard."

We talked for awhile about Dennis's philosophies on music. He loves Reggae, but for business purposes he concentrates on R&B. "Reggae will always be an island rhythm. Bob Marley has taken Reggae wide. Ziggy Marley has taken it even further. UB40, which is a white and black mixed group, has taken it big. But Reggae will never be as big as R&B, so dat's what I mostly do."

"It makes me feel happy to know that you are using your talent, Dennis. You're getting what you want in life, but you're contributing so much to life also. You're bringing joy to others. People need to develop their talents. You've got to aim big. You're not going to get there if you don't."

"My modder always told us dat. You have to blame my modder for dat. She is always strong. Success has never gone to my head and I pray to God dat I will remain de same way. I'm not looking at women after my shoulders. I'm not in dat kind of ting you know. I'm looking forward to my career and to dis year."

"Do you dream much when you sleep?"

"Not very often, but when you called dis morning I was about to get a license plate number in my dream, heh-heh. I dreamed I had an accident. Dis guy just drove into my back and admitted he was wrong. I was about to take his number and de phone rang. It was de first time in a long time dat I remember my dream so clearly."

"Shoot! Hope you don't need that number later! Do you think dreams are prophesies?"

"I tink to a large extent. What I get is feelings, vibes. Dis is what I live by, and dey're usually right. Like if I have a relationship wid you and you're fooling around, if I tune into you spiritually I can sometimes know. I don't know what is wrong, but I search and I usually discover what is wrong.

"I tank God for dat and I'm careful. If I meet somebody, I can feel dem and I can know if dis is a good or a bad person. I tink all of us can do dat, but we just don't exercise it.

"A couple of years ago, I was driving real fast wid a guy. For some strange reason I felt like I had to slow down. I didn't question it. And sure enough, around de next corner a guy was coming in on my side. I just laughed and said, 'See? Dat's why I had to slow down.'

"Women have come up to me and want to have a relationship wid me, and for some strange reason I just can't give myself to dem. And den I discover dat dey are sleeping around wid six, seven, eight men. And I just laugh.

"One of my philosophies in life is 'don't force anyting.' I try, but dat is different from forcing. I make it flow, because nature and God has set up everyting in perfect timing you know. De whole universe is in perfect synchronization, so don't step out of line. It just makes tings happen most times you know. And it works dat way. I mean, we are really here to work on tings, but don't do tings and buy people off."

We spoke for awhile longer about his immediate plans. Then he asked me all about my life and the book. I really enjoyed my morning with Dennis.

He's a most interesting person, and not afraid to live his own truth. He understands how important it is to be able to be your own friend and live happily with yourself.

I went to the beach party again tonight. As always, it was magical. Part of the entertainment is the African Fertility Dancer. His name is Uriel and he's gorgeous! He does an incredibly sensuous dance and goes throughout the audience shaking his fertility wand over the heads of the women. It's great fun.

Uriel performing African Fertility Dance

Uriel's costume is exotic and erotic, guaranteed to arouse the fire in any woman. His body is in perfect shape, and he is clad only in a black and white zebra lined G-string with a white tail, ankle pom-poms, and a feathery headdress. His face is painted and glittered, and his entire body is covered in a luscious smelling oil.

He told me he would be happy to do an interview after his show and agreed to meet me at some picnic tables as far away from the crowds as we could get. As I waited for him, I let myself soak up all the beauty around me. The night was warm and the tree frogs and waves were singing in harmony. The stars seemed close enough to reach up and touch.

I've known Uriel for years. He's one of the sweetest men I have ever met and I cherish our friendship. I remember when I got transferred to Acapulco while working for Apple. The last time I saw Uriel before I left he told me that every time he did the Fertility Dance he would do it for me, as an ode to our friendship. He reminded me of that again this evening, and said that he has never forgotten that promise and he still thinks of me whenever he dances. What a romantic soul he is! Thanks, Uriel. My life has been extremely fertile, filled with love and magic.

I heard Uriel come up behind me and turned to see his radiant, shy smile. Reaching out to him I said, "You are so wonderful. I love you so much. Great show tonight!" He held me close for a few minutes and rocked me gently in his arms. There was such a strength in his gentleness. I sensed his innocence and his deep love of mankind. He's humble, shy and soft spoken. To me he's a precious flower that always seems to be blooming.

Uriel had just showered and smelled of scented soap. He was clad in red spandex dance wear that was pulled down to his waist. His hair is short and he has huge brown eyes with unusually long lashes. His smile lit up the night as we started our interview.

He told me he's been dancing on the north coast for three years now, but he first studied dancing in school for five years. He started out learning all the traditional dances like Cumina, Pocomania, Quadra, Ghetto and various others. Then he won a scholarship and studied at CDC in Kingston for three years.

I was intrigued, as I hadn't realized that Cumina and Pocomania actually have ritual dances. I was under the impression that everyone just did their own thing.

Uriel said, "It's a possessive type of dance. When you go through it, you go into de spirit world. I've got away into Cumina already. It's de drums. De drums talk to you and you sort of get into de trance. And if de person who is playing de drum doesn't understand it, den you're in trouble. Because if de person doesn't know how to get you back out, den you'll be dere and you could die."

"Wow! So how did you feel when you were in this trance?"

"Well, at first when I started—when de music got to you, right? It's like, you're dancing and you feel de beat and everyting, den someting just suddenly takes over and you go into a trance. And you do weird tings, weird tings...You climb de wall, dance on your back..."

"When you're in trance, do you have control over anything that you are doing? Do you even know what you are doing while in trance?"

"No, no no! You have no control! Dis is like um, de voodoo ting. You don't know what you're doing, but it's happening to you."

"How does the trance end?"

"Well, de person have to beat de drum in a certain way. De person dat is beating de drum play Cumina. De right person, he knows how to get you out of it. It is special. He pulls you right out of de trance."

"Do you know where I could go to one of these ceremonies?"

"Yeah, you can get someting like dat in Portland. Or you can go to Runaway Bay and ask for Miko Blanco."

I've seen Miko perform and the man absolutely spooks me! I get goose bumps every time I'm around him and I can't look him in the eye. It didn't surprise me to know he is into Pocomania. I should look him up, but I don't know if I have the guts. I don't know what it is about him, but my spirit tells me to stay away from him. Maybe I don't know yet how to protect myself from someone like him.

Miko and Uriel were both in a recent TV mini series called 'Passion and Paradise', which was filmed in Jamaica. Uriel was one of two guys who blew fire during a trance dance ceremony. I was enchanted with the show. To my delight I discovered that I knew several of the characters who played bit parts.

Uriel said, "Do you remember de part where de girl was writhing on de ground? Well, she was actually in a trance. She wasn't acting. Dey were doing a ceremony. And dey beat off de head of a chicken and de blood was all over de place. If you want, I will give you de phone number for Miko and you can talk to him more about it."

I asked Uriel about his childhood and religious upbringing. He is one of nine children and was born in 1957 in Linstead, in the parish of St. Catherine.

"I grew up in Angelican community, and went from dat to de Catholic. When I was smaller I was a Boy Scout and went as far as a Queen Scout. It taught me a little of everyting, of surviving and stuff like dat. Dat's where I learned to swim. It's good for de body."

"Do you remember your dreams?"

"Yeah! Okay, for instance I might go to bed tonight and dream someting. I wake up in de morning and I can tell you exactly what I dreamed from start to finish. I don't pay dem any mind you know, just let dem pass by most of de time."

This surprised me. It seemed to me like his dreams would have great significance, what with his trance dancing and all. "What about waking dreams? What's your big goal in life?"

"Well, I did a half a course already in Computer Programming in Kingston. I would like to go to de States and finish de odder six months."

"Great field. There's a big demand for it. I have a brother who does that and he's doing very well for himself. But what a switch from dancing! You're not going to give up your dancing, are you?"

"Not really, but I've always worked odder jobs. I worked wid de library service for about two years, den worked in accounting at a bank. But I didn't like having to sit all day, so I started back dancing. I had a new home and stuff, so I go to dancing because it sort of keeps me occupied, keeps my body in shape and stuff like dat."

"It sure does! How did you become the African Fertility Dancer?"

"When I came to Ochi in 1986 I was just a routine dancer. I danced wid de rest of de group like dey are doing right now, de limbo and all dat. Keith, who was de Fertility Dancer, went away, Carl saw my potential and said, 'Alright, hey, go through it. Learn to dance it.' I did, and from dere I took it over."

"Oh, and you're so good! What I really like is how you make eye contact and smile. The women just melt."

"Okay, you have women out dere, right? You have to show dat, um... It's like I'm a king, right? And dey are my ladies. So I have to show dem dat I am de mon, when I just get started. And after dey get to know me, den all de smiles come."

"Can you tell me more about your childhood?"

"It was a sort of strict one, because I had to stay in a lot. What really happened is dat where I lived we had all dis violence going on all around us. My fodder and modder didn't want me to get into all dat, so dey kept me in to get away from it.

"But dat didn't work, because I sort of got into it anyway. But after awhile I thought about it and said, 'Dat ain't gonna get you anywhere because you're gonna get deeper and deeper. So forget about it and do someting constructive.' What I was doing didn't make sense, so dat's when I started getting back to myself. And for dat I am most grateful, dat I came around again.

"If somebody doesn't have de experience of someting, den de person doesn't know what is going to happen. So experience is good. Den you can advise someone else not to do it! Give dem pointers and stuff like dat. You're not telling de person directly not to do it, but you're telling dem what will happen if dey do. And if dat person is tinking, de person can take what you say and analyze it. Eventually dey will see exactly what you are talking about."

"When you misbehaved, how were you disciplined?"

"Well, sometimes I would get a beating or a thrashing, or for a week or so I would not get to watch TV or go to parties."

"Oh, you had TV. So you come from a pretty nice home, huh? What did your father do?"

"He was a mechanic. He used to operate cranes and odder machines and also service dem."

I remembered my own childhood and had to tell him what happened to us when we were naughty. "When my sister and I misbehaved, Daddy would make each of us stand in a corner facing the wall, so we could think about what we had done. He'd shout, 'Now I don't want to hear a peep out of either one of you!' So we'd stand there and whisper softly, 'Peep, peep.' We'd be having a great time because we thought we had pulled one over on poor Dad!"

Uriel and I had a good laugh over this. We talked a bit more about childhood and he told me his favorite game was Hide and Seek. That was one of my favorites, too. My father used to play that with us and he instilled a great sense of humor and adventure in me. We wanted to be just like Dad. Mom was fun, too. She taught us so much and made a big deal of every little thing we accomplished. Both of my parents are artistic and adventuresome. I realize now how fortunate I am to have such great parents. No matter where I've been or what I've done, they've been pillars of support for me spiritually.

"Uriel, do you have any superstitions?"

"Well, let me tell you, de voodoo ting dere...I sort of believe in it. Once someting happened to me. I went to somebody and de person tell me dat somebody's trying to do me someting. Deep down I didn't really believe it, but I got a guard for dat anyway, you know? But it got lost when I was doing de movie 'Passion and Paradise.' It just disappeared! I don't know where it went."

"What was it that disappeared?"

"A ring dat protect me from evil and crime."

"So that makes you kind of nervous now, eh?"

"Yeah! You know I don't really understand how it got mislaid or what. But when I come back from de movie and take a shower and went to put on my tings it was gone! It's spooky!"

"Do you know where I can find any obeah people?"

"Dere's a lady somewhere in Mo-Bay here. Miko knows about her, so you could ask him. Obeah is pretty common in Jamaica. For instance, somebody do someting, and de person says, 'I'm gonna obeah you.' Dat person doesn't take it serious, but it really is serious if someone says dat, because de person goes somewhere and does someting.

"To me, though, I tink it's all in de mind. If you believe it, it will happen. If you don't, I don't tink it will trouble you."

"So, do you think someone can have a spell put on them?"

"Yeah, of course."

"So, for instance, if someone put a spell on me and I didn't know it, then I might start getting sick or something?"

"Yeah, if it is strong enough."

"Do you think I might be able to shake it off with my own power?"

"Sure, sure. All you have to do is believe in de Almighty."

"Okay. So that brings up another question. What do you think is going to happen to you when you die?"

"Ohhhh! Dat's anodder story. All I know is dat when I die I am going to Hell."

"You're going to Hell??"

"Hell is um, de grave to me. You're going to go dere and den when Christ comes again, you're going to rise from de dead."

"At that time, do you think you'll be in spirit form or have a body or what?"

" I'm going to have my body. And everyting dat is bad is going to fade away. Dere will be no more badness, all good. Heaven will be right here on Earth.

"To tell you de truth, how I see it, God gives everybody de chance to do what dey want to do, wrong or right. It's up to you to change from de wrong to de right. We must make our own choices how to behave and tink.

"Do you think that some people are going to suffer for all eternity in a burning Hell?"

"No, I don't believe dat. I tink what is going to happen is dat de people who were good in life—okay, you have dis ting, de United States President, and congressmen and stuff like dat, people scattered all around. I tink de people who did de right ting are going to govern us. De people who did de wrong tings coming on down. Dey are going to take care of us. One person is going to say, 'Okay, we're going to plant rice today.' He passes dat down to odder people dat is between us and him. So it's someting like dat. You have somebody dere to take care of you."

"Do you know the difference between Revival and Pocomania?"

Pocomania's a sort of feast like. You celebrate someting. Dey set de table and cook rice or someting. Dey have drinks, candles, everyting cover de table. Everyting's supposed to be clean, white as ever. Den dey start, do de dance. After dey finish all de dancing, den dey eat. It's like dey're doing ceremonies and all dose tings. De dance is like a sacrifice. Everybody partakes of whatever.

"Dey can use de dance to take an evil spirit out of somebody. Or possibly an evil spirit could enter. When dey go into trance, dey don't know what is going to happen."

"So why would they do that? That's pretty scary!"

"Well, you see, what dey call it is de person's destiny. So if dat really happens, de good spirit or de bad spirit, dat's de person's destiny. It's someting unpredictable."

"Revivalists are similar, but it's more of a blood sport. Dey spill a lot of blood, like cut off chicken neck or neck of a goat. Dey cut de throat and use de blood all over de place. Dat invokes de spirit."

"Do you know anything about Cumina?"

"Cumina is something used to take spirit out of somebody. Say somebody does something bad to you, puts a spell on you, well you want to reverse dat. So you dance Cumina and everyting is reversed just like dat!"

Uriel told me that all three religions are pretty common in Jamaica. When I told him that people keep promising to take me to a ceremony and then backing out at the last minute, he said that many people are afraid of them. He said that there is a possibility that I would be able to partake in a ceremony if I went, but generally they don't just accept a stranger in. They guard the ceremonies and rituals.

A laugh escaped him when I mentioned duppies, but then he turned serious and said, "When I was small, I used to see stuff like dat because I was born wid a caul, a ting dat covers de face. I don't know if dat is de right pronunciation, but it's a white, transparent ting. It's someting like a second skin. People born wid dat often see duppies easier.

"When I was small, say about ten on up, I used to see a lot of dem. Dey were like transparent tings. You could see through dem. Dey were like cows wid fire in dere eyes, headless horsemen, guys wid chain, a lot of chain over dem, and stuff like dat. Where we lived, we were about say two chains from a graveyard and I used to see all dose tings frequently."

"Were you frightened when you saw them?"

"My heart started palpitating and my head sort of expanded and I felt a chill all over."

"Did you feel threatened, like they might hurt you?"

"No, I don't tink dey would've done dat."

"You didn't think they were after you, then?"

"No, because all of dem dat I saw were going about dere business, you know. Like just passing by."

"What do you think causes them?"

"Well, I tink dey are just wandering spirits, trying to find dere resting place, stuff like dat."

I suddenly remembered that Harris had told me the same thing about being born with a caul and seeing duppies. Uriel and I talked a bit more about our lives and personal plans before I left. I think he is such a fascinating person and has a nice balance within himself. He possesses the logical and analytical mind of a businessman, yet he doesn't allow it to rule him. And he also understands his need to express his intuitive, creative, artistic side.

My friends and I are really going to miss Birgitta when she moves to Mexico, so we're trying to see as much of her as we can before she leaves. After the beach party tonight Deedra, Howard, Birgitta and I went out to the disco at Wyndham Rose Hall. What a comical group they are!

Saturday, February 17

I'm really beginning to understand the great pull and mystique of Jamaica. It has been fully brought to my awareness now how very real obeah, trance dancing, spirit possession, duppies, etc. are on this island. The people are all big bible readers, but what amazes me so much is that even Christians acknowledge that obeah exists and many fear it. The stories these people told me are absolutely wild, but they swear they are true. Who am I to say they are not? It certainly provides food for thought. We know so little about this universe we live in. Even the famous and well educated people tell me the same things as the poorer people. Jamaican culture fascinates me endlessly and I have great respect for all who call Jamaica home.

Grandma Sweet and Grandpa Dudley

I hiked up to Rose Heights today and spent a few lovely hours with the children and Grandpa Dudley. Their home is so modest, yet has such a warm, loving energy. I turned off the road, walked about fifteen feet down the hill, and unwound the wire that was holding shut the gate on the rickety old fence. As I greeted the roosters and Lassie the dog, I glanced around at the coconut trees, the rusty old rain barrel, and the pieces of zinc which rested against the porch. Drinking water is obtained from a faucet in the yard.

The house is pink and blue and the front porch has maroon and beige tiles on the floor. Someone once told me that the reason island houses are all painted in bright colors is to keep the evil spirits away. The porch is made of cement and blocks and is also painted pink.

Grandpa Dudley looked extremely comfortable perched there on the porch rail as we talked. He was barefoot and had one leg of his torn blue trousers rolled up to his knee. On his head was a straw hat with a brown hat band. He sported a moustache and goatee, and also wore a beautiful smile that danced all the way through his sparkling, brown eyes.

Some of the girls curled up at our feet, listening to our stories and giggling. Coretta also read and wrote in her lesson books. She takes school very seriously. Dawn and Grandma Sweet were gone. They had taken little Sharon to Cornwall Regional Hospital because she has Russian Measles.

Grandpa told me that he keeps his boat at River Bay Beach near Seawind. I asked him to tell me about his life as a fisherman.

"Well, in de night I leave. And I go to sea from eight-thirty to sometime in de morning. I come in at nine or ten o'clock. And when I come in, I carrying de fish and I sell de fish to de people. Den I clean my boat, look after my line, fix myself up and come home and rest.

"And sometimes I go back in de night and still fishing, sometimes three times for de week. And a next day now I skip dat night and I do trap fishing. And dat is in de morning, and I come in and look about if some of dem is mashed up."

"Are you talking about lobster pots?"

"Yeah, de big lobster pots. And if some of dem get hurt, I carry dem in and fix dem up and carry dem back out. And I draw dem sometimes three or four times for de month."

Lobster pots are huge hand made containers. They have a wooden frame and chicken wire netting and are set into the sea. Lobsters and certain fish can find their way into them, but not out.

"What kind of fish do you catch?"

"I catch snapper, yellowtail, grunt, wrenchmen, moonshine snapper, and when I fishing wid de line, I catch snapper and yellowtail. And I catch godlight. Dat is de fish dat comes in de winter most of de time. And in de trap now, we catch parrotfish. We catch grouper. We have two quality grouper, one in de deep and one in de shallow at certain times of de year. We catch it in de pot, too. We catch some of what we call mutton snapper, in de pot and on de line.

Dose big fish. And sometimes we catch marlin when we troll in de morning. Or kingfish."

A long time ago I had gone out to sea with a fisherman in the evening. I was amazed that he didn't use a fishing pole. He merely baited his hook and dropped the line in the water, holding the other end with his fingers. I asked Grandpa if he uses a pole.

"Just fish line we use. We go out in de night and carry our little dipper, what we dip for bait. Any time we find some small fish, like piper, we dip it up. And we might find some little someting what we call shrimp. We dip it up and put it on de line and sit down dere in de night until we feel a bite."

"How do you feel when you're out at sea at night? You go out alone, right?"

He smiled broadly. "Yeah! I go out alone. I feel hoppy when I go out dere! And sometimes I hear de music in de hotels, and I hoppy about it by shaking my legs!" His joyous memories bring much laughter to him now.

"So you're never afraid out there?"

"Noooo! Sometimes when I don't catch fish I just rest back and I get a little doze. And I just wake up back and start fishing again. I don't frightened."

"Have you ever gotten caught in a storm out there?"

"Well, sometime we feel de breeze and we can come in. For anytime you see de boat turning to land by de breeze you can leave de sea. For wind out in de sea coming in, and you can have difficulty to come in."

"So you must know the area very well."

"Yeah, you must know de reefs and everyting."

"How long have you been doing this?"

"Well, about nine years straight, since I leave de airport where I was working in de fly kitchen. I do twenty years dere. And after I leave, I had a little shop here, but it just go down. And I make up my mind to go to sea. My fodder is a fisherman from Black River, St. Elizabeth. And my brodder. So I have de habit in St. James to do de said work for my living, for de loss of my odder ability."

"Is fishing very profitable?"

"Well, if you catch de fish you can be hoppy, but sometime it very slow. I sell it on de beach, same place. People come and buy it. So dat is my living."

"I'm fascinated by how you feel at sea at night alone."

He laughs hard and says, "You know, sometime we just draw back and sit in our seat and take a doze and we tie de line on our toe. You strap it on your toe and take a doze, and de fish just come bite you and squeeze it up and you grab up de line. Oh yes, I love it!"

"Do you have a lantern or a motor on your boat?"

"Oh yes, a tilly lamp. I did have one motor, but I had some trouble wid de propeller. I want oil seal for it. De engineers say it cannot pull it yet. He trying to soak it, for it's a split pin in de foot. It's not a screw, it's a split pin and it get rust so he have to soak it out. So until now, about five months, he don't pull it off yet. So I have to row by hand. I love it, too, but you know, I cannot go dat far."

He told me he sometimes goes near Holiday Inn, which is about seven or eight miles away, a long way to go in such a tiny boat. And he is often out for at least twelve hours.

"Don't you get tired?"

"No, we carry food and water. Sometime two of us go. But me personal, I go alone. I love it, but you know it very slow now. In de fifties, at which case I was at de airport, I always do my day off fishing. I love fish! I eat nutting but fish, roast, boil, any how."

Grandpa told me that part of the reason fishing isn't as good as it used to be is because the harbor was dredged out so a nude beach could be put in. The mud and feeding places of the fish was destroyed and replaced with sand. It upset the ecology and the livelihood of the local people. Sounds a bit like the rest of the world. This, all in the name of progress of course.

I asked where he got his boat. "We have a mon in de country who dig boat out of de cotton tree. Cottonwood is very light and buoyant, won't sink. Dem boat is very dear now, very dear. He did sell me my boat for $900 JA. Dat is a twenty-two foot boat. He say dat right now it cost $1500 JA."

I seem to always encounter loud laughter when I first mention duppies to a Jamaican. Maybe they're just surprised that I've heard of them. Grandpa was no different. After he settled down he said, "You see we used to hear about it from de country. Our foreparents and our modder always told we dat duppies under de cotton tree. Dey always be at de cotton tree, for in de old slavery time dey always like to be in shade, to have a cool time. Cotton tree is big and it very cold. Dem say anywhere you see a cotton tree grow, water is dere. Oh yeah, a river under dere."

"What exactly do you think a duppy is?"

"Well, duppy is a kind of spirit. De Devil put himself in dat form."

"So you don't think it is somebody who has died?"

"Yeah! Sometimes it's his person. De Devil will just form like him. I see dem already! Oh yes, I see dem."

"What did you see?"

"Well, sometime dem turn like a dog, a puss, all dose tings."

"Could you see through it?"

"You not see right through him. Sometime his shadow. Sometime he don't have a head. You know, him just grow tall. It's just a picture like you see.

"Once when I was at Black River, me and my modder was coming into Newton Town. Over on de left side you see de burying ground. On de right side a mon named Dr. Stewart did have big property. In de evening on dat street when we was coming in I just see a dog leap into de air and jump on de gate and disappear and I never see him again. I say, 'Mama, Mama, look right dere Mama!' Mama say, 'Bwoy! Hush up your mouth! I see it before you! Hush up your mouth and come on, come on, come on!' She know it was a duppy.

"I see plenty more duppies after dat. Dey just a shadow in front of you. I not afraid, but my head grows. My head feels different, light, like I'm not on de land."

The children giggled uncontrollably when they heard this. Evidently they haven't had the duppy experience yet. I said, "Do you think they're going to hurt you?"

"No, I just afraid of live mon, not dead ones."

"Have you ever heard of a duppy hurting or harming anyone?"

"Well, as to de old saying in Jamaica, if dem set for you, dey will catch you. De bible tell you about evil spirit. But if dem not set for you, dey not going to hurt you.

"Sometime dem just passing by and you see dem. Sometime you do not see dem, but de place what dey pass is a very heated place and your head just grow. You can feel dat somebody was just dere.

"Sometime when I go out here in de morning going to sea, I stand up dere (he points down the road) and just see a flip—somebody going down de gully and just go crossways up dat road by dat ackee tree. Sometimes dey late, for dey is hurrying. Heh, heh, heh!"

We started talking about dreams and Grandpa said that a lot of his dreams come true. "It nice if I see white people in my dream. Dat's good luck. And green and red is my lucky color cuz I love it. Now if I see de color black, I don't leave my home. Dat's bad luck for me."

"If you could have any dream in the world come true, what would you wish for life?"

"My first wish is live my life for de Master. He gives us strength and health to live. You might don't have a bunch of money to spend, but de Master give you health and strength to see anodder day. So dat is my first choice. He made me hoppy and I'm not telling you no lie. So I feel for de Master first and money after."

"Do you think there is a Heaven and a Hell?"

"De churches say you have a Heaven and you have a Hell, but I feel as Heaven is down here. Is your soul is heaven. And from you live, if your soul is right, you have God. According to de churches, dem say when you die you is going to Heaven. But I feel dat Heaven is here now."

"What about Hell?"

"De Master did turn out one of de best mon at his right side. De one he turn out is one of his best angels. And he caused dis on us. Sin. And is he want to torment de master. Remember when he on de building, him say, 'Master, if thou be de son of God, come down and worship me.' "

"Do you think people actually go to Hell?"

"Dey is resting all right now. When de time cometh and de trumpet blow, de churches say dey are going to rise again. I no know. Is dem told us.

"If you do good now, when you die you sleep in peace. You don't torment on de earth, like how you are to see some duppy now. Some of dem torment sometime. You die quiet, you just sleep in peace, like my sweet modder-in-law did. You die kicking and screaming, you torment."

Grandpa said that he doesn't love the way Americans use money for greed, but the one thing good about American money is that it has the words 'In God we Trust' imprinted on it. I couldn't leave without asking him about obeah.

"It demon spirit. It dangerous! Some people it hurt!"

"What happened to them?"

"Dem die! It coming to friends of mine a good while now." He points to a neighbor's house. "Dat lady over dere, one day her daughter just stand up and say, 'Mama, Mama, someting lick me in de head!' And from dat, blood start come out of her nose. Yeah, just like dat, and she die after. Dey go to a doctor, and doctor told her dere was no reason dat dat should've happened. She don't have no hemorrhage."

"Do you think there's a way to protect yourself from it?"

"Well, yes, depends. Some say it can if you get like De Laurence ring. Him from Chicago. Dangerous mon."

He said that his wife, Sweet, knows a gentleman way in the hills who works for De Laurence. He's very evil and when people don't pay him he puts out spells to burn down their homes.

Grandpa knew a man who had a daughter in the hills above them. There were houses all around, but only this particular house burned. Dudley is certain that a duppy was set on it, since the man owed money to the obeah man. It also wasn't logical that the fire didn't spread to the other houses.

Not only that, but wherever the daughter went to live after that, the home would soon burn the same way. Finally a Catholic priest performed an exorcism on her and it hasn't happened since. Evidently the duppy had attached itself to the girl. Grandpa knows this girl and said she is fine now. This all happened about six years ago.

Grandpa also knew of a house near Holiday Inn where a ghost was. Things inside the house would fling all over by themselves. The outside of the house was pelted with stones by an invisible being. An exorcism was finally performed there too, and as Grandpa said, "Yes, de priest have his good luck dere, too."

Dawn and Grandma showed up at this point, carrying frail little Sharon. She looked ill and flushed, and sat down and rocked back and forth in an effort to relieve her belly ache and head ache. My heart went out to her.

Dawn was as sweet as ever, but her problems and concerns were evident to me. She walked slowly, shoulders slumped and she forced a smile. Normally she's energetic and always smiling. They had had a long, trying day. When they finally arrived at the hospital, they had to pay five dollars and then sit and wait until a doctor was available. Then they had to travel all the way downtown to get three prescriptions filled. It cost $100 JA, which was the family's grocery money for next week. I wanted to cry. I had only $20 JA to last me the rest of the weekend, and the banks were closed. I silently vowed to bring Dawn some money on Monday. I love this family as my own.

Dawn loves her children and parents so much and works hard at home to provide for them. Then she bartends on Union Street until the wee hours of the morning. I don't know how she keeps going. Bless her heart!

When I left them, I decided to stop and check in with Daniel God since I was in the vicinity. Interspersed with the new information that I received was a lot of repetition of what he had previously told me.

Daniel did tell me that since I had last seen him, Mother Heart had chopped down the plantain tree with the seven yards of red cloth tied to it. "Dat mean when she chop it down she chop me down, cuz I condemned her evil and lying."

This incident took place three days after I had left there. "What happened to you, Daniel? Did you feel different?"

"Sick! Sick! I got a belly dat just runs every time I eat someting. Sometimes I lie, too weak to move. But I know it's demons. But de spirit dat is inside of me will deliver me."

"How do you fight the demons?"

"Prayer. I know how to pray, Debbie. I'm innocent. Modder Heart's granddaughter's boyfriend has two babies wid her. He chopped his grandson in de head wid a machete, busted de head in two! Dis happened at home, three days after dey chopped de tree down. He did it to chop me down.

"He used de child's spirit but God turn it back, Debbie, cuz de child still live. Every evil she has set on me has turned back on her. She can leave her property, but I don't want her to. I can thrust her away. I can kill her. Her body is free to roam around, but I've captured her spirit of evil. I don't want to hurt her cuz she must pay her debt. God will call her on de judgement day."

"Do you talk to her anymore?"

"No."

"Well then, how do you know what she is doing?"

"De spirit showed me! She turns into frogs and bats sometimes. She's a vampire. You know, she do de De Laurence."

I asked him if he thought it would be dangerous for me to talk to Mother Heart. Daniel seemed stunned that I would want to and said, "Dangerous?

Dangerous? No, but—she will talk to you wid de tongue of an angel and de heart of a Jezebel. You have no use for her, neither."

Mother Heart thought that Daniel would die when the plantain tree was chopped down, but instead the spell turned on her. "God took away her power. Her grandson and grandson-in-law are her bodyguards since her husband left her. De three of dem try to work wid island powder now. Her time is up. She can mix up de powder and evil, but it has no power any longer."

He told me now how she had worked with the frogs once and sent them into someone's home. The man tried to shove them out with a broom, and as he did so, one side of his body became paralyzed.

I told Daniel that all of his talk of spells and things was making me feel a bit uneasy, and I feared that by dwelling on it so much I may be an easy target. By now, I was feeling a bit spooked and vulnerable. I still was amazed that I was here listening to this, rather than back home going out with my friends on a Saturday night. Talk about doing a reality check! I realized that there is a lot more 'reality' in our world than I had ever allowed myself to confront. I was clearly drifting into different realms, and I knew I had to be careful. After all, I'm the one who preaches on the power of our thoughts. Time to get a grip, girl.

I told Daniel that I will probably be in Jamaica another month or so, and asked him what he thought I should do. I didn't necessarily intend to take his advice, but I was curious as to how he would advise me.

"Debbie, you must be careful now. When you go back to de States and someone asks you who you are, you must say, 'I am a missionary. I can read your heart.' "

"What advice can you give me as far as my own spiritual quest?"

"You are seeking de spirit of truth dat hide from de world. And you have found it."

Daniel told me that all trance dancing is performed by obeah people and that he knows of a church down the road which performs such rituals. He said that the woman who runs it has sexed another woman and has powers. He knew that my curiosity would take me there to explore, so he offered to accompany me. Services are on Sunday and Wednesday nights, so I told him I would definitely be back to attend.

By the time I left, I felt totally drained. The man spooks me. I hiked home through the sunset, twilight and night feeling completely exhausted, yet filled with all the beauty around me. My walks through Jamaica will always be a part of me.

Sunday, February 18

Last night a bunch of women who work in tourism gathered at the Rep house where I am staying. It was great fun to have 'girl talk' and just kick back after my strange afternoon with Daniel. Some of the things that made an impression on me throughout the course of our conversation last night were the following: "If we allow people to intimidate us, they will. Wake up!" We had a discussion on how corrupt many of the police are in every country. "They buy into the illusion of power, not the reality of it!" Few seem to believe in politics anymore or the government. There is simply no respect. The government itself has caused this lack of respect.

Birgitta, Deedra, Sara, Carolyn

We spent a lot of time swapping stories and laughing about our experiences as Reps. It was good to find balance by looking at life humorously. Let's face it, humans really are funny creatures!

The group last night consisted of Jamaicans, Americans, Canadians and Germans. How's that for an international group? The motto of Jamaica is "Out of many, one people." We felt our oneness and it was magical. I love my sisters of the world. They are strong, independent women, yet in the same token, they are nurturers.

My friend Mooney came over and cooked me dinner tonight. What a treat, especially considering how little I've been eating at all. He brought his famous rum punch, which we sipped as he cooked chicken and rice. He first marinated the chicken in all kinds of spices, tomatoes and scallions. Then he fried it and covered it with a sauce made from the marinade. He added coconut milk to the rice, and we feasted royally.

Monday, February 19

It's 5:00 PM. I'm standing with hundreds of Jamaicans under a shelter at Montego Cooperative Credit Union. The vendors quickly moved their stands off the street when a barrage of rain suddenly hit out of seemingly nowhere. Every overhang in the area has people stuffed under it.

I'm in the heart of Sam Sharpe Square in Montego Bay. People who have tried running even across the street have been totally soaked in a matter of seconds. The rain is so intense that it sounds like I'm standing under Niagara Falls. Other sounds include the deep Patois of friends chatting, and as always, Reggae blaring from several shops.

There is a madman playing in the street. He is barefooted, very dark skinned, has dreadlocks, and is wearing a ragged brown shirt and a tiered, frilly, maroon skirt. He's swishing his skirts back and forth as he dances merrily through the puddles. The rain isn't bothering him in the least, even though it's so thick and blinding. The air has turned cool, but still hangs heavy with humidity.

I wonder about this man/woman who others call mad. I see that he is happy and celebrating his own truth. I agree with him that it's fun to dance with the raindrops. So why aren't I out there with him? I fear I've become a victim of society. "It's raining! Run! We might melt..." When we allow the raindrops to touch our skin, we feel their rhythm and hear their song and we become part of it, allowing an internal cleansing to occur as well.

I'm standing by Sandy and her mother, who are vendors. Thirteen year old Sandy has a ponytail and is wearing a pink T-shirt, magenta skirt, and black shoes with missing laces. Her mom is smoking a cigarette and wearing earrings in the shape of a dollar sign. Their vending stand has black coral jewelry, cheese snacks, cookies, Craven A and Matterhorn cigarettes (sold one at a time), hard candy (sold by the piece), Red Stripe beer, a wooden bird and little straw baskets.

The streets are flooded. It has been quite awhile since Mo-Bay has had rain and this one isn't quitting. It hasn't let up at all in over an hour. No one seems to mind. They just patiently wait it out. "No problem." They'll get wherever they were going whenever they get there.

Later: The rain is finally letting up some. People are running through it now, with shower caps, plastic bags, washclothes and towels covering their heads. It's colorful and somehow seems festive.

Sandy insisted on putting a braid in my "tall" hair. She put pink and white beads at the bottom. A little school girl just stopped by to purchase some candy. She had a pair of panty hose slung unself-consciously over her head to keep her hair dry.

I had been on my way to tape Pearl Harbor's stories about Peter Tosh and Trench Town. But it's getting late and will be dark when I reach home now, so I'll save it for another day.

Tuesday, February 20

I did a lot of meditating yesterday as I feel like I've pulled too much away from my spiritual being. I must remember my reason for being here and seek that, or else chaos results in my mind and emotions.

I'm really tired of living out of a backpack. The thought of leaving Jamaica is very painful to me, yet it will be so nice to go home. I miss my family and friends in America. When I return there, I'll miss my Jamaican family and friends. It's a price I must pay for the adventuresome life I've chosen.

My finger is permanently crippled. It didn't heal right and I can't bend it. My penmanship has always been rather sloppy. If I so choose, I can now use this as an excuse. Ha-ha! The doctor here, when trying to console me, told me that if this happened all I had to do was have surgery on it back in the States. Did he think surgery was free? America does have good health care, but it's unattainable to many of us because it's unaffordable. I'll just learn to live with this. I can adapt to almost anything.

Later: Deedra, her boyfriend Gary, Sara and I are on our way to the south side of the island, the untouristy side. I'm so excited and hope I get a chance to tape some people. Right now we are crossing the mountains and I feel like I have come home. My surroundings have taken me into the wild, untamed jungle of my psyche. I feel so alive because I see myself, my elfin self, in all of this. Infinite reflections as I remember who I really am. Now I understand.

Here lies a contrast of the majesty and power of Mother Nature and the quiet simplicity of the villages. Country folk are very friendly and fit. They live in harmony with the surrounding beauty. They are part of it.

We just passed the Peter Tosh monument in Bluefields. Peter Tosh was a famous Reggae star who was gunned down in Kingston one night when he went out to purchase some chicken for his family's dinner. I love his music and remember crying broken heartedly when he died.

The music of Jamaica really expresses the people and their culture. It seems that everything is dancing with us as we wind our way down the road. The cows, goats, egrets, pigs and donkeys roam free out here. Road side fruit stands are everywhere, laden with pineapple, coconut, bananas, papaya, star apples, and countless other wonders of nature. Grandpa Dudley was right when he told me that Heaven is right here on Earth.

We just passed a small country home. Out in the front yard was a lady sitting in a home made wheel chair. The wheels were made from old bicycle tires. She has no legs, but looked elegant in her red dress and white turban. I wonder what she was thinking about.

We're in Black River now, and just stopped to stretch our legs and grab a drink at Waterloo Guest House. It's a grand old building and is land marked as being the first place in Jamaica to have electricity. There is a sign posted on the door with the following information: "Pre-Easter Fair at Black River Primary School, Grand Raffle, First Prize = One Calf, Second Prize = Gold Earrings, Third Prize = One Laundry Basket."

Later: When we arrived at Treasure Beach Resort we pretended to not see the "Only Registered Guests Beyond This Point" sign, and we boldly walked right past. No one was around to question us anyway, We headed down some winding old stairs surrounded by vibrant flowering trees and bushes, out to a wild, crashing sea and a soft, brown sandy beach. To our delight, we had the entire beach to ourselves.

Off to the left was a forest of palm trees and a long, curving shoreline. To the right was more beach and volcanic rock cliffs. Exotic vines decorated the sand dunes behind us. What a glorious day! We were children again and screamed in delight as we charged into the soft, warm water. Even the ocean floor was soft and sandy.

It was like floating in a vat of champagne. We felt intoxicated as the sea foam massaged us, tickling us and kneading our bodies all over. The sea was erotic today, a magnificent lover and a cherished friend.

We danced out far to where the water was about chest high, and watched excitedly as the huge walls of sparkling, aqua water headed toward us. Then we laughed playfully and beckoned the waves closer until the five foot walls would finally crash upon us, sending us tumbling around. Sometimes we would allow ourselves to be lifted up like ballerinas and we'd ride those waves in great, graceful leaps, dancing across the stage of life. I couldn't help but wonder how anyone could be afraid of the sea, not this sea...

The sky added to the magic because all day the sun shone over the water, yet the sky above the shore was very dark and stormy. The wind was so intense it looked like it was going to uproot the coconut trees. Mother Nature had definitely cast a spell on us, a good one.

It took enormous willpower to finally leave, but we knew we had a long drive back and everyone else has to work tomorrow. School had gotten out and all along the road we now encountered happy, laughing children, waving and playing as they walked home. They looked adorable in their uniforms, with their school bags on their backs. Many held hands as they walked along. The earth was red here, and there was cattle and cactus. It reminded me of Arizona. The children looked so tiny against the mountains, which disappeared into the clouds.

Suddenly a huge, vibrant rainbow appeared, arching all across the mountains. It had a shimmering aura like none I've ever seen and the sky behind it was black. It took our breath away, so we stopped for a moment to observe it. We could see the sun shining off in one direction, and rain far away in the other direction. Within moments we were in the midst of the torrential rains ourselves. It rained so hard that it somehow seeped in and covered the entire floor of the car! We were at a total loss as to how this could happen, but it merely added to our adventure.

Later when the rain let up, we bought pepper shrimp from the vendors at Middle Quarter. Several ladies approached our car, holding out bags and pans and begging us to buy. Each insisted that hers was the best. They were happy because we each bought a bag for $20 JA. A bag held about twenty good size shrimp from the Black River. Pepper shrimp is boiled, then marinated in hot sauce and scotch bonnet peppers. To eat it you simply pull off the head and tail, and the shell if you want to. It's excellent if you like spicy foods. One must be careful to keep his fingers away from his eyes afterwards though, as they will be full of fire for awhile.

I had devoured all my shrimp by the time we arrived at a place along the sea where we were again barraged by ladies as we rounded a bend in the road. This time they stuck pans full of fish and bammy right into our open windows. It was irresistable! The fried fish was covered with onions and peppers. Bammy is a bread made from cassava, and is soaked in coconut milk before it is deep fried or baked.

Fish and bammy, Scott's Cove

These ladies enjoy their work, each claiming to have the "biggest and best parrotfish, snapper," etc. Their fires burn on the seashore, and the smell of the food is exquisite. I was wishing I could purchase something from each of them.

We drove on a bit further and then stopped to eat as we watched the sun drop behind the sea in Bluefields. I spoke with a man named Lance while we were there. He doesn't believe in duppies because he has never seen them. He practices no particular religion, but believes in Heaven and Hell. "If I live a good life, I will go to Heaven. It's simple."

Lance has six children by three "baby mamas." Two are in the States, one is in England and three are in St. Elizabeth. He has a hearty laugh over this and it's quite obvious that he considers himself quite the stud.

As far as obeah goes, Lance knows that it exists, but he believes that it's merely a way to cheat people out of their money. On the other hand, he thinks highly of bush doctors, who he believes work with herbal cures.

I also spoke with a man who calls himself Chef Christopher. He was frying spiced turbot over an open fire on the beach, and also had a pot of fish tea cooking. I asked him what was in the fish tea. "Pumpkin, yam, banana, cho cho, carrot, fish, water, scallion, thyme and pepper. I boil it and den add flour and cook it down to de thickness I want. It's very nice, mon."

Christopher is twenty-six and has a five week old daughter, his first child. He doesn't believe in duppies either, although several of his friends claim to have seen them. And like Lance, he doesn't practice any certain religion, but he believes in God. He thinks when you die, the "breath of life" leaves and your body becomes simply a carcass.

I had to cut the interview short because it was getting dark and we had to leave. But as we were leaving, Christopher asked me if Sara was my daughter. (Thanks a lot! I'm not that old!) He said he wants her and asked when she will be returning.

On the ride home, Gary told me that he was born in Spanish Town. He said that his Mom was on her way to Kingston where she planned on having the birth. Gary, however, had other ideas. They had traveled as far as Spanish Town and he said, "Mom, I like it here. Let me out!" So she did.

Soon after, Gary's Mom went to the States and he was boarded out to a teacher who also raised three other children. She was a harsh disciplinarian and often beat him. I asked Gary when he became intersted in girls. "As soon as I first saw them!" He said that by age nine or ten he was seriously interested, but he was so shy that he would shake like a leaf in the presence of someone he liked. Kissing was out of the question. He couldn't even make eye contact. He was afraid he'd drop dead if she even said hello. The girls were probably equally shy. Gary is a very handsome fellow.

He now lives in Montego Bay and is the Senior Dispatcher for Green Light Tours. Gary puts in a lot of hours and likes his job, but has a dream of becoming a commercial airline pilot. I think he'd make a great comedian.

1

SPIRIT SONGS

*"Throughout the course of our conversation
she was moving in and out of trance state. To
receive information, she would close her eyes
and cross her arms. Her whole body would jump
and shudder as though she had been struck by
lightning."*
— *Debbie*

Wednesday, February 21
I moved from the Rep house over to Deedra's tonight. And what a night it
turned out to be! We went up to the Garden of Eden so Deedra could meet
the legendary Daniel God. I was amazed and amused to discover that he had
perfumed himself in the scents of ganja and liquor. I have heard him preach
on the evils of ganja, but come to think of it, I've never heard him mention
liquor. He certainly doesn't want me to know that he has these habits. (What
would de Fodder say?)

Even more ironic is the fact that Deedra had asked me to have a beer with
her before we went up there. I had replied, "Oh no! Daniel would condemn
me. If I'm not in his graces, he'll stop telling me his stories."

This is a perfect example of the illusions of our earth plane. Daniel believes it is so important to be pure and not "sex" anyone. Because I have no children, he assumes that I am "pure." Since he never directly asked, I never told him. I, on the other hand, assumed that he didn't drink, but I never asked. Ha! He drinks, and I sex, and we both are just doing the best we can as we travel down the highways and byways of life. Who are we to judge each other anyway? I bet neither of us will go to Hell.

Upon reflection, maybe Daniel was just trying to get up the courage to take us to the "obeah" church. Daniel told us it is a Pocomania church, but I had doubts after visiting it. My understanding was that Pocomania works more with the dark forces. This entire ceremony was praising God for two hours.

Lighthouse Tabernacle Congregational Church

When we arrived at the Lighthouse Tabernacle Congregational Church on Mount Faith in Rose Heights at 8:30 PM, service was already in progress. Two men were beating drums, and two women and two men were beating tambourines. Everyone was singing loudly and off key and to his own beat. Even the tree frogs outside were singing more loudly than usual. All of the women had their heads wrapped in turbans.

I had a distinct feeling that no tourist had ever been here. The church was a small, zinc walled hut and tonight only seven members were in attendance. But what a zealous group they were! Intense emotion prevailed the entire two hours that we were there. The energy was dynamic. These people were sincere. Of this I had no doubt. Most of these people were elderly and had several teeth missing, but their spirits were more alive than most of the young people I know.

Each of them took a turn screaming about their love of life and "de Lord" and then leading a song. The rhythm never stopped, and I could sense the vibrational shift of movement into the spiritual realm.

When we first entered, a woman handed each of us a pillow to place on the hard wooden bench beneath us. Reverend Samms gave us a warm greeting and said, "Our visitors seem to be from a foreign land. Instead of being out seeking entertainment, dey chose to be somewhere to hear de word of de Lord. We hope dere hearts will be richly blessed. When dey depart for dere homeland, we pray for God's guidance and blessing. I am quite sure dey will have someting to share wid somebody in dere hometown. We over here in Jamaica chose to love and serve de Lord.De reason "—and here she suddenly starts singing loudly— "He is coming back again!" Everyone cheered and joined in. During her entire speech, everyone chanted an affirmation after every sentence that she spoke.

We were asked to come up front and introduce ourselves. Deedra went first. I went next, feeling conspicuous and nervous. Every phrase we uttered was met with a loud "Oh yes!" from the group. Then Daniel got up, and pointing to me he said, "Dis little bird is searching. She desire to find de truth. She takes my religion and she asked me to take her to see yours. It's my duty to bring her here. We will all learn tonight."

Then, of course, he went on a rampage of bible quotations. I did notice that his demeanor was very meek compared to usual. I could tell that he felt intimidated by these people.

While all the dancing and chanting was going on, I took a close look at the interior of the church. There were no doors anywhere, and I thought it odd that the floor was painted a bright red. A lit kerosene lamp dangled from the center of the ceiling. I was curious about a vine shaped thing. It had a ring at the top and a paddle like stick with a circle at the other end.

There were a couple of tables with bottles of clear and bluish purple liquids in them. On the floor were old paint cans full of flowers. The tables or altars also had the following on them: red and white candles, a cup and saucer, a white bowl, a wooden paddle with 'Revelation' painted on it, a watch, and a jar full of clear liquid in which was someting that looked to me like a dead snake. It was about one and a half inches in diameter and made my skin crawl.

After about two hours of chanting I became very aware that this was all we were going to be allowed to see of the ceremony. They would continue on this way until we left. I realized that all of the things on the altar were going to eventually serve a purpose, but we weren't privy to it.

So we all gave thanks and left. Everyone thanked us sincerely for coming and I was touched by that. I felt like laughing and crying all at once as we walked toward the car. It came to me with clarity that every night things like this are going on in our world.

On the way home, I asked Daniel about the significance of the items on the altars. He told me that the clear bottled water next to the basin was a very bad sign because it was there to feed the Fallen Angels. "Dey lie to you! Dey are obeah people! Debbie, dey are demons!"

I asked about the dead snake. Daniel said he hadn't seen it, but, "Dey use island powder! When people was sick, dey went to dem. And if dey want to do evil to people dey know how to do it. God doesn't do dose tings.

"De bottle wid de water is a bad sign, Debbie. You see de white rose in de glass? If you put dat at de end of your bed wid a bible, you get nice visions. But your hands and your heart must be clean before God. Especially a woman.

"Did you see de old black woman sitting beside de boy knocking de drum?"

"Yeah?"

"She's an old witch! She killed her babies' daddy! She live right at de bottom.

"Our bodies must be de temple of God. De three of us could've mashed up dat church tonight you know. But we was cool. And dem would listen to us you know. So dat's why I take you dere, to prove it.

"Dis body not mine. And dat one is not yours, Debbie. It belong to God. Daddy made you, but for God's purpose, not for de Devil's work. Be careful what you eat and drink. Mon will try to trick you. You mix your own food and drink.

"You see de white candle and de red candle? Dey write your name on de red candle, turn you bad, and suck your blood. Dangerous tings. I got a book which came from Chicago. It's called 'De Head of all Iniquity and Witchcraft.' A boy lent it to me but I gave it back. I get it so you can see it."

We dropped Daniel off at home and as he said good-by he asked God to take care of the two sisters, Mary and Martha, (referring to Deedra and I.) Once we were alone, I asked Deedra what she had to say about the evening. She burst into gales of laughter and said, "It was definitely an experience! I think the church people were really sincere and wondered what Daniel was doing there. Who knows? They might be obeah people. They certainly wouldn't do their rituals in front of us."

I don't know what to think anymore...

Thursday, February 22

Everyday is a new adventure. This morning I took a minibus to Trelawny where I met Mooney. We hitched a ride with a buddy of his over to Salt Marsh. Mooney told me about a lady who runs a Revival Church there. Her name is Rosetta, but people call her Tine-Tine and many believe that she is an obeah practitioner.

When we entered the grounds, we were greeted by George, the caretaker. He asked us to wait in the church while he summoned "Mammy," as he calls Tine-Tine. The interior of the church was amazingly similiar to the church we were in last night. A feeling of awe came over me and I had a distinct sensation of being watched. I strongly sensed the presence of other beings, even though I could see no one with my physical eyes. Even Mooney seemed uncomfortable.

We sat down on the small wooden benches which were covered with pillows. I noticed several drums near the altar. The floor of this church was also red, and a red and white cross hung on the back wall. On the altar was a red cloth with a white cross on it. Along side of it were several plants and bottles of various colored liquids. A bare lightbulb and a yellow paper bell dangled from the ceiling. A mirror hung in the front of the church, along with an alphabet and a chalkboard. In the center of the church was a deep hole. It looked like a well of some kind.

I saw the same vine type thing with the circle and handle that I had seen last night, so I asked Mooney about it. He whispered that it's called a supple-jack and said that it's used to beat people who are really bad. (I have no idea where he got this information.) He may have made it up.

After awhile, we were led into a small, green room and invited to sit down. Tine-Tine entered and the moment I saw her I liked her. Her outfit consisted of navy socks, a black and white polka dot skirt, a purple flowered shirt and a purple turban. Wisps of grey hair peeked out from underneath it and a cigarette dangled in the corner of her toothless mouth.

She smiled and greeted us, then sat down across from me and prayed. Separating us was a table with a yellow cloth on it. There was a basin of water with a Leaf of Life and money in it on the table. When Tine-Tine stopped praying, I asked her about it. She asked me to drop $5.50 into it and told me that the spirit told her to put it there. The purpose of the water and Leaf of Life was to cleanse the spirits of the people who dropped money into it. The table also held a vase of plastic flowers and a bible.

Tine-Tine was a fascinating woman. Her normal demeanor was kind, gentle and soft spoken. However, throughout the course of our conversation she was moving in and out of a trance state. To receive information, she would close her eyes and cross her arms. Her whole body would jump and shudder as though she had been struck by lightning. Then her eyes would flare and a loud, masculine voice would excitedly shout something. This was always met with a giggle on her part, and she calmly explained to me, "When dat happens, dat is not me talking you know. It is de spirit talking through me." Tine-Tine is so used to this happening that she just accepts it the same way we would accept the interruption of a cough or sneeze in our own bodies.

I asked her to tell me about her church. "It's Sixty Revival Church. Dat mean dat sixty guardian angels from de rank of glory arranged dere flight for all de earth to guide you in going out and coming in."

She asked me what religion I am, so I briefly explained my situation. "Do you believe de spirit of God moves in you?" she asked.

"Of course."

"God will guide dose who believe in him, but anyting can guide dose who don't believe!"

She talked a bit more, then suddenly started singing and clapping and informed me that the spirit was coming. I asked what a supplejack is for. She explained that three times a year there is a spiritual school held in St. Anns. People come from all four directions of the world to learn their lessons and their purpose in life. Everyone takes exams and moves onward at their own level of growth.

"Someone will say to you, 'Go ask for a glass of spiritual medicine.' You will feel it go into your heart and a tree of life will grow widdin you. Everyone gets an outward sign. Some are drawn to de supplejack as a spiritual staff. Some are drawn to de sword, or to chalk, or to paint,or to a turban. Whatever your spirit calls for is what you will get. It's important to meditate on whatever Pslams you are drawn to. You will contact your spirit and learn what you were meant to do, such as a doctor, preacher, whatever."

Tine-Tine said that over five thousand people are expected to be in attendance at the next spiritual school, which happens to start a week from Thursday. She repeatedly asked me to come, guaranteeing that I would feel the spirit through my dancing. I already have. When I dance alone, my energy becomes vibrations of spirit and I commune with the higher realms. I must remember to dance more often. It is a form of prayer that I used to use a lot, but have somehow strayed from. It is a gift, my personal link to the beyond.

Mooney had told me that Tine-Tine has special powers. He once saw her parading in full uniform through the streets of Salt Marsh. She was banging her drum and telling people to get out their funeral clothes because someone was about to drown. The next day a seven year old boy drowned. I said to her now, "I heard you help people with their problems. How do you do that?"

"When people come and tell me dere problems, dey must believe dey will get an answer." She said this gently, but then she suddenly shook with tremors and once again that fierce, masculine voice shouted, "Your problems will be solved!" There was a very authoritive note in that voice.

She giggled, then told me a few stories of people who had come to her. At first they didn't make any sense to me, but I finally understood what was happening. A man who had lost something came to her in the hopes of finding it. The spirit directed him to throw five stones into the sea. He did this, and five doves immediately flew up out of the water. Soon after, he found the missing item.

Another time, two men who were seeking employment came to her. The spirit directed them to each gather two Leaf of Lifes. They were asked to give one to the church, and boil the other and drink the tea. This they did, and within two weeks they returned to tell her that they had both found a good job.

Tine-Tine said, "It's funny! De answers are really so simple. If you believe, den you will get de best."

What I derived from all of this is that the things that were being asked of these people were merely a lesson in learning to trust that a higher force (or God) will help us. If we do what we are asked, then we are showing that we trust, thus allowing the spirit to assist us in fulfilling our needs. We need to listen to what is being asked in order to find fulfillment and purpose. Many of us have difficulty asking for help and learning to trust it when it does present itself.

Tine-Tine told me that the reason I came there today was because I had heard a message from the spirit to do so. I asked her what she knew about Pocomania. She said that it is not a form of Revival. She heard that on certain nights ceremonies are held in which human beings are burned alive. Their bodies are used as sacrifice amidst a lot of singing and dancing. "Me no know. I only telling you what I hear."

While we were discussing this, Massa George entered the room, cradling a beautiful baby girl. We all jumped up and made a fuss over her and I learned that she is Tine-Tine's granddaughter. Tine-Tine told me that from now on I must call her "Grandmodder." She invited me to the Sunday service, and then we all made small talk before leaving. I marveled at the range of new friends I had made since my arrival on the island.

Mooney and I hitched a ride back to Trelawny with a gentleman from St. Mary. I had planned on hanging around Trelawny for awhile, but when James offered me a ride all the way to Oracabessa I decided to take it. Public transport can be so difficult.

I made the most of the ride by asking my usual questions. My curiosity about these people seems unquenchable. James told me that he is a car rental representative, but he didn't want to tell me for which company. He wasn't sure if they would want their name used in my book. I smiled inwardly at this, but admired him for the respect he was showing.

James is also a mechanic and a farmer, so he keeps very busy. His farm has cows, pigs and chickens. He has four children, but not by the same "baby mama."

"De reason why I am busy is because I like to be independent. I don't want no push around."

His childhood was rough because his parents were very poor, so poor that he couldn't attend school as often as he wanted to. They couldn't afford to send him and his five brothers and one sister. He said he is grateful for his fast brain because he was able to grasp things fairly easily even though he had to miss so much school.

James has heard of duppies, but never seen one. He thinks it's pointless to think about death since we don't really know what will happen. Fearing it is a waste of time.

If he had the money, he would tour the world, but Jamaica will always be his home. He's happy right here.

"If you could have anything in the world, what would your big dream be? Pretend there are no boundaries, no barriers, nothing to stop you."

"What would I like? Uhhhh... to walk and talk wid God."

I mentioned that many people would've said they wanted lots of money. "Money does nutting! You have money today. Tomorrow you don't have any money. As a matter of fact, put it dis way: If you die now, you cannot take any money wid you, ha-ha! I like to have someting, but not to be rich. You have too much money, you just worry about it. I just want to serve God."

We talked about Hurricane Gilbert. James said he took the weather reports seriously enough to "button up and nail everyting dat I could," yet he didn't get too upset because he realized that a hurricane is "an act of God." It was meant to be. Because of the precautions he took, not much damage was done to his property. On the other hand, his neighbor didn't heed the warnings and lost quite a bit.

We had arrived in Oracabessa, so I thanked James and hopped out of his vehicle. While walking through town, I passed the police station. On a whim I decided to go in and check it out. I explained to the sole officer on duty that I was just curious, and asked him if I could look around. He was sitting in a small room behind the front desk, and to my surprise he said yes. Behind that room was a poor kitchen and an old toilet and shower.

I walked boldly out back where a separate building housed about five jail cells. The doorway was merely a steel gate. I peered into a dingy cement hallway. There was a wall on one side and cells on the other. A young boy of about seventeen was in the hallway and walked up to the gate when I looked in. I asked him if he was a guard and he told me he was locked up for stealing.

I realized then that all the cells were filled and the hallway was also being used as a cell.

Suddenly I saw faces and hands pressed up against the cell bars as everyone tried to get a look at me. "What's it like in there?" I asked. A myriad of angry shouts echoed back. "It's horrible!" "It stinks in here!" "It's a hell hole!"

I had my own face pressed up against the gate in an attempt to get a better look, when the policeman gently tapped me on the shoulder. He led me quietly away and informed me that I wasn't allowed to speak to them. I had kind of figured that, but I acted innocent.

Oracabessa Police Station, built in 1890

The officer had a gun tucked into his pants with the barrel pointing directly at his "privates." I shuddered to think how painful it would be if the gun suddenly discharged. I barraged him with questions and was told that these are the local lock up cells. Many of the prisoners are repeat offenders. He said that all are fed three square meals a day which is provided by the government. I was willing to bet that the food was stale and awful and I had my doubts about how often they were really fed.

I told the officer that I had heard that the cells in Mo-Bay are pits dug in the ground and that people are tossed into them and left without food. He assured me that this couldn't be true because such treatment would be illegal.

Bibsey and Sunshine were happy to see me again, but they knew I was coming even before I did. Last night Sunshine had a dream that I was in her bedroom looking out of her window. She awakened feeling certain that I would show up today. She also informed me that I'd been gone fifteen long days. I missed them, too!

Friday, February 23

My heart went out to Bibsey when I saw her yesterday. She had developed a horrible, painful white growth over one eye, but had no money to go to the doctor. I gave her some, glad that I was finally able to help her out for a change. She has been so good to me. I'll never forget it. It was hard to leave, but I packed up everything I had left in Oracabessa, as I probably wouldn't be returning until my next trip to Jamaica.

I caught a minibus back to Mo-Bay and my ride was both frightening and humorous. The driver must've had a death wish because he was a maniac on the road. A man in the back of the bus kept screaming, "Slow down, driver!" This was met with rapid screaming and cussing in Patois from the driver. The conductor said, "Bwoy! Him worried for his life!"

"Yeah, so am I!" I thought.

Other passengers laughed like it was all a big joke. While all of this was going on, we were being blasted out of the van by gospel music coming out of someone's boombox. In the midst of all the arguing, I could hear the lady next to me singing all those gospel songs in such a sweet voice. It was as if she didn't even hear the arguing. She was definitely in a different world.

Of course the more the man screamed. the worse the driver drove. He had to prove that "him de boss mon." I don't scare easily, but even I was praying up a storm at this point. I was relieved when I reached my stop. I stumbled off the van, and the other passengers threw my backpack out the window as the driver roared off, leaving me standing in a cloud of dust.

I had a very strenuous hike up to Coral Gardens. My backpack was too heavy to be lugging around in the intense heat. I prayed that I wouldn't pass out. I know that I promised Deedra that I will go camping with her in the Blue Mountains, but this afternoon I definitely lost my enthusiam for the trip. When I finally arrived at Deedra's apartment, I guzzled water and jumped into a cool shower, then kicked back to rest for awhile.

Birgitta is leaving for Mexico tomorrow, so she, Deedra and I went to our last beach party together tonight. It was fun, but also sad, because I knew it was the closing of a very magical era that we had shared in our lives.

After the party, we went to a concert on the Great River. Entertainers included Lovindeer, Chalice, and Stevie and Ozzie. I met them all and did a short tape on Lovindeer. I was going to finish it at the end of the concert, but somehow it just didn't seem that important. I was physically and emotionally worn out. I had pushed myself as far as I could for one day.

Saturday, February 24
I really wanted to camp on Burwood Beach before I leave Jamaica, but I've lost my enthusiam for that, too. I think the reason is that I am now in a position of knowing that I am forced to say final good-byes to people as I travel through the different areas. Who knows when I'll return and what Jamaica will be like when I do... .

It makes me feel melancholy. Sometimes I wish I didn't love as much as I do. It makes the farewells all but impossible. These people will always live in my heart, but I already miss their laughter and hugs and all the good times we've shared.

It's not only the people that I will miss, but the land itself and the sea. It is a part of me and feeds my soul daily. The island speaks to me constantly and holds me in its loving arms. I feel safe here and at home. I have received so much and have a deep need to give back now.

Sunday, February 25
How I hated having to say good-by to Birgitta! Poor Howard! His heart must be breaking. He loves her so much.

I'm very homesick today. I'd love to be relaxing with Mom, Matt and Grandma. I slept in today, and am going to read and write all day. I need to relax and replenish my energy so I can make it through the next few weeks.

I must take inventory and see what else I want to accomplish before I leave. I'm getting very low on funds, so I'll have to be careful. Living out of a backpack and trying to move around the island without a car has taken its toll on me. But it has also been very good for me to experience this. It has taught me to appreciate myself and my life.

Monday, February 26

What a great day! Yesterday Carolyn Jobson left a message with Deedra to have me come to her house this morning. I was feeling ill and tearful, the usual PMS symptoms, so I didn't really want to go. I just didn't feel like talking to anyone, but I forced myself to go and I'm so glad.

Carolyn is so sweet and feels that this book is important. Her encouragement keeps me going. A friend of hers named Lynda Lee Burks is visiting her. Carolyn wanted me to meet her because she has done editing and knows something about the publishing business.

David and Carolyn left for work (they operate a tour business), and Linda and I had a wonderful day visiting on their huge front porch. The house is on a hill and we had a fabulous view of the mountains and the sea. This home feels very Jamaican. There are lots of old wooden floors and a lot of character here. I felt like I had traveled back in time a hundred years.

I was surprised when maids came out to see if they could get us anything. I've never been comfortable with maids. I remember when my dad and step-mom came to visit me in Jamaica. They loved the condo we were in, but they refused to allow the maids to cook for them unless the maids would join us for meals. It was great fun for all of us.

To my delight, Lynda was very excited about what I am trying to do. She offered to help me in any way possible. She said she would love to edit the manuscript, and even offered to help transcribe the tapes. I need that kind of feedback in order to have the guts and discipline to finish this. I realize that the real work hasn't even begun yet, and won't until I am back home.

I'm trying to prepare myself for what lies ahead. I will need to work full time to support myself while I write. I can't really expect anyone back home to be excited about this, because they have no idea what it's all about. I'm very aware of how difficult it is for new writers to get something published, but if I dwell on that then I won't find the stamina to keep working on it. So, I'll take it one step at a time. If the Creator wants it published, then it will get published. My job is to just do it!

Lynda is a wonderful lady and her friendship is such a gift right now. I was starting to feel so discouraged, but she has recharged my batteries. The magic is coming back, along with the belief that I can actually finish the project.

Carolyn brought us lunch, lobster and calalu. She knows that Deedra and

I are planning on heading to the other side of the island soon to camp in the Blue Mountains. While we enjoyed our feast, Carolyn casually extended an invitation to stay at her father's house in Mamee Bay as we journeyed over. I feel pampered and spoiled today. I've been fed well spiritually, emotionally, mentally and physically. Everything is irie. "Yeah mon. Praise Jah!"

Tuesday, February 27

Late yesterday afternoon, Deedra and I traveled back across to the south side of the island to spend the night at the Waterloo Guest House. We're taking advantage of every opportunity we can now, because we know that our time here is limited. Deedra is leaving her job and moving back to the States. Since she had use of a company car yet, we had to go for the gusto!

Waterloo Guest House, Black River

This is a time for us to celebrate life. We shared a bottle of wine as we watched the sun set over the sea, and then we treated ourselves to a fabulous Jamaican dinner. Afterwards, we went into the little bar to socialize. Directly outside the open doorway was the narrow street. And right next to the street was the sea. We wandered out there after dark to look at the stars, and to our amusement the four men in the bar followed us.

The bartender had heard me say that I enjoy the music of Gregory Isaacs, so he cranked up the old juke box and sent that music all the way across the street to us. Before we knew it we were all dancing wildly with the sea. It was a magnificent night. I felt fully the gypsy in my blood as my long skirt swirled around me. We felt the harmony of the universe and became one with it. Joy pervaded. I know Heaven exists. I've been there.

We took time out here and there to chit-chat. I don't remember ever laughing so much in one evening. We were all so happy that for some reason everything seemed incredibly funny. And laughter is definitely contagious.

The sea sang gently to us and the little fishing boats danced in the distance as we talked. Two fellows did most of the talking. One was named Phillip and the other was named Carlton, but his pet name is Lollipop. Everyone calls him Lolly. He has a beautiful spirit and dealt with his basically shy nature by acting like a comedian. Much of what he said is not going to be printed here (due to its graphic nature), but boy did we laugh! I couldn't help but love this man. He's the pearl in the oyster.

"What do you think of duppies?"

Phillip piped up, "Duppies? Evil spirits. When I was a little boy we lived in an old house. We had a helper dat used to work for us, and one night when I was about ten years old he called me into de backyard to come and see someting. It was like a fog, a mist, someting white, not natural. It went up a coconut tree. I never forget it."

Someone said, "Lolly, you ever see duppy?"

"No mon! Rasta no see duppy. Dem don't exist. We believe in natural vibes, you know, natural creation."

He said he thinks that when we die it's the end of everything. I said, "Do you think Bob Marley is dead?"

"Bob Marley asleep mon!" I asked how come Lolly would cease to exist upon death if Bob Marley merely went to sleep when he died. They were both Rastas. Everyone laughed, but no one had a response. Talk turned to Haile Selassie. No one knows where he is buried.

"So what is going to happen when you die?"

Lolly replied, "De gift of Jah is life. I is life, so I just live. I don't tink of death, because I don't know. Hey, life is sweet, you know? Really nice. Especially when I meet a nice daughter like you. I don't believe in de duppy business."

"Well, I saw one, so what am I supposed to think about that?"

"No! You were smoking a spliff!"

Everyone erupted into gales of laughter. "No mon!" I said, but I realized Lolly wasn't going to take this subject seriously so I let it go.

Lolly told me he loves Patois, but can't usually speak it around foreigners because they don't understand it. Then he said, "We are one people, one blood, no matter what dey call de creator. No matter if we creating mixed breed, we are all one blood still and should be loving each odder."

Then he got silly and said that when he saw the two daughters (Deedra and I) with no men, Jah told him to come and talk to us. "I thought maybe you was a bit shy. Most of de time women depends on mon to say hi. De women never want to say hi. Maybe if I do she'll be impressed a little bit."

We're all laughing hard. Something about Lolly's mannerism is so humorous. He says, "Now it makes me feel like we're having a little party!"

"We are, " I said. "Deedra is quitting her job and moving forward in life, so we're celebrating new beginnings.

"What is your big dream in life, Lolly? Pretend there are no holds, no limitations. It can be anything you want."

He sounded very happy as he said, "Love, mon! Love! Love for de whole world, mon! Because dis is Jah's creation. Babylon mess it up but Jah say, 'Ye do I walk through de valley of shadow and death. Fear no evil.' Have faith. If people get frustrated and miserable dey can't even find dere own way. You can see dat people get confused. And people even try to turn demselves into evil baldheads.

"I mean, look at de beautiful creation. Why can't people live as beautiful people? I tink den dat God would smiles wid us everyday and give us even more life to live. Dis earth is good, but some of de people are corrupt really. I personally no love dat. But I have to live my own life, de true life.

"If people really have love, I tink dey have all tings. To love is everyting. As long as you have love, no wrong can go wid it."

Lolly was born in St. James and has one brother and five sisters. I asked about his childhood. "I don't tink I can remember too much about my childhood because I don't tink behind me too much. I always tink forward."

Lolly asked me if I have any children and told me that I was very selfish when he found out that I don't. His friends all chastised him for this and he

224

graciously appologized. I wasn't offended, just amused by all of this.

I asked what he was spanked for as a child. "Maybe when I hold de little girls and share my nature."

"How old?"

"Maybe four, five."

"You don't mean sexual things, do you?"

"Yeah. From my understanding, I always want it."

Phillip told me that when he misbehaved his parents would make him take off his clothes because they knew it would keep him in the house. Also, when he went to Sunday School (Methodist Church) everyone else would get candy but he got none. One time he and his buddies stole money out of the collection basket and went and bought candy. They got a whalloping for it.

He told us another good story. "My modder was a teacher, taught shorthand and typing. She used to also have a private school at de house. So anyway, one evening when I was about four, I took one of my modder's panties and put dem on and go inside de school. She was dere and was so embarrassed! Dat was de first and de last and de only time she beat me."

"Do you remember why you did that?"

"I just wanted attention. I was bad. De first time I had sex I was nine. It was wid de helper. I watched my odder brodders, den made my own negotiations." Phillip said he has four brothers and they were all hellions.

We were laughing hard at this point, and suddenly Deedra asked me if I've read a book called "The Lunatic" by Anthony Winkler. Gasping for air, I replied, "I am the lunatic!"

Then Phillip told us he used to put mirrors on his shoes and stand next to the girls so he could look up their dresses. He even did it to the teacher.

Later we finally got a bit more serious and the subject reverted back to spiritual things. Phillip said, "Everyting in life is a cycle. What goes around comes around. I tink we possibly come back."

Someone mentioned the Anti-Christ, but no one seemed to know much about the term. "He's supposed to be someone who performs miracles and tings. Him seem like de Christ, but can deceive people."

It was getting late and most of the group said good-night at this point. As they climbed into their old truck, Lolly said to them, "Jah bless and guide and keep you and protect. Irie, baby!"

I asked Lolly what he thinks of the stars. "Dey are beautiful. I tink when I look at people I can see de stars in dat person." He said this very shyly, as though he was sharing something sacred to his heart. I was deeply touched by this. What a gift to be able to see that kind of beauty and light in people. He revealed a lot about himself in that statement.

I told him that when I was a little girl I used to think that the sky was the floor of heaven. I thought that the stars were merely holes in the floor in which the light from Heaven showed through. It was, and still is, magical to me. That light forever calls me to itself.

Lolly asked, "Where do you tink Heaven is?"

"Here and now. It's a state of mind and a choice we make."

"Yeah, so your happiness is your heaven. Natural vibes. Good vibrations. You could be a Rasta because you have so much good vibrations."

Lolly said that Rastas are frowned upon by many Jamaicans because of misconceptions. People assume that anyone wearing dreadlocks is a Rastafarian. This is not so. Many are just troublemakers, so it gives the whole movement a bad name. I asked Lolly when he became a Rasta.

"From de time I small, about twelve, my heart was Rasta. My grandfodder would give me money for a trim, but I would go buy a book or someting."

He told me about some friends who taught him to speak German. When I asked him where his friends were from he replied, "Moscow, Germany."

We stepped inside the bar for a bit and encountered some locals. When I tried to interview them I realized they weren't as eager as most people. After all, it was the middle of the night and they didn't know me, or what my motives were. They were a bit leery and managed to interview me before I even realized what was happening. Ha! The tables had turned. This was insightful. We ended up friends. "Respect, mon!"

Lolly and I went back outside. We were alone now and danced some more under the stars, celebrating the beauty of creation. What a dear soul he is! I hated having to say good night, but it was time. I headed dreamily to our little room in the hundred plus year old guest house, and drifted into a peaceful sleep. Deedra had long been asleep, off in that magical place beyond our consciousness. Before I fell asleep I looked at her and wondered where the night had taken her.

8

HIGHS AND LOWS

"Him could do tings like make your arms rot off.
Dey got oils dey mix. It can make girls rush you,
oil dat can make a mon stay wid you forever. Dey
got oil to make you lose a job, oil to get you a job,
all different kinds of oil. When mixed right, dey
call it obeah."

—*Mike*

Wednesday, February 28
I love the south side of the island. Deedra and I made the most of it before returning to Mo-Bay yesterday. We started the day with a lovely breakfast out by the sea.

Then we went on the Black River Safari. This is a touristy thing, yet it's low key. Not many people know about it. It's also something the locals can enjoy. As a public relations gesture, we were invited on the trip for free. What a delightful surprise!

The small boat moved slowly and silently down the river, allowing us to really observe the natural beauty of the mangrove trees and dense jungle beyond. The vine-like roots of the trees grew down into the water, casting wild reflections. We saw several different kinds of birds, and also a few crocodiles.

I don't think I'd care to swim here, although the locals do.

The safari was magical. On the return trip we encountered heavy rain which I enjoyed. The river literally got up and danced for us. It cast a mood all its own.

I really admire Charles, who runs the safari. He has tremendous respect for nature and ecology. Like us, he's concerned about the rumors he has heard that people are thinking of turning the south side of the island into pure tourism. That would be tragic. Not only would it upset the ecological balance, but it would force the local people to move and lose their homes. Land would become scarce and prices would skyrocket. The people are happy with their life style. Their very way of life and a precious part of the culture would disappear. Some would call this progress. I would call it greed. I pray it doesn't happen.

Before heading home, we decided to explore YS Falls. Someone offered to guide us to them, but we thought it would be more fun to find them on our own. We did get a bit lost, but it just added to the fun. I let Deedra lead us, and there were a few places I had doubts about following. We hiked through fields with cows, jungle, and even crossed rivers.

The heat got us, and we were so thirsty we got giddy. But then we stumbled upon some coconut trees. We managed to crack the coconuts open by pounding them on a rock, and the water inside was truly a nectar of the gods.

What a thrill to finally find the falls, which are large and clear, pristine and untouristy. It was getting dark by then, so we couldn't stay long, but we did jump into them and refresh ourselves. I would've loved sleeping there, but Deedra had to get back for her last day of work. Thus ended another day in paradise.

Well, that was yesterday. Today we were back in the world of people. I didn't feel well, but forced myself to hop into a crowded minibus and go to Ochi. I ran through the pouring rain to the place I was supposed to rendezvous with Milton to do an interview. After all that, he never showed up. I had no way to contact him, so I finally gave up and came back to Mo-Bay feeling angry, irritable, discouraged, hurt and worn out.

Thursday, March 1
How can so much happen in the course of one night? I slept in my sleeping bag on Deedra's floor, where my physical body remained all night, but my spirit

traveled far and wide... through terrifying nightmares and strong warnings of impending danger. I'm taking these warnings very seriously.

One dream was of being trapped in a room with a murderer trying to break in. I had other disturbing dreams, one of a boating accident, one of driving a car off the road into a river. On and on they went, all night.

Anyway, I woke up feeling so lost and frightened that I knew I must meditate. I went up to the top of my waterfall, felt the cool mist cushion my body, and then saw myself getting smaller and smaller as my spirit rose higher and higher above it. Looking beyond the falls, I could see forests. The sensation was wonderful, as I needed to get away from the emotional torments that had been plaguing me.

When I asked who the guiding force is that has been helping me with this book, I saw a lady that I have seen before. She has blond, fluffy hair, piercing blue eyes, and always wears white. I usually see her hovering off to the left side of my being.

The first time I saw her was last Spring. I was sitting at the dining room table when I suddenly became aware that I was not alone. I felt some negative entities and ordered them away. But then I saw the lady. She was quiet and serene and seemed to be hunting for something over by the window. I watched her in stunned silence, but decided to not interfere.

I've seen her several times since then, but finally spoke to her this morning. These messages came back. I have heard them before, so I know I must heed them. "Remember to be objective. You are the channel for this. It is not your purpose to get so physically and emotionally involved. You don't have to suffer when you go through hardships because you have the ability to rise above them. When you understand how unimportant these things really are, then you can laugh about it (things such as being stood up after traveling seventy miles on a crowded minibus to interview someone, etc.) Things are unfolding as they should. Don't take it personally. Just trust that you are being guided and remember that you are not alone."

Well, that's quite a challenge for me, learning detachment. I'm not too good at that yet, and I can see that I'm creating my own experiences as a result. But I'll try to be gentle with myself, as I'm doing the best I can.

I looked down at the waterfall and was drawn into the essence of pure love and bliss. I allowed myself to remember and know it again. The experience was something I couldn't bear to let go of, but I knew it was time for me to go back into my body on that kitchen floor in Montego Bay. I didn't want to, as I sensed the difficult and challenging times that lie ahead.

When I was fully conscious in the physical realm again, I realized that I had tears running down my face. I sat up and couldn't stop the deep sobbing that flooded me even though I was embarrassed. Deedra was in the room making coffee, and I'm sure she wondered what was going on. I apologized, explaining that I had had bad dreams and just needed some time to pull myself together and do some writing.

The selfish part of me wants to live eternally in the meditation I just experienced. But I can't. Not now. Not yet. I have things to do here.

Deedra just came up and hugged me and asked if I'm okay. I said yes, then burst into tears again. I can see that it's not going to be an easy, carefree day. But, I'm going to jump into the shower and get on with it.

Deedra at home

I feel like there is a negative force hovering around me. It's starting to make me angry. "Enough! Go away!" I cry out loud. I've never let them beat me yet and I'm not about to now. I'll tread cautiously today and in the near future, because I strongly sense a warning to be careful. If I remain in touch with my spirit, then I know I will be guided and avoid whatever potential danger lies ahead.

Friday, March 2

Yesterday, Deedra and I went downtown and bought all kinds of good Jamaican food. We came home and made fried plantain and pumpkin soup. Although we were having a marvelous time, it became even more fun when the power went out because we were forced to cook in candlelight. I should do that more often. Come to think of it, it would be a very romantic date thing to do, especially on a cold, winter night.

My emotions are going wacky. I'm out of balance, feeling terribly lonely and depressed and I hate it. I wonder what is causing this. Even a trip to Cornwall Beach today failed to cheer me up.

We met a character named Mike on the beach and I decided to interview him. He's twenty-seven years old and for the first half hour all he would talk about is how wonderful girls look in their bikinis. Then he tried to convince us that, "But I goes for personality more dan good looks. I doesn't go for riches because I'm not a male whore." He's already been in love five times in his young life.

I finally managed to change the subject. "What do you think happens when you die?"

"If I repent, den I'll go to Heaven."

"What if you don't change?"

"I'll die as a lost sinner and be possessed by demons for all eternity."

"You're not worried about it?"

"Well, a bit."

"What do you think anyone could do that would be so bad that they would go to Hell?"

"Stealing. Temptation towards a woman. Killing."

"What have you been doing that is so bad?"

"I tell a couple of lies."

"What do you think Heaven is like?"

"I never got no dreams about it, but I tink it's someplace where we all could live as one, socialize, love each odder, tink about happiness, nutting about sex on your mind."

Mike obviously feels guilty about his own sexual activities. The fact that he loves women so much, yet thinks that all good things will be found in Heaven except sex, was a very revealing statement about his inner conflicts.

"What about UFO's?"

"Dey exist, but nobody knows where dey come from or go to. I saw tings moving in de stars." He thinks that by the year two thousand they will be common sights on Earth.

"Do you believe in obeah?"

"Yeah! It's a real high scientific power. It can do tings you wouldn't believe!"

Mike told me about someone who stole tires off the car of an obeah man. A spell was put on him and soon after he tied a rock around his neck and jumped into the sea and drowned.

"Some of dem don't kill demselves, but go crazy on de street."

It is common to see madmen wandering on the streets of Jamaica. Most are harmless, but certainly not capable of functioning rationally in society. Mike feels certain that most of them got that way from an obeah spell that was cast on them.

I asked for the name of the obeah man that he knows and if he thought it might be possible to interview him. Mike replied, "He's from Montego Bay, but believe me, you don't mess wid dem kind of guys! You know what I mean? Stay away from dose guys! Just try to be good and don't be bad.

"Him could do tings like make one of your arms rot off. Dey got oils dey mix. It can make girls rush you, oil dat make a mon stay wid you forever. Dey got oils to make you lose a job, oil to get you a job, all different kinds of oil. When mixed right, dey call it obeah."

"Do you think that people are aware of a spell when it has been put on them?"

"Sometimes dey know. Sometimes dey don't know. Westmoreland and St. Thomas have most of de obeah people here. In Haiti, dey got heavy science. It very dangerous. If you mess wid somebody, somebody will mess wid you bad. We got a ting called 'a blow for a blow,' like 'an eye for an eye.' Den dey put your name on someting dey call watchman paper. And dey put it on a tree dey call de cotton tree. And dey hold down your life. It make you do bad tings.

"Sometimes if a mon has a case in court, he will go to an obeah mon or a Bush Doctor. Den he will win de case and go home free even if he was guilty. You know what I mean? Some guys charged wid murder even get off de case."

Mike had to leave, but promised that if I come back tomorrow he will tell me about a forty-eight year old woman that he fell in love with. It's clear that he can't stay away from the subject for too long. I hope he treats this woman well.

It rained for hours late in the afternoon. The last thing I felt like doing was going downtown tonight, but I felt like I had to. Deedra and I want to have a party for the kids before we leave and I needed to see Dawn to discuss arrangements.

Harris was at Sir Candles waiting for me. Pearl Harbor had told him I was coming. He looked exotic with his long locks hanging down under a white T-shirt that he had bound around his head Revival style. We had a great talk. He was excited about my interview with Gregory Isaacs, and encouraged me to keep working on the book.

Harris begged me to not go camping in the Blue Mountains, insisting that it is far too dangerous. He understands that I've been off working on this book, but said he becomes very concerned for my safety when he doesn't see me for awhile. I was touched when he said that he misses me and prays for me all the time. It's nice to know someone cares, and I can use all the prayers I can get!

We spoke of a dream he has of opening a food shop near his house, so that his children could all move back in with him. Only some of them are there now. The others stay with Grandma Sweet. Harris said that Kimoy is a dangerous child because she refuses to obey. He never had this problem with the others. But he dearly loves them all.

Pearl Harbor showed up and told me what it was like to live in Trench Town when he was young. Bob Marley and Peter Tosh used to come in and eat at an Ital shop where Pearl Harbor cooked. Ital food is all natural food, grown and prepared with no preservatives. Rastafarians believe that it is a means to the greatest physical health possible. It also brings about harmony of spirit because that which is eaten has come from the earth which God (Jah) has created.

"Peter Tosh had many brodders. One get killed. Two do bank robbery. One into political affairs. Peter was a very good carpenter, very fit. He was good in karate and was an acrobat. He liked to ride bicycles and play guitar.

"Bob Marley was a guy dat used to play a lot of football. At dose times, dey was looking about dere careers, stepping up to music step by step. I knew dese guys, and later dey became famous. I didn't get to know Bunny Wailer dat much.

"I, Pearl Harbor, used to work in an Ital shop and fry dumplings, make carrot juice, soursop juice, all different herb juices. Dat's what de dreadlocks like to eat and drink. I did five years of Ital eating. De spices and coconut milk dat you put into de food makes it taste like it has salt. Everyone would go for it, especially de corn and dumplings. We put corn meal and flour togedder and fry it. Very sweet in Jamaica.

"I had locks when I was thirteen or fourteen. My modder and fodder did want me to trim it, but when dey would give me some money I would take it and go cook some Ital food. I was on de Rastafari side of society, so I use dat money to cook for I and my friends.

"I showed dem dat when my mind tell me to cut my locks I will cut dem. But if my mind tell me don't cut, I won't. So if you give me de money to cut, I will use it for a different reason. My friends appreciate dat.

"Due to de Babylon system people get carried away, brainwashed in education. Now if you are a locks, you can step in certain society. Bob Marley reached to a certain stage and died. Peter Tosh reached to a certain stage and died. Now I'm looking for Dennis Brown. It going to happen to him. Whenever a black mon rises up and starts to say anyting dat people all around de world can understand and realize what really is, den he gonna go down. Right?

"Bob Marley speak a lot of reality. And what happened? Jamaicans say dere's a lot of ways to end a dog dan to put a rope around his throat. You can hold his stomach and hang him. You can hold his feet and hang him. So de truth of de death of Bob Marley is not going to really come out in de public. But I know it widdin myself, because I was looking for it."

"You don't think it was cancer that killed him?"

"No. De first ting dat I heard was dat uranium gas was in de microphone dat he was using. I tink it slowly poisoned him. I heard dat first. Den I hear cancer. I tink dis happened in Germany because of de reality tings dat he speak. De Babylon system doesn't feel dat he should tell people dat de cow can't jump over de moon. De dish can't run away wid de spoon."

"What is the Babylon system?"

"De Babylon system is de kind of brainwash dat take you away from de reality part of life. Dey put it in dere teaching. It bad. You know dat if you walk and hit your foot you're going to feel a lot of pain. But dey want to tell you dat you won't feel any pain. Just drink a little of dis and de pain will leave.

"De Babylon system is a very much corrupt system. Dere is no individual to point a finger to. It is a certain group of people who congregate demselves in dere segregation. De good tings, reality, won't rise in front.

"For instance, dey try and say we can't use natural cure, or put our own bush medicine togedder. Dey say we must run to de doctor first. Dey don't want us to use it, but to get it from de doctor."

Pearl Harbor went on to say that, basically, greed is the main motive in the Babylon system. The governments, doctors, lawyers, etc. work together making laws which benefit their greed but don't serve the people's needs. There is no true compassion and concern for your brother. He even said that a lot of the churches do the same thing.

In this day and age, only blind people can't see what is really going on. There is so much power and corruption involved that yes, many of those who do rise up and try to stop it are gunned down. Or they just 'happen' to die in some kind of accident. So a solution isn't easy.

But I believe a time of peace is coming and that the tables will be turning. This is most definitely an interesting time to be visiting the planet.

"Each of us have to tink, to know what is right, what is wrong, and what is inbetween. Dere is three ways, de good, de bad and de indifference. You must always look three ways, not one or two.

"You must see all sides. You don't just picture someting one way and say, 'I'm sure dat is de right way.' You have to go in de self-conscious mind and represent yourself wid some questions. Inner mon speaks wid inner brain and den comes up wid an answer. And if you picture it more dan one time, you'll find dat you find more dan one answer to de question. For example, a mon drowned. Why he drowned? Did he get tangled, muscle contraction, suffocates or what? You have to look more dan one way at all times.

"So de Babylon goes through all dat research just to say to de people of de world, 'Dis is de way a nation go, dat all of us can get an income from dis direction.' So dey look at de left and de right biz. Dey give us de left right, and dey keep de right just to achieve de vanity.

"Dere's a lot of Jamaicans who don't come to de self conscious dat de cow can't jump over de moon. Dey teach dere children. You see me? I've got four children and I'm not going to tell dem dat de cow jumped over de moon. I'm not going to tell dem dat de dish run away wid de spoon. I'm not going to tell dem horse head and cow fat. Dat is old time slang for dem lies. If I tell dem dat, den in later days to come, dey might realize dat, 'Hey, my daddy was telling me a lot of bullshit. I'm gonna kick his ass out for telling me dose tings.'

"No, I'm not gonna do dat. I'm gonna try to teach dem de right tings, de tings dat I know is possible. My oldest one is six, and even if he come to me and ask, 'Daddy, how I come to Earth?' I'm gonna tell him dat both people have sex, getting pregnant, and den from de hospital he born. When he comes older, I can tell him dat it pussy. But for now, at six years old, I just tell him about sex."

"Pretend I'm your son and I have asked you. How would you explain it?"

"I would just say, 'Me and your modder have sex.' Maybe he's bright enough to ask, 'What is sex?' Den I tell him to ask me again in a few years and I will tell him. 'And from de sex, pregnancy comes, just like how you see de goats and de cows and de horse have dere young ones. Dat's how you come.' He must walk on de street and see some tings, because it is not everyting dat someone must have to tell you. And it is not everyting dat I can tell him. He gots to learn someting outside.

"Because Marcus Garvey, which is a prophet for Jamaica, say, 'What is hidden from de wise and foolish, now, now in dispensation, reveal to de babes and suckling.' So dere is nutting dat we can hide from de younger ones. Right?

"Now de Babylon system would say to us dat dere is a lot of tings we shouldn't tell de kids. If dey find we tell our kids or maybe a hundred kids dat de cow can't jump over de moon, maybe dey eliminate you, right? All because you are educating de youth to reality. Babylonian say you must keep dem in de darkness. Dat's how dey play dere game. Dey don't want de people of de world to see reality side of life. Dey want to teach dem what dey want to teach dem to do.

"If it costs my neck to step out and tell de truth, I will do it, because dere will and dere should be, someone who will take on my message. Bob Marley die leaving a lot of messages behind. Ziggy Marley, his son, stepping up wid de message. Peter's son doing a lot of music too, mon.

"Let me tell you someting. De younger brain right now tink more swiftly dan de older brain. Dey go into dere self conscious mind and find de truth."

He said he believes that the less we sleep the better, because when we sleep we are close to death. When we are wide awake we can think and talk and learn and teach. With our eyes wide open we realize we are well.

"Each brain cell holds tings. So de brain have to be moving. De Babylon system don't want to know dat you don't go to bed."

Pearl Harbor said that the police want to haul people away who stay out all night, even if they're doing no wrong. They want to charge them with loitering, and the reality is that they are merely thinking and reflecting. The reaction of the police to such innocence breeds violence in people.

"De police are taught to harass people in training school. Dey don't know dat de cow can't jump over de moon."

Pearl Harbor went on to say that he believes that human eyes are more accurate than a traditional lie detector test. He said that if one tunes into his intuition and looks directly into the eyes of another, he can see the truth. It is also important to hear what is really being said, not what is coming out of a person's mouth.

Sometimes people don't want to know the truth. They prefer to live in a world of illusions, thinking that it's easier. It takes courage to face the truth head on, but doing so ultimately provides growth on all levels, not only personally, but globally.

Pearl Harbor has a brother who is in prison in St. Catherine for murder. The murder was committed in self defense and was politically oriented, but Pearl Harbor said that the police don't ask questions, just look at facts (Babylon). The questions would reveal self defense, whereas the facts indicate only that he did kill a man.

It's almost pointless to try to visit someone in a Jamaican prison. One must fill out countless forms and then go through an intense question and answer period. If you are finally approved for a visit, then you are allowed only two minutes, this talking through a hole in a glass window.

Considering the fact that it takes most visitors close to a day of travel, besides all the rest of the hassel, it's obvious that this system definitely discourages the visiting of inmates.

Because of this, Pearl Harbor went to see his brother only once. He couldn't justify spending fifty dollars for transportation when he really needs the money to feed and support his four children. This has created a problem with his brother who thinks that Pearl Harbor just doesn't care about him. He is vexed and wants revenge.

Pearl said that everyone in his family except his mother knows that his brother killed that man. Her brain refuses to accept it. In order to not cause her more strife and high blood pressure, he knew he must do something. So he went to an obeah man in Westmoreland who commanded him to do certain things.

He told me he couldn't reveal them all, but some of the things were: write his name three times, then cut down a banana tree; then write his name five more times and put it in a bible. Pearl Harbor is convinced, without a doubt, that he saved his brother's life by doing these things and the other things that were asked of him.

His brother was sentenced to hang, and now the sentence has been changed. However, Pearl's brother has now turned on him. I can't help but wonder about these obeah powers. Someone always seems to have to pay a price, have harm done to them. His brother was saved and may soon be out, and now Pearl fears for his own life, thinking that he may become the victim of the brother he helped save.

In 1983, Pearl went to an obeah man who gave him a small, shiny grey seed and told him to carry it with him always for protection. When he pulled it out of his pocket tonight to show it to me, he dropped it. Sheer terror covered his face as we searched for it. I had seen it bounce and knew we would eventually find it, which we did. But I'll never forget the fear, and then relief, on his face. He was somewhat embarrassed about admitting his beliefs, yet shared them with me anyway, because it is his reality.

Deedra showed up to give me a ride home, so I thanked Pearl Harbor and said good-night to everyone. It had been a very interesting evening, to say the least.

Saturday, March 3

I woke up feeling depressed yet again, and cried as we packed for our camping trip to the Blue Mountains. What is wrong with me??? I'm so hard on myself.

I'm upset because I haven't finished reading all the books I brought with me and because I haven't done more writing. I need to be more objective and remember my purpose here.

Later: Well, here I am on Union Street again. It's a hot, humid night and a half moon is hanging up above. I'm sitting outside on the balcony at Sir Candles, observing the night life below me. On the corner are vendors selling fresh fruit, jerk chicken, soup and hot roasted peanuts. The aromas are heavenly.

Watch your step on the sidewalks as there is garbage here and there. I can't smell that though. Little dogs are out looking for a good time tonight, too. They are all so scrawny I can count their ribs. Wish I could feed them and let them love me, as I know they would.

Yes, it's Saturday Night Live on Union Street in Montego Bay. Here is the scene across the street outside of Peter's Bar: A tall, slim man in blue shoes, jeans and a muscle shirt is heavy into Reggae dancing on the sidewalk. He is also wearing black beads and a gold watch. He dips now, dips now, then blows a whistle and jumps, changing beat. Soon others join him in dance. A small boy pulls up on his bicycle and everything is "just cool."

The feeling here is laid back, relaxing and comfortable. The only thing I have trouble with is how loud the music is. I bet it can be heard in Janesville, Wisconsin. My ears are tickling.

Couples are strolling slowly down the middle of the street, laughing and drinking white rum or Dragon Stout. I keep hearing "Pssssssst! Psssssst!" I call that the famous Jamaican mating call, as it is always a come on.

The dancing is loose and disjointed. People are doing 'rub-a-dub,' which is exactly what it implies. Even people dancing alone make the erotic movements in the hope of attracting a passerbyer. A hefty, bald man is dancing with an eight foot length of sugarcane. Another man is unselfconsciously scratching his privates as he meanders down the street. A broken water pipe is flooding the street, but no one pays any attention to it. A man in a dress hat and brown pants is holding himself up against a wall across the street and peeing.

The ladies of the night have come out of the woodwork and are dancing provocatively down the street, sporting red and gold hats. They slither along with their hands running down their hips and it's clear they have no underwear on. Yes, the night is in full bloom.

I can hear laughter from inside and turn my attention now back to Sir Candles. Inside the doorway is a sign which says "Welcome to Sir Candles." When exiting, one sees a sign "Thank you for your patronage. Sorry you have to leave, but please make it Sir Candles again."

Sir Candles Nightclub, Harris and author

Hanging in the bar is a 1988 pin up calender and a Craven A cigarette ad. Dawn must keep track of every drink she sells in a notebook, as there is no cash register. An American war movie is turned up full blast. Harris is watching it. I am puzzled by the way gentle spirits always seem to be drawn towards violence. When I asked Harris about it he replied, "So dat if I see a sityation like dat I know how to deal wid it."

As he watches it, he laughs. It is not any kind of reality to him. When I watch it, it is all reality to me. So I can't watch it.

As I sit here I am thinking. I have things inside of me that are so special and so private that I think they will go with me to my grave, never even to be revealed in my writing. If this is so, and it is, what about all the other people around me? Each of them must carry his or her own secrets. No wonder life is so amazing and magnetic. Heaven must be all of these secrets combined.

Harris and I go outside and talk. I ask what he has to say tonight. "Well, I gots to say dat I'm glad you are here wid me tonight. We have human feelings for each odder, and we both have to get our goals dat we are trying to make. And both of us is just de right persons to get tings to where dey should be, wid de help of de Fodder. And you already know dat is special enough, can never break or change."

"That's great. My immediate goal is to try to finish my book. What is yours?"

"Well, my goals right now is to try to get tings togedder, to try to set up someting to make my own money, don't work for no one. So I'm just hoping and praying dat I get to set up a little cook shop, to get tings going so dat tings can be copacetic, to keep me moving along as life goes on.

"Right now I'm checking around to see if I can get any work, like plumbing or painting, to really get a portion of funds to start it. Cuz I have everyting at dis time dat I would like. But on dose tings it's only to get dose foods and tings togedder, and get a little car, dat I could do it more distant and more copacetic."

"Copacetic? I never heard that word."

"Well, normally dat word means tings in de right and proper way."

Dawn told me that Harris used to do ceramics. When I asked him why he quit he said that money is tight in Jamaica right now and people just can't live in that fanciness. They need their money just to buy food and other necessities. He says he knows he would be filling a need by cooking. And he knows he is a good and clean cook.

"Harris, I would like you to describe me. What is Debbie to you?"

"Debbie, to me, is a person dat I see from a long time when we just met, a person dat is genuine towards tings, a person dat really from de spirit, takes you de right way. She would never let you down any way you move around, as long as you don't do wrong. If you make a mistake, we can both understand de mistake, dat no one is perfect right now.

"I know de Fodder put de blessings on de both of us to make tings go de way it should go, cuz we're not dealing wid wrong tings. We're dealing wid right."

"This may sound like an abstract question, but what is life to you?"

"Life? Well, right now life to me, it's looking to know dat I just live and have tings, not material, but tings to my comfort. To know dat I don't really go out dere and steal. I don't go out dere and beg. I don't go out dere and piss.

241

I can have tings to my little convenient, to live, until de Fodder ready to do what he want to do. Cuz de Fodder is de one who know what to do.

"We are only guests, but he de one who manner to life. If him say you have to go, you have to go. And if he say you are to stay, you have to stay. So I'm just relying, praying, and asking de Fodder to do what de best he can for me. And to do what he can do for each and everyone also, to make we are more better in certain situation and certain condition dat we are in right now."

"What is death to you?"

"Death to me I can't really understand, because I don't take it for nutting. It can be, if someone take acid, a downfallment for people."

"A downfall? How do you mean?"

"Well, I mean dat de time has come for dat person to really vacate off de Earth. But it might be good or it might be bad, but his time has just come. And from de time it come, he just has to go. He can't resist. Some people die because of tings dey do wrong. Dey die even before dere time. I heard everyone has to die. I'm not just saying dat.

"But I say, I will just keep praying to de Fodder to really keep me through many decades of life. If I have to die, it's just that way, but I'm doing my best to really stay alive. Cuz life is de best and it's very good. Don't matter how you might be in life, but it's good to see you living, talking to people. It's very good."

"But what do you think death means?"

"Well, death just means to me dat de body of you is de breath. God leave de body, so you are no longer a human person on de Earth, but your spirit is still moving around. Cuz de spirit never die. It's only de body fade away."

"What do you think happens to the spirit?"

"De spirit move around and can be good spirit or bad spirit."

"Do you think when your body dies that you are still going to relate to your spirit as strongly as you do right now?"

"No, because de body is de carcass at dat time. So de body does disappear. After a time, de body does melt away, so de spirit can't relate back to de body. De spirit just keeps moving around until it probably takes in a younger born. Or it takes into anyting, a cow, anyting. A good spirit will take into someting good. But if you are a bad spirit, it will take into anyting dat not really good. So de Fodder know how to really mind dose tings."

"Do you feel comfortable with your spirit? Do you feel like you really know your spirit? If your body died, would you still be comfortable with your spirit?"

"Well, I'm not really looking to die at dis time."

"Do you think your body and spirit are separate?"

"No, dey are togedder. Normally sometime I would lie down and close my eyes, right? And den I would pause myself to know dat, suppose I would die, how I would feel, and how my spirit would feel. And I don't feel no way, cuz de feelings don't really takes me like I feel when I would feel when I wants to do someting good. It's just a little farce you know, like someting fade away. It doesn't contact de right way when I do dat ting."

"What do you mean, contact?"

"Like trying to really take de feelings of death wid de spirit."

"So you feel really strongly in tune with your body?"

"Yeah! I feel in myself to know dat I will continue on for a long time, no matter how life is rough and tough. I know dat one day de goal will reach where it should reach. I'm not guessing about dat. I know it!"

"Like you said earlier, sometimes we need each other to guide each other. I firmly believe that. I know that the people who have guided me in my life have been very important."

"Okay, I'm gonna show you now. When you told me, I will just sits back and relax and listen. And den my mind floats toward my body and tinks to react towards it, to know dat yes, Debbie pinpoints at de cup. And de cup is really right towards my life's movements. It's like when you rewind back to someting to really get de feeling of it.

"Like when you are playing music and de music really gets to you. You take up de change of head and start all over again to really get de feeling of it. Well, normally den I would go to de purpose of my mind force to know dat's why Debbie said I must really keep myself in tune wid dat, and pick it, and run it through my mind force. And if it really move to me I will know dat yes, dat verse is really right towards stepping dat way. I really keep myself in dat way."

It's obvious to me that Harris goes within to determine the truth of what is presented externally. "I would like you to describe yourself now. List maybe five things that you like about yourself."

"I know dat, number one, I'm a loving person. And I like to see everyone, whether you are white or you are black, try to get yourself togedder to know dat we are all one human! We are not because of color. We are steel and concrete. We are all one red blood.

"And I would like to know dat we try to brace one anodder to good, not to bad. And I would like to know dat whenever we are living wid de people, I live right wid dem. Dey don't have anyting bad to say. I don't do anyting dat's wrong, even though no one on earth dat's human is perfect. But I try to do de best dat I can to really cope wid de Fodder.

"And I would like to know dat I reach out of de standard of poverty, not go on de street beg or tief. I'm asking de Fodder everyday to keep me away from dose tings, and to know dat I'm a person who can listen to anyone. I'm very humble and very calm you know."

Harris believes in patience. Haste makes waste. In other words, stealing may be a temptation, but in the long run it will work against you. We talked some more and got on the subject of judgement and criticism.

"Examine yourself before you really criticize odders, pass remarks to de next one. Cuz if you don't examine yourself first and den you process towards someone else, it hurts. Look at you own self first.

"Like dey say, you must pick de demon out of your eyes before you pick it out of someone else's eyes. Dat mean you must first look at yourself to see if you are doing right, before you curse de next person. How do you know de person is doing wrong? Dat person dis. Dis person dat. No one is perfect more dan de Almighty.

"But if I'm doing de right procedure, den de Almighty should keep me and guide me through de decades of life. De Earth is getting very polluted. All over de world is getting polluted, people fighting for power. And normally, tings is getting closer and closer to odds, a day of wipe out. Both people black and white suffer, poor and rich, old rulers, everyone."

Harris talked about how countries often work against each other instead of in the best interst of all. The same thing happens within countries. "And sooner or later, dere is going to be a stampede for tings dat are not right. Cuz all dat is going on all over de world, is one and only one mon dat have control. And when he gets fed up wid what is going on he is going to destroy what he want to destroy. So dat mean dat all of us is going to go. Some still gonna be around, but it is only de fittest of de fittest going to survive. Dat mean if we don't try to live a certain way, we aren't going to make it. Yeah, sooner or later, de Fodder going to wipe it all out."

Harris said he would like an opportunity to go to America for a while to earn some good money so that he could come back and start his cookshop. He loves Jamaica and wants it to remain his home. He has reservations about America because he heard it is a very violent place. And he heard it is definitely not safe for a man to walk alone at night because another man might rape him. Harris heard these things on the news and from foreigners. This is his perception of America. I wonder how many other people see America this way.

We got on the subject of rum. "When you drink de white rum, in de morning it would give you a back feed, make you feel weak in your joints and tings. When you drink de JB now, you wake up in de morning and you feel strong like you could really push down all de burglar bars. You know, it don't give you any low feeling.

"Like you drink one JB, it really put you in de right feelings of how you want to feel. When you drink two or three white rum it make you feel antagonized, but de JB keep you in de right feeling. In de morning you get up, feel bright, de same way, no hangover, no bad feelings."

"How old are you now, twenty-six?"

"No, no! I'm thirty-four years old. I'm not a little young lad. I'm stepping up in age, but age don't really matter. It's just how you keep your structure, how you mind to yourself. Cuz sometime you have some people, twenty-five, sixteen, eighteen, don't look like. Look like a person forty-five or fifty, cuz he don't keep his structure in good tune. Got to keep your body in good tune.

"Age don't really matter. Age is just a number. So I don't really care about dat. I know dat I'm still fit and living and strong. Dat's what I care about."

"That's right. You just radiate this sweetness. Do you know that?"

"Yeah."

"Everyone who is around you feels it."

"But that is normal, Debbie. I am loving and nice to people. It's just because I know how to move wid people. And I have to respect a lady cuz a lady make a mon hard. It's de mon first, but de lady do de greater part. Cuz de mon just dilly into de lady, okay? And de lady keep it for nine months. And for someone to keep you for nine months to put you on Earth is a great job.

"So I have to really cater for a lady. I move wid lady more dan wid mon, cuz normally a lady can really tell me what to do if I doing wrong. When I move wid mon, mon say, 'Bwoy, come let us take dat and dat.' And probably dey get on top of my mind force cuz de both of us is a mon. Lady's mind force can't get on top of my mind. We must both link wid mind force.

"Dat mean if I wid a lady and she would say, 'Bwoy, come let us go and steal some,' my mind force can come to her and say no. But probably when I am wid mon de mind force will say, 'Yes, all right, we go.'

"So dat's why I more cling to ladies, cuz I know if I'm wid fifty ladies I'm de strongest mind force of de group cuz I'm de mon. And de mon always to be a ruler. So I just try to stay dat way. A lot of ladies come and check me and dose tings, cuz when I'm wid dem I'm not giving dem no bad feelings."

"I understand what you're saying because there are a lot of men that I am leery of. For instance, earlier this evening I approached a man just to say hello as a friend, but right away he started making moves on me. You know, he said things like 'I always needed you and wanted you.' I was insulted because I know he says this to every woman he meets.

"But you're genuine and sincere. You're sweet, honest and protective and you speak to women respectfully. There is something about you that we can trust because we sense that you won't hurt us. Your attitudes are right."

"Normally, right now I'm gonna tell you, okay? Around here are a lot of ladies I turn down a sexual mode. Cuz it's not really every lady I see dat I would want to go to bed wid. Cuz it's de ruin of me, not de lady. Cuz it's a lot of different blood, and dat's de ruin of de mon. And you don't know what's coming around. And I don't normally use protection. If I have a lady I will make sure she use protection. And I have to know who I'm dealing wid.

"So I don't really go around and run around. If I'm moving around wid fifty, just one out of de fifty. It's an affectionate touch. And I know dat living dat way is much better. Women come around and drink and tieve, and dey get vexed when I won't have sex wid dem."

"How interesting that you should say that, because women go through that all the time. Men act interested until they find out you won't have sex with them. Then they get really upset and try to make you feel like you're in the wrong. They throw such a bad feeling at you!"

"When I was at Cornwall Beach I could've had a lot of women. Where

I work out dere dey check me very much because I don't go around and talk and harass.

"I just go around to watch my work, and several times de mon at de bar or my boss himself come to me and say, 'Bwoy, see dat girl over dere? She wants you.' And I returned back to de boss and say, 'Look, I'm not here for looking at girls. I'm here to do some work.'

"And if my spirit don't take de person, I just can't be wid de person. So normally, at de time, I don't want to get in contact. You know? Cuz some guys sweet to one, fly out next week, one odder come. One fly out de next week. New girl every week. No, no, not me! Dere's a lot of men like dat. Bwoy, dey get demselves in trouble!"

"That's right! Do you know what I hate? I used to be torn between it, because when I lived here, I knew who these men were. I call them the Leech Boys. They were everywhere!

"My clients would come to me in a daze and say, 'Oh my gosh, Debbie! Somebody loves me! I'm so happy! I can't believe this is happening!' And I would think to myself, 'It's not happening. Oh! What am I supposed to do?' I knew the guys were playing games with the women and that they were going to burst their bubble eventually.

"I thought, 'Is this my job? Am I supposed to get involved in this? Should I tell them what is really going on?' I realize now that most of them probably would've chosen to not believe me even if I had. On the other hand, I wanted to look out for the welfare of my clients, so it was really tough wondering how to handle it.

"They would say, 'Debbie, what do you think of this?' I knew they wanted positive feedback, so it broke my heart! I wanted them to stay as happy as they were because everybody deserves to be happy in life. But what was happening to them was so unfair, because it wasn't real. These men would use the same lines on woman after woman. It was really hard for me to deal with!"

"Dat's de tings I don't like. If I'm moving moving wid someone, I have to have proper feelings for dat girl. I have to love her. Don't like to know dat I'm wid her just because I can have sex."

Harris and I spent the next few hours talking about politics and then about our friendship and all that it means to us. I will miss him when I leave the island.

Sunday, March 4

Harris and I talked until 6:00 AM. I then slept for three hours in the 'cell.' It wasn't a sound sleep, as I was awakened several times by the roaches which kept falling off the ceiling.

I finally got up and stumbled down to the beach, where I spent the day swimming and reading. Deedra met me there and we had a terrible time trying to get home. There is a gasoline strike on now, so the taxis and minivans aren't able to fuel up. It seems strange to see the streets so empty.

Due to lack of sleep, I was feeling dizzy, sick and exhausted. I need to take Harris's advice and tune up my structure. We walked two miles, which seemed like twenty to me. I was ready to lie down and pass out on the street. Then we waited a few hours in the hope of catching a taxi. We finally gave up and walked over to Wexford and had dinner there so we could catch their free shuttle home.

This is life in paradise? For a moment I forgot where I am...

Monday, March 5

I do need to start taking better care of myself. I'm running out of enthusiasm and energy. I had been really looking forward to traveling with Deedra, but I'm burnt out.

When loaded with all my belongings including my tent, my back pack weighs thirty-three pounds. The idea of toting that around for a week in the intense heat doesn't excite me anymore. Experience has taught me that it's not fun. Deedra is so enthused. I wonder how long that will last, ha-ha. Of course, it will probably take her at least a week to get tired of it because the experience will still be unique.

I'm asking for guidance and protection as we journey. I still have an uneasy feeling about it... .

Tuesday, March 6

I can't believe that I didn't even want to get up yesterday. It ended up being a truly magical and joyful day. The weather was heavenly and our luck turned around completely.

It started when Gary arranged a free ride for Deedra and I on a very comfortable Green Light bus. What a luxury after the last few months of overcrowded minivans! It seemed almost like a different world.

We found our way to Carolyn's father's house in Mamee Bay. No one is staying there right now. But the gardner, Harry, had been told to expect us and was there to let us in. I love the energy in this house. It's obvious that this family is very, very creative and talented.

Carolyn's brothers, Brian and Wayne, are musicians. Wish they were here because I'd really like to meet them. The tree frogs seem to sing extra loudly here. That's good because I love their music.

Once we were settled at the house, we caught a cheap taxi into Ochi and shopped for gifts for my friends in Oracabessa. Then Trevor and the new Rep, Daniel, met us and took us sailing on PJ's catamaran (again free). I've known Captain PJ for years and love him dearly. I used to sail with him on his beautiful boat called the Heave Ho.

We had an exciting reunion yesterday, complete with lots of hugging and dancing. He's very handsome and had my heart fluttering. And it felt grand to be on the sea again. What a special celebration! I couldn't stop smiling.

Later, Deedra and I hiked up to Evita's Restaurant and had not only a great dinner, but also a great view of the bay all lit up at night. While we were up there, we ran into an old friend of mine named Konrad. I knew him from when we both worked at Plantation Inn. This was the day for meeting handsome men I tell you! I always had a secret crush on him, but never let him know. He was shocked to see me and ran up to give me a big hug.

Konrad is now the Resident Manager of Sandals, a wonderful all-inclusive resort in Ocho Rios. To our delight, he invited us to come and spend an entire day there before we leave the island. We're definitely going to try to fit that into our schedule. An entire day of free pampering (free food, drinks, water sports, entertainment, etc.) definitely sounds like my cup of tea. I believe that play is the best health insurance in the world.

We weren't finished being surprised yet. God gave me such a gift yesterday. He gave me the company of many dear friends who I hadn't seen for years. I harbor so much love for them always.

There is a place called The Little Pub in Ochi, where I used to take my clients every Tuesday night when I was a rep. We'd have a special dinner and fabulous entertainment. It was always fun, so Deedra and I headed down there last night. The people at Little Pub are like family to me.

Baldie

Keith Foote, the owner, was happy to see me and said, 'I'm gonna buy you a big, fat drink!' and he sent a bottle of wine over to our table. My dear friend Guy is still playing in the band. On break he ran over to me and kept kissing and hugging me. He said he heard that I went to Tokyo and he thought he would never see me again.

Baldie, the singer at Little Pub, said the same thing and shouted, 'Oh my gosh! Coconut Woman, is it really you?' I adore Baldie. He really knows how to get a crowd going and it's impossible to have a bad time in his company. He has always called me Coconut Woman and it became my pet name on the island.

What a marvelous day and night this was! I had been feeling so lonely, and suddenly everywhere I went I was kissed and hugged and treated like a queen. It did wonders for 'tuning my emotional structure.' Praise Jah!

9

PSYCHICS, RASTAFARIANS AND CINDERELLA

"I know personally that I walk with angels. I even know one or two of them in that I have seen them. One in particular has been around in the last three or four months."
—*Arianne*

Wednesday, March 7

More magic...so much magic... Monday night on a whim I asked Trevor if he would be interested in seeing an old psychic up in the hills. To my delight he said yes. Trevor is a Rep and has a company car, so our transportation problem was finally solved.

Tuesday is his only day off, so yesterday Trevor, Deedra and I headed to Oracabessa in the hopes of finding Bibsey and Sunshine. We ran into Sunshine right along the roadside. She was walking to the sea to take a swim, but quickly abandoned the idea in favor of seeing Kuz. Unfortunately, Bibsey was unable to join us because she was working at the polls. It was local election day.

I enjoyed the ride up there. It's always fun to explore new territory. The feeling of love and serenity was so intense in that area that I wondered how I would ever be able to make myself leave. We parked the car on the narrow dirt road and hiked the rest of the way in. I wondered how these people get around. They must have to get some groceries and things.

I realized that here I was seeing the Jamaica that only Jamaicans see. No wonder they love their island so much. The trees, flowers and fruit were lush and vibrant. Everywhere I looked I encountered a mystical sort of beauty. I was completely entranced and enchanted. It was the kind of experience one usually only knows in fantasies or dreams. Everything was real and yet nothing was real. The energy was such that I felt like I had moved into another dimension.

Off in the distance I saw a Rastaman sitting under a tree meditating. A gorgeous little boy with dreadlocks was standing near him, watching him intently. I wanted so much to take a photograph of them, but I didn't. It would've been an extreme invasion of their privacy. I wouldn't want someone traipsing uninvited through my bedroom with a camera while I was engaged in my own morning meditation.

As we approached a little house, I could see some brown-eyed children running joyously through the grass. Their laughter was like music coming out of the hills. When they saw us, they ran up to give us kisses and hugs. The only one of us that they had ever seen was Sunshine, but when they saw us they saw love and responded to it automatically. I realized then that they live in a world of love. They haven't been exposed to a world which teaches mistrust and fear. No wonder they don't carry it around.

Next we greeted Kuz's sister, a petite elderly woman wearing a purple dress and straw bonnet. Her head shook back and forth uncontrollably, yet she smiled warmly and welcomed us.

Kuz was sitting on the front porch floor soaking up the hot sun, her legs straight out in front of her. The first thing I noticed was how tiny she was. Her beautiful granddaughter brought her some bread and butter and she ate it like it was a feast. It was obvious that everyone deeply loved and respected Kuz.

Sunshine introduced us and told her we would all like a reading. Kuz charges $10 JA and a small flask of rum for her readings. She doesn't drink, but uses the rum and herbs to make medicine to help people. There are no traditional doctors up here.

We were taken into a room in which the wooden walls were painted blue. The floor was a dark wood. On one wall was a picture of the Sacred Heart of Jesus. Right next to it were two pin up girl calendars. Christmas cards were strung on a line across another wall. An open door led out back with a view of fruit trees and a river down the mountainside. Looking out a window, I could see a banana tree with a finger of bananas hanging invitingly.

Kuz finished her lunch and then went into her room, donned a red hat over her long, greyish white hair, and shakily walked out and sat down at a kitchen table. This little woman was only about four feet, six inches tall and weighed about seventy pounds. The table was covered with a lacy netting that looked almost like a curtain.

I found Kuz to be deep and sincere. There was nothing phony about her. She said that in order to do a reading she must see with the eyes of God, not her own eyes. The messages come to her through the angels. I remembered that Sunshine had told me Kuz can't do readings when it rains, and I gave thanks now for the lovely day.

I had the first reading. Kuz opened up a bible. To my amazement, her eyes roamed over the words on the page as if she was reading, but what came out of her mouth was all about me. Every once in a while, she would look up at me. Her eyes were so intense that I felt like she was looking right through me, like she knew everything about me and could actually see my soul.

Her Patois was heavy and Sunshine had to interpret some of what she said to me. The reading was a serious one, yet was interlaced with humorous things, teaching me to remember to laugh as I journey through life. Kuz told me things that none of the others in the room had ever known about me, so I knew that she was tuned in. Then she offered advice regarding future events. Whether or not I took it was, of course, my choice. I was impressed with the reading, but prefer to keep what she told me private. I felt much love for this woman.

Deedra went next, and finally Trevor had his reading. When we were finished, Sunshine spent some time with her. I felt serene and blessed and had no desire to ever leave this place. I felt truly like I was in heaven. It's good to experience the magic of life.

We visited for awhile longer and then finally had to leave. Before we left, we loaded the trunk of the car with sugarcane, grapefruit, and mint leaves (for tea), a generous gift from Kuz. Then as we headed down the road, a little boy seemed to appear out of nowhere and flagged us down. We bought a huge finger of bananas from him for $4 JA.

On the way home we discussed our readings. Kuz had done well on all of us and we were grateful for having been given the opportunity to see her. She told Sunshine to get some Oil of Love and wear it. Trevor and I were instructed to get some Lucky Charm Perfume and wear it on our forehead, stomach and heart for protection. (Evidently Deedra wasn't in any danger.) Sunshine told me I could find this stuff on the back shelf of any witch doctor's office. The problem was, I didn't know any witch doctors!

Later, we took Konrad up on his offer to visit Sandals. He was happy to see us and invited us to stay for dinner, so we had a free gourmet five course meal. Talk about getting pampered! Konrad told me that he heard I married a Jamaican. I'm getting a big kick out of all these stories I keep hearing about myself lately. Sounds like I'm having a great life, only I'm missing half of it, ha-ha!

We ended our day by cruising down the White River in a little fishing boat. It was dark except for the torches burning along side of the river, and the light of the stars overhead. Then we headed up on shore in the middle of the jungle and saw a fabulous show. This was all arranged for us for free, courtesy of Carl Young, who operates the excursion. Thank you dear Carl! We enjoyed every moment!

Thursday, March 8

Luck was with us again when we left Mamee Bay yesterday. I went over to Arawak Hotel to say hi to my old friends and one of them gave us a free ride into Ochi. What a treat, especially since we had our back packs and all to lug around.

We stopped at the market in Ochi, then hopped a bus to Oracabessa. Deedra refused to stay at Bibsey's, only because she has no bathroom. I laughed hard at this, but agreed to stay at Nix Nax Lawn, a local guest house run by some Rastafarians.

Once we were settled in, we walked to Race Course so I could say good-by to Bibsey's sweet parents and give them a gift. I just hate these good-byes. They break my heart, but they can't be avoided. On the walk back, I saw a lot of other people I know and realized this area sure feels like home now.

At sunset time, we gathered Bibsey, Sunshine, and some children we know and headed for the beach. It was time to have a going away party and honor my friends who have been so kind to me. We built a huge fire and cooked chicken, potatoes, fish and breadfruit. We swam in the clear, warm sea and sang and danced in the bright moonlight. It was clearly a celebration of love.

The only thing that marred the evening for me was my fear. I'm still bleeding from the rectum and a thought keeps surfacing even though I try to bury it. What if something is seriously wrong and I'm dying? I love life so much and have so much I want to accomplish yet. How could this happen to me now?

My friend Leroy, who used to run a little restaurant on the beach near here, showed up at our feast. I was thrilled to see him, but needed to tell someone what was happening to me so that I could cope with this fear. I found myself telling Leroy of all people!

He took me aside and gently and confidently told me to not worry, assuring me that he knows I'm okay. He said that I just need to clean myself out and he knows how to mix a brew that I need to drink for five days straight. He said his girlfriend had the same problem and it cured her. It's an herbal mixture and is drunk like tea.

I'm afraid to try it, but maybe I should. The problem is that we are leaving and I can't wait for him to find the herbs and mix it. This really concerns me, because Kuz also told me that I need to clean myself out. Is something inside of me that will fester or grow if I don't?

Friday, March 9

We said good-by to our friends in Oracabessa yesterday morning, and I was in tears as I boarded the minivan to Kingston. The first thing we did when we arrived was to look up a lady we used to work with. Her name is Arianne and she is very lovely. We found her at the Institute of Jamaica, where she works.

Arianne and her boyfriend Jimmy are having their house renovated and are currently living with Jimmy's boss, so we obviously couldn't stay with them. She did help us to find an inexpensive local place in an area called Harbor View. We're staying at the Caribbean Villa, which is right on the sea.

We were tired, so once we were settled in, we spent the rest of the afternoon on the black sand beach. The sea is wild here and the beach is full of rocks and driftwood. It has a mood of its own and was just what the doctor ordered.

I love our hotel. It's laid back and homey. There is a cute little outdoor bar and patio, with plenty of music, where the locals gather for dinner or just to visit. While sitting out there, we could see coconut trees and a full moon. An outdoor theater next door had an American war movie playing.

The place definitely has its own character. Beyond this area are a few roofless cement rooms. One of them has an old iron gate which is rusted shut. I wandered out there and looked through it to find huge waves crashing about five feet away. A goat skin was hanging on the gate drying. Someone told me that it will be used for making a drum.

Our room is certainly quaint. The walls are pink and the floor has maroon, beige and white marbled tile on it. The lacy curtains on the window are ripped and hanging funny. The ceiling has several holes in it, but the twin beds are covered with clean sheets with little roses on them.

Our furniture consists of an old dresser and two night stands, all of which are falling apart. There is a mirror with half of the backing off and a lamp with no shade. We do have a fan in here, but it's filthy.

The bathroom door is falling off its hinges. There is no waste basket and no hot water. We turn on our faucet from the pipes underneath the sink. On top of the sink is an old bar of used soap.

Yes, nothing but the best for Coconut Woman and her friend... Believe it or not, we like it. As long as it's clean, we're happy. Let's face it, we couldn't have an adventure like this at the Hilton.

Arianne met us today and we ran around downtown Kingston for awhile. I needed to find a place to buy more microtapes. I found some, but they cost me four times what I paid for them in the States.

I've learned to wear skirts in Jamaica. One seldom sees women in shorts, especially in the city. Deedra had shorts on today, and everywhere we went men made comments about her sexy legs. We also kept hearing, 'Hey Whitie, you want a Blackie?' While men were telling Deedra about her lovely legs, they were telling me about my lovely breasts.

The funny thing about it is that they don't say it vulgarly, but more as a sincere compliment. One gets the feeling they are trying to be nice. I don't think this would go over as well in the States, ha-ha! We both have a great sense of humor anyway and always laugh off things like this.

We stopped and rested for awhile at William Grant Park, which is right in the hustle and bustle of the city. In the center of the park is by far the largest cotton 'duppy' tree that I have ever seen. Thank goodness it has been preserved! Vendors were everywhere, some sitting right on the sidewalks. Several of them had bathroom scales, and for a fee they would let you weigh yourself. People use their creativity to earn a living any way they can. No stone is left unturned, and everything is seen as opportunity.

The feeling of downtown Kingston is festive. Amid the laughter and shouting and hustling is lots of music, lots of color, and lots of little shops and restaurants.

I had told Arianne about my visit with Kuz and asked her if she had any idea where I could purchase some Lucky Charm Perfume. To my surprise, she did. "Who believes this stuff works?" I asked. She laughed and replied, "Almost everyone in Jamaica!"

I was excited when we entered Marsh's Drug Store. Sure enough, there was a special shelf in the back which held all kinds of tonics and oils to aid every problem imaginable.

For $9 JA I was able to purchase my Lucky Charm Perfume. It came in a plain, small bottle with a white screw cap on it. The label was red and white and showed a drawing of a turbaned seer with his hands over a crystal ball. The words 'luck' and 'love' were written on the ball. In the background was a fireplace. A fire was burning and spirits were coming out of the smoke. The top of the label said, 'Lucky Charm Perfume.'

The content of the bottle was a brilliant orange colored liquid. The scent was pleasant and clean, but unlike anything I'd ever smelled, so it's hard to describe. Since I was into it this far already, I finished the job by doing as Kuz said, crossing my head, stomach and heart with it. I had nothing to lose, and... who knows what to gain.

When we finished shopping, we hopped a minvan to an area called Yallahs, where Arianne lives. It's breathtakingly beautiful here, all mountains and sea. How could anyone not move in spirit here? Jimmy farms for a living. He and Arianne have a darling, chubby fifteen month old son named Tau.

Jimmy and Arianne make a striking couple. They are both exceptionally good looking and both have long dreadlocks. Arianne usually keeps hers covered, but not always. They are serious Rastafarians.

257

Jimmy has incredible huge, light-brown eyes and his locks hang to his waist. He was too shy to let me interview him, but was very interested in what I am doing. While we were there, he cooked us some Ital food. The meal consisted of seasoned rice, fish, vegetables and fruit, all in a fruity gravy, and also a carrot and lettuce salad. It was delicious!

Arianne told me that while she was at work she called Rita Marley to see if she could arrange an interview for me. Unfortunately, Rita is out of town right now. Arianne said she is sure that Rita would be interested. I would be thrilled if I could meet her. I have such respect for that family. Rita, (Bob's wife), sings also, and all the Marley music is so positive and powerful.

While Jimmy was cooking, Arianne and I took a stroll and I asked her all about her beliefs. As we walked along the beach, we could see the farm where Jimmy works, and behind that the glorious mountains. What a heavenly place to live. They grow coconut trees, corn, onions, calalu, pumpkins, and raise goats and cows.

I asked Arianne about her youth. "I was born in Kingston and schooled there until I was seventeen. Then I went to a university in Canada. After that I traveled to England, where I spent three years. Totally, I spent twelve years out of Jamaica.

"When I returned to Jamaica in 1985, I moved back and forth from Montego Bay to Negril for awhile. I finally ended up back here, living in Yallahs and working in Kingston."

Arianne worked with Deedra and I for Apple Vacations at one time. This is how we met her.

"Do you have any favorite childhood memories?"

"Yes, going to Dunn's River Falls before it was a tourist attraction. We usually went there for a picnic at Easter. It was an annual family outing. There was no walkway like there is now. I remember going down the very steep, muddy embankment, trying to keep my balance while carrying all of our picnic goodies. We were always alone there because most people thought it was too dangerous to go all the way down. Going there now is a bit of a disappointment for me."

Arianne speaks very proper English, unlike most Jamaicans I know. "Another good memory is of a time we went to visit friends in St. Elizabeth. There were a lot of children around and we all went out and collected peenie wallies. Peenie wallies are huge fire flies. We had about twenty or thirty jars full. We walked all over using them as lamps. That was great fun!

"When I was a child, I remember digging in a pile of sand at school. I didn't know that the sand had been dumped on a concrete slab that housed a drain. I dug down and happened to find the hole for the drain. I could reach my little hand all the way down into it and I thought that I had found the exit of the Earth. I thought it led to the outside of the Earth and I was so excited! I carried my secret around for a long time until somebody else finally found it and told me it was merely a drain. I think it was my brother." We laughed hard at this, including Tau.

Arianne and Tau, Yallahs

When I asked about discipline, Arianne told me that her family just taught her to live up to her obligations. She was taught to be prompt and stick to her word. She only remembers getting one spanking. That happened when she was told to not ride her bicycle until the flat tire was repaired. She tried riding it anyway and was discovered.

Arianne has two brothers. Both of her parents are professional people. Her father is in business and her mother is an entrepreneur. When she was a child, the family went to church only on holidays. Arianne's father had been a strict Catholic, but had an experience while living in England which moved him away from it. While there, he went to Mass one time and the priest refused to allow him to receive Holy Communion because he was Black. This happened in the fifties. After that, he wasn't too concerned about organized religion.

Arianne said that her mother likes to go to church for show. It's what is expected and gives her a certain image in the community.

Her father is a roots man, and very much into music. He was a child protege and by age twelve had completed every level of piano training available. However, he wasn't allowed to take the final exam because of a ridiculous rule that one had to be sixteen years of age to take the test. So this was very discouraging to him also.

"Arianne, tell me what it's like to be a Rastafarian."

"Well, spiritualism and Rastafarianism go hand and hand. Rastafarianism isn't really something one learns. It's an inborn spiritual perception. I personally believe it's in your bloodline. I believe one is put into every family.

"Within my family, my first cousin is also a Rastafarian. He's even more deeply spiritual than I, I would have to say, because this is a man who does not speak. As you know, Jim doesn't speak very much and my cousin speaks even less. He just lives completely within himself and for the day of repatriation, which is what all of us are looking toward.

"We feel that as Africans we've done a lot to build the western world. We feel that if all that energy - if you think of all the wealth and ability that's even in just the United States amongst the Black communities - we feel that if all that energy was spent rebuilding Africa, then Africa would be a great nation once again."

Arianne feels that Africans were a highly civilized people who lived peacefully. She spoke of some of their accomplishments, like the building of pyramids. She thinks Europeans were jealous of them and wanted what they had and that's why they decided to come and take them. If they were so advanced, why was it so easy to capture them? Arianne believes it is because of their peaceful nature. The idea of being vindictive or war like was foreign to them.

Tau started crying here. Arianne looked at him and said, "When you were speaking I didn't try to come and interrupt you, remember? Where is a bird? Tau, go and call a bird to come and teach you. Look at the sea."

Tau was restless, so we took him inside to visit with daddy while we finished our talk. Arianne continued, "The real idea of Rastafarianism is peace and love throughout all mankind. We are in 1990 now, in what is commonly called the space age. People want to go towards higher ideals now, but it's still the simple virtues of life that matter. And many people aren't working toward that. If we can't live peacefully and in a loving fashion towards all people, then I don't see how we're going to be able to go out and find new civilizations and make anything work.

"There are a great deal of people with dreadlocks who are not Rastafarians. In order to decipher who they are, we look at the spirit of the person, not the hair. Frankly, I feel that if you got two hundred people together who said they were Rastafarians and asked them what it is, you wouldn't get two identical stories.

"You can ask some simple questions to find out the level of people's understanding on this. Ask them why they are known as Rastafarians."

"What is your answer to this?"

"Emperor Haile Selassie I was crowned Emperor of Ethiopia. His family name was Tafari. He was prince of his province. The word ras is an Ethiopian title which means the equivalent of prince. So we are Rastafarianns in that we follow his example on Earth. We know him to be the temple of the living God, also known as the Christ.

"So if you want to ask us outright if we see him as God, I would have to answer outright affirmative, without any apology. Because I know that the spirit that he carries with him is the spirit of his ancestor. It has been proven without a shadow of doubt. I have documents to prove it. They came from respectable sources. He is of the line of the man who was also the living embodiment of the Christ. In his first appearance, he was called Jesus.

"Also, Haile Selassie has been written up and spoken of many times in the bible. So even if he came in a totally different race or appearance, we would still know him to be that man because we were told that he was coming on Earth again.

"Many people in the outside world know that Jamaica is a very important place spiritually on Earth. And many people know too, including the Pope, that here is the home of a very peculiar and special people. I'm sorry that you don't read the bible more, because it speaks of us in volumes. But one needs to have the eye to see and the ear to hear."

We sat down under a mango tree in the yard. Arianne had pulled out a document called "Rastafari International News of People of Truth and Rights." In part it said, "Heaven is not necessarily beyond the heavens or skies, but anywhere that God choses to do a little personal presense and unveiled glory. Thus the Garden of Eden, the first home of God, was the original Heaven. Of course it was the sin of man that forced away His personal presence from the Earth, and hence, from Eden."

Arianne went on to read about the New Jerusalem, and how people have interpreted this. There were a lot of bible quotes in the document. Finally she asked, "Do you have any questions?"

"Yes. I want to know if there is such a thing as a church that you attend."

"In the Rastafarian culture we speak of, 'In our Father's house, there are many mansions.' We are always referring to the bible because that was the original history, science, geography, even recipe book for that matter. The bible is really a book of life. We don't look at it the way the church looks at it, which is to use it as a weapon against people.

"As far as assemblies are concerned, the various areas are a bit different. And then everyone is familiar with the twelve tribes. To my eyes - and this is just a personal opinion as being a member of the twelfth tribe of Israel, but not a member of the house of twelve tribes - to my eyes it's an organization which has been formed that's intent on convincing the Jamaican authorities that we're harmless. We don't seek to convince anyone of our position. We're not trying to gain acceptance and we're not being rebellious either. We just wish to be allowed to live our lives in the way we choose. We know that everyone has a constitutional right to live the life they please and not be persecuted because of their appearance or their tradition.

"We don't like to use the word belief either, because we feel that the word belief suggests that you have a doubt. And we don't have any doubt in what we're doing.

"I've mentioned that we have twelve tribes. One of them is the Ethiopian Royal Congress, who are the Bubba Dreads. They're the ones you see that make their living selling brooms. That is a very honorable living because everyone needs to have a broom to keep their house clean, from the highest to the lowest, right? So even though some may look at them and laugh because they just make and sell brooms, the fact of the matter is that everyone needs a broom. They're quite strict. They spend a lot of time chanting and praying.

"The various mansions now are like your body. You have your eyes and nose and mouth and limbs and torso. On one hand you have five fingers. On the next hand you have five fingers. But even though those ten fingers all look alike, they are completely different. The thumb on your left hand certainly wouldn't want to have to try to tell the little finger on your right hand how it should function. Much less, the nose couldn't tell the knee how it should function.

"So we, knowing that there are many bodies of the one all encompassing being that has a job to do, are living in a loving spirit as much as possible with all other artists. But of course some mansions are now trying to go on a political road, to which we show our strong disapproval. We wish not to involve ourselves in any politics while we are here in Jamaica. We want to wait for the time when we are rebuilding Ethiopia. Those skills will be needed then.

"We're not going to jump into the foolishness of politics in Jamaica. Because when all is said and done, none of the politicians here really like to see us in existence, although they like to feed off of our spirituality and they glory in the fact that tourism is so great. They would never admit that the reason tourism is so great is because Rastafarians are here.

"Because I can assure you that if the Rastafarian culture did not exist in Jamaica, the tourist population would not be as large as it is. Without Rastafarians there is no ganja. There is no Reggae music. There is no vibrancy really. I think the authorities are well aware of that.

"So they use us, but at the same time we can still function outside of them. They use us, but at the same time they don't want our children to go to their schools. They want our children to cut their hair to go to school."

This is an issue that has always bothered me. "As if that has anything to do with getting an education!"

"Right! Many have had to go to court just so their children would be allowed to go to school and keep their dreadlocks. Housing is another story altogether. And jobs. You could be qualified to the eye teeth, but unless you encounter someone who is tolerant, you don't get a job. And then the authorities turn it around and say we just don't want to work.

"Everyone turns around and says, 'Well, if you would just cut your hair, you wouldn't have these problems.' But why should we be forced to bend? Suppose someone would say, 'I don't like wearing make up.' And then the rest of the world would say, 'Well, if you wear make up we'll see to it that you have a house and a job. But if you don't wear make up, you're not going to live anywhere.' And we don't have any antidiscrimination laws in Jamaica, so we're just stuck with it.

"But you see, they want us to cut our hair. They tell us we can still be Rastas and cut our hair. But that's just making it comfortable for them because they don't want to be faced with the fact that the African culture has positive aspects and is alive and well here. They want us just to emulate European life style completely and forget about Africa as much as possible.

"I'm sure if you ask a simple man on the street if he wants to go to Africa he'll say. 'No, no, no!' and be quite adamant about it, because of the sort of media coverage it has been given. If you tell people right now that South Africa is an industrialized First World Nation they would be amazed. When people in Jamaica hear Africa, they see underdevelopment and lack of civilization.

"This was the whole colonization process. It was to teach Africans to hate themselves. That way they would always be looking to the European man for their worth."

I said, "That is so comparable to the plight of Native Americans in my country! They take them off the reservations and put them in white schools. They tell them that where they came from is not important. And everything they were taught at home is so different from what they are told in school regarding their history. It's shameful and sad."

"I don't know why the European man has that sort of mentality, because all other nations get along perfectly. But he just always wants to divide and rule."

"Yeah. Why do they always think that they are better and that their way is the only way that is right?"

"Because they have an inferiority complex." This makes us both laugh.

"So much is lost because of that. It's really a tragedy. When I was talking about churches earlier, I was referring to actual buildings with actual ceremonies. I've heard they exist and that it is legal there to smoke your ganja for ceremonial purposes."

"We don't call them services. We have assemblies at certain times of the year, holy times. We have celebrations or feasts and they usually last between a week to a month. We are a secret society so we try not to reveal too much really, because we don't want to be completely swamped by what is known as culture vultures. We have to keep certain of our mystique to ourselves. There are those looking to destroy us, and the easiest way to destroy is to know your entire story. But yes, we do have assemblies where we chant and meditate."

"Do all Rastafarians smoke ganja?"

"We don't. Many don't. Some do."

"Do the ones who smoke believe they can meditate better?"

"Yes, but the reason why we have stopped is because we realize that we can maintain that meditation without smoking. It angers me that people are always saying that the only reason we want to grow our hair like this is so we can have an excuse to smoke ganja. We want them to realize that it's far beyond that.

"If you go into number six in the book of Numbers you will see that Sampson was also a Rastaman. You saw what happened when he was trimmed. His spiritual powers were completely gone."

"I thought you made an interesting statement earlier. You said that Christ had dreadlocks."

"Yes! Christ was a Rastaman. That's what the whole persecution was about.

"In fact, just last week in the *Gleaner* I saw that it has come out that in the 1950's the British parliament asked His Imperial Majesty, by a letter, to deny that he was God because they feared that the Rastafarian movement was growing too large in Jamaica at the time. Now I say to that, why would you ask a man to deny his divinity on this unless you suspect there could be some truth to it? And if anyone knows, it's those people.

"Anyway, His Majesty made no comment. He didn't even answer the letter. And they named all names, Lord this and Lord that, who signed the letter asking for this public denial of his divinity.

"Now, as far as I said about Christ being a dreadlock, he came from the line of David, who was the son of Solomon, who was born of an African woman and an Israel man. Israel are people of color anyway. Even in the bible Solomom says, 'I am black, but comely.'

"So being born of people of black skin, his ancestors, naturally Jesus would be a man of color as well. And he was living a very humble life, which means no vanities such as combing his hair. Yes, he kept himself clean, but he wasn't too bothered about wearing shoes and things like that.

"You know, the Romans always show him as blond with blue eyes and long hair, but in fact he was ruddy with uncombed long hair. And the people he walked with were just as disheveled in the eyes of the Pharisees. And this was the whole grounds for the crucifiction, because here was this homely man who said he was a king. He wasn't looking like the people of the day who shaved their heads. Thus the word 'baldheads,' right?

"Of course when they crucified him, they found out they had made a great mistake. They tried hard to right it by bringing Christianity into the world, but it was still their version of Chrisianity."

"I want to ask you what you think is going to happen when you die?"

Arianne sounds absolutely shocked at this question. "Die???" Pause. "Well, we don't see death. We see everlasting life. We know there are those about us that have put down their flesh, but the wages of sin is death. So we feel that the more and more you live towards a righteous life, the less likely you're going to have to lay down this temple. Perhaps if you do have to lay it down because you haven't lived righteously enough, you get another one immediately.

"Your spirit can't die unless you're in iniquity work. Life is a continual renewal, so we don't speak of death."

"Okay. I have a few other things I would like to ask you that doesn't necessarily have anything to do with your Rastafarian beliefs. They're things I'm asking everyone. What is your reaction to duppies?"

"Well, the spiritual world is all around us even as we sit here speaking. I'm sure there are many who are sitting here listening to us. Big and small. Some here are really afraid that perhaps we can see them, and they're doing everything in their power to conceal themselves. Others are not concerned because they're just existing along with us.

"Duppies. There is a whole book that could be written about duppies in Jamaica. There are so many types that people seem to know of and speak of, Rolling Calf, this kind of duppy, that kind of duppy. I don't even know the names of some of them, but there's a whole long list of them.

"I think that there are many, many dimensions of life and anything is possible. If you never knew how you came onto the Earth, and one day someone told you the story of how a man planted a seed into a woman, you would probably think it was a lie. It sounds so impossible.

"Scientifically, they explain the process of birth and try to make it sound so matter of fact. But if you really sit down and go into it within yourself very deeply, it is an impossibility that it can happen. But it does.

"I know personally that I walk with angels. I even know one or two of them personally in that I have seen them. One in particular has been around me a lot these last three or four months. I don't know them by name.

"My mother told me that when I was a child I used to have many imaginary people that I spoke to. There was one person in particular that I spoke to all the time. My mother said she came home from work one day and I was on the veranda crying and crying. Nobody could soothe me. When she asked me what was wrong, I told her that a lady who was my friend who was named Kenancy - and I think that she's still around me sometimes - anyway, I told my mother that she was coming to visit me, and I saw her step off a bus at the top of the road. She didn't look when she was crossing the road and she got run over. I knew that I wouldn't see her again. My mother said that I never again spoke of her, either. Before that, I used to tell her everyday when she came home from work what Kenancy did and said that day.

"So as far as duppies are concerned, the spiritual realm is all around us. Jamaica is a very spiritual country, you know."

"I want to ask you about obeah. How big do you think it is on this island?"

Arianne burst into peals of laughter at this question. "You're asking a Rastafarian about obeah? Well, the most I can tell you is by giving you a simile. Bob Marley said in one of his songs, 'I am a duppy conqueror.' We don't really pay the duppy world any mind. The practice of obeah is to use the spirits of iniquity to perform works. And, of course, you know that there can be no good in that as far as we can see.

"So we see and we feel and we know that obeah is powerless against us because our weapon is truth and rights. So as far as your question regarding what I think of obeah, my answer is, 'Not much!' "

"Do you think it's practiced much on the island?"

"Oh yes! It's practiced greatly throughout the island, from the highest of the high, from leaders of the political parties right down to the man that can't scrape together a few cents for his next meal."

"Do you think there is power to it by people who let themselves be affected by it?"

"Naturally, if you believe it you're going to be affected by it because you'll always be living in fear of it. So it would be able to take you over quite easily."

Arianne asked what other kind of response I've had to this question. She was amazed when I informed her that most people from the States believe that obeah is not practiced much anymore on the island.

"What??? It's practiced heavy! In fact, you are in the obeah parish right now, St. Thomas. Every Tom, Dick and Harry out there can tell you of someone in their family or themselves that has had some experience with it. It works you know, when people are fearful of it. It's powerful!

"It's practiced by the guys who are driving Mercedes Benz and by the guys that are pushing hand carts. It's practiced heavily and it's big business."

"Have you ever heard of somebody named De Laurence?"

Arianne laughs again. "Yeah. This is his parish, mon! I know right now that if you go out on the street and mention his name, people are going to show you a crucifix and run away. Even the most educated people will tell you that it works. That's why a lot of people find Rastafarians so unusual. It's because we just scoff at it. We refuse to be afraid of it, so people realize that our power must be much greater. We know we shall win because we are confident that good wins over evil."

"What do you hope to accomplish in your life? What is your big dream or goal?"

"I want to go to Africa and see at least one of my children schooled there. That is my goal and I think it will happen."

"Do you have any idea how?"

"Well, I'll continue to hold my skills so that when I go there I have something to offer. And of course, I'll save. I have a few contacts there."

Arianne told me that Rastafarians cannot currently go to Ethiopia because it's Marxist rule now. The world was told that Haile Selassie is dead, but Arianne doesn't believe that it's true. There was never a funeral, and he was an Emperor. The story is that he was being transported from point A to point B and he asked to stop and pray in a cathedral they passed. He entered and was never seen again. Rastafarians feel in their hearts that he is still alive.

"Do you have anything else that you want to say?"

"Well, just try to live as good as possible and as clean a life as possible. A clean life doesn't necessarily mean that you mustn't enjoy yourself. You know, a lot of people think we don't party and we don't dance. I tell you we were the inventors of party and dance! But a clean life means always carrying around the best thoughts possible.

"I'll tell you, before I was carrying my dreadlocks I was very frustrated by what I saw going on around me. I was always complaining and I was unhappy. You know this because you used to work with me.

"But you see, as I put this on now, this is like lamb's wool. When I put this on I was able to realize in my heart who my true friends are. And I'm really happy to see that you and Deedra are among them. Our hair functions like a spiritual antenna. It can pick up vibes. That's why I keep mine covered when I'm out. When you're combing your hair all the time, the comb is agitating the membranes which pick up information.

"Have you ever noticed in America how there is a constant thing to get women to perm and curl their straight hair, and black women to straighten their hair? It's because they know that the power is in the curl. What other way is there to make a woman feel always uncomfortable than have her hair be in constant worry? If you're constantly worried about setting your hair and if it looks good enough, you're never going to be able to build confidence in yourself.

"They tell us that our hair, in its natural state, is ugly. And they coerce us into spending lots of money to change it. If it's straight, we're told it should be curly. If it's curly, we're told to straighten it. All you really need to do is love yourself, and then everyone else will love you."

"Before I wrap this up, can you just tell me a little bit about what you do at your job at the Institute of Jamaica?"

"Conservation of artifacts, which is the restoring of aging artifacts for the museum. The ways in which we do it are mechanical as well as chemical. At the moment, I'm the only person doing this work in Jamaica. Throughout the Caribbean, I think there are only five or six people doing this work, because it's a new science.

"It's interesting work, because many of the artifacts are hundreds and hundreds of years old. Mostly what we try to do is retard aging. The work is ongoing and we must inspect the pieces again every five or six years."

"What kind of artifacts do you restore?"

"Everything. Paintings, ceramics, woodwork, textiles, very delicate things like masks that have feathers and shells and things on them. We even have some Arawak earthenware bowls that are hundreds of years old. We have some fabulous things."

It was time for bed, but I certainly had a lot of food for thought. Arianne is a strong, independent woman and has no qualms about speaking her truth. I learned much from her.

Saturday, March 10

Arianne stopped by our hotel this morning on her way to work. She brought spice buns and cheese for breakfast, so we provided the coffee.

I had told Jimmy about my experiences with Daniel God. He relayed them to Arianne. She told me that both she and Jimmy believe that Daniel was very wise to not "sex" Mother Heart, because they, too, believe that she could've gained power over his spirit and taken part of it.

Jimmy says of his relationship with Arianne, "I am the eyes. She is the mouth." In other words, he observes, but she speaks for them. Arianne says he is a priest in their order and holds many powers, some of which must be guarded carefully so they aren't treated sacrilegiously by society. I understand this. I'm learning to keep silent in my heart the things which are most personally sacred to me.

Arianne also believes (as do I) that your thoughts and emotions while you are pregnant really affect your baby. She also believes that if you carry around negative and evil thoughts your baby will be born ugly.

Unfortunately, this was all the time we were able to spend with our friend, because we had to keep on moving. Deedra and I hopped a bus downtown. I knew I was still in Jamaica when a small boy stepped on and went around trying to sell the passengers a roll of toilet paper.

I was advised by several people to try to meet with a lady named Olive Lewin. She is a well known Jamaican journalist and historian and has a great interest in the culture and the arts. Olive writes a regular column in the

Gleaner. We weren't able to reach her by phone, so Deedra and I decided to try to track her down.

We started by going to the Art Gallery. When we didn't find her there, we hopped a bus to the Little Theatre. Olive wasn't around, but I learned that there is a Jamaican Ballet Company that has performed all of the great ballets.

Viewing Duke St., Kingston

From there, we walked and walked, and walked some more. But it was worth it, because we finally made it to Dumfries Street and had dinner at our favorite local restaurant, Zapatas. Jamaica's version of Mexican food was fabulous!

We were exhausted by the time we got back to our hotel, so we treated ourselves to a glass of ginger wine and kicked back in the old ruins behind our room to listen to the song of the sea as we watched the full moon rise above it.

Sunday, March 11

I've got to put a lid on spending, as I'm almost out of money. I must think before I spend and eat. It's so true that less is more, because I feel so much better when I eat in moderation. Actually, I believe that moderation is the key to success at anything. Extremes in any direction leave one unbalanced and ultimately prove to be a pitfall. There are no shortcuts to learning our lessons.

That's why we're having the human experience, to learn and grow.

Later: Deedra and I spent the day at Cable Hut Beach, a glorious place with black sand, a wild sea, coconut trees, and mountains rising majestically in the background. It's so fun to look up to a mountain top and see palm trees swaying instead of snow.

All day we were surrounded by happy, laughing Jamaicans and lively music. I saw several little Rasta kids who were so cute they stole my heart away. As we watched a particularly stunning sunset, we ate fish and festival.

I felt gleefully joyous and so alive as my gypsy spirit roamed free. At the risk of looking silly, I had to dance down the beach in the moonlight. The waves danced back and forth with me and I communed with the water sprites.

At 10:00 PM, Deedra made me leave. Good thing one of us has some common sense. After all, we are in Kingston, the crime capital. We waited an hour for a bus back to the hotel. I was embarrassed when I first boarded because the bus was filled with bible toting people who had just come from church. They were dressed to the nines and here I was smelling of the sea and wrapped only in a sarong.

I thought about it though and realized that I, too, was coming home from church. I had done a lot of praying on that beach. My ceremony consisted of prayer, meditation, dancing and singing, just as theirs did. So much energy is generated in dance... .

Monday, March 12

Deedra had heard of a place up in the Blue Mountains called Maya Lodge, up on Jack's Hill. We headed up there today. I would've preferred heading blindly out on our own, but Deedra realized it would be foolish to go out and hike all day in mountains unknown to us.

Maya's Lodge provides hiking guides and a base from which to operate. It's very primitive up here, so of course I love it. It's located two thousand feet up, off Jack's Hill Road. I'm so at home in the wilds. We set up camp, which consists of my little orange two man pup tent, and we built a fire ring for later. We're nestled in a very private spot surrounded by bamboo trees. Bamboo, when singing in the wind, sounds like the creaking of a wooden-masted sailboat.

Deedra needed to rent a sleeping bag, and the man running the lodge kept us waiting around all day. I wish I felt otherwise, but I don't like him. He's a white Jamaican and he's extremely arrogant. His staff are all Jamaicans, warm, kind and wonderful. But he treats them like he's the proverbial "white master" and they're his nigger slaves. It nauseates me. At one time today, I saw him take off in his station wagon. He took some of his staff with him and made them climb into the back of his station wagon and sit in the middle of the produce, rather than letting them sit on the seats.

He seems to be on some kind of ego trip, definitely a control freak. It would've taken just a few minutes to issue Deedra her sleeping bag and help us set up a guide for tomorrow, but he kept us sitting in his office for a long time while he made phone calls.

This character is definitely a left over hippie from the sixties. Some people get stuck in a time warp. His office is also his bedroom, and I really didn't care to spend time there. As we waited, I observed him. He has a white beard and wore shorts and a cowboy hat. As he talked on the phone, he kicked his feet up on the desk and smoked a huge spliff.

A red light burned in the room, along with candles. New Age music was playing, and his walls were plastered with posters of scantily clad Jamaican girls. I'm certain he was trying to impress us, but it had the opposite effect.

Anyway, earlier when we tried to see him we got tired of waiting and finally just took off on a hike alone. It was magical. We hiked up steep mountain sides and found a great spot to spread a blanket, watch the sunset, and drink some Roots Wine. Deedra left at early dusk to give me some time alone.

I had trouble tearing myself away from this heavenly spot. I could see Kingston twinkling way below me, and I could see the pinks and blues of twilight from my vantage point. However, as soon as I left my perch and headed back into the trees I discovered darkness everywhere.

It was a bit eerie as my sense of balance was lost. I had no idea where to step among the steep ridges. At night the mountain looked entirely different and I hadn't paid much attention to landmarks on the way up. I have a little flashlight with a very short battery life, but I used it to try and find my trail. And of course, I was soon very lost! The peenie wallies were my only other source of light, and they look like the stars so it was even more disorienting.

I was suddenly aware of lots of noises in the bushes, things fluttering, hooting and hissing. I figured it would probably rain sometime during the night, so I began thinking of how I could keep my tape recorder dry. By now, I assumed I'd be stranded until morning.

I slowly felt my way along and kept calling for Deedra. She couldn't hear me, and when I realized that she couldn't see my light either, I turned it off to save the battery for an emergency.

Some nature woman I am! I must be honest and admit that my knees started knocking together as I thought of all the stories I'd heard of people meandering out for a hike and never being seen again. It was certainly an interesting experience. Here I was, face to face with God. Even so, I wasn't ready to die yet.

I felt terribly embarrassed because I knew that Deedra would be worried and possibly send out a search party. I realized that in my excitement about being there, I had behaved very foolishly and irresponsibly. Now others would be worried.

Camp site, Jack's Hill, Blue Mountains

I wandered around for awhile longer, trying to find my way back up to the summit, and I suddenly saw a light circling way down below me. Stopping dead in my tracks, I heard my name coming to me on the wind.

Relief and laughter flooded through me as I called Deedra's name and happily swung my micro light in an answering circle. She somehow started upwards and laughingly told me that she had also gotten lost returning to our camp. That eased my bruised pride.

Deedra swore she was on a trail as she led me down an incline that seemed like a straight drop off to me. I was terrified, but felt it was my only choice at the moment. I made it and sure enough I finally flashed my light right on our dear tent. I was ecstatic! Home sweet home!

An odd thing had happened though. Earlier, we had built that nice fire ring, but it had completely vanished, rocks, wood, tinder and all. We couldn't believe our eyes! Who even knew where our tent was? And why would someone do that?

It gave us a strange feeling of being watched by unseen eyes. But suddenly I started laughing and I couldn't stop. Deedra joined me. We had only been here a matter of hours, and already both of us had managed to get ourselves (separately) lost, and it seemed our camp site had been invaded by duppies!

Yes, I love it here. But what kind of a gypsy am I anyway? I semi-panicked when I got lost in the mountains, even though I've always said that I wanted to be lost. (Be careful what you ask for as you will eventually get it!) I'm disappointed in myself. I guess it would be different if I had started out alone. But knowing that people would be worried about me really bothered me. Other than that fact, being out there alone all night would've been a great spiritual adventure.

Later: Well, we found out that "he" only allows campfires in designated areas. We're visiting with staff now and sitting around a fire we've built out of bamboo logs. It's awesome in that the flames are leaping ten to twelve feet high. There is a huge moon again and it looks wavy and mysterious through the heat from the fire. The light dancing on the tall, dense brush of the hills around us looks fierce and jungly.

The cook, Adassa, is here with us. "He" refused to take her home tonight and thus, is forcing her to spend the night as it is too far to walk. She wanted to go home. I can't believe how cruel this man behaves.

To me, Adassa is magical. She is a short but huge woman, and one can almost read her life by looking into her eyes. Tonight she was clad in a pink and purple scarf, a pink shirt, a bright yellow, orange, white and black flowered skirt and dirty tennies.

She sat down by the fire, crossed her arms over her more than ample bosom, and began singing some gospel songs. Her voice is incredibly lovely, and what emerged from her was pure emotion in sound.

Between songs I talked to her and discovered that both of her parents are deceased. She has six brothers and sisters, but never sees any of them. It's obvious to me that this woman is very lonely, but finds great comfort in her relationship with God.

She's kind and motherly and was concerned whether we would be warm enough tonight. The mountains get much cooler than the seaside at night. She asked me if I will be sleeping in my "tall black pants" and advised me to keep my head covered for warmth.

Adassa

Suddenly Adassa said, "You see like how we sit here now? It seems as the way Cinderella always did sit around de fire, wid her feet among de cinders.

She only use wooden shoes for her feet. Her stepmodder used to treat her very rough. So she used to make de fire, cook de food, clean de kitchen, and do all de hard work in de house. She had to wash de dishes and scrub de floor.

"So den now, one night she was by de kitchen door. Dat wasn't her modder you know, dat treat her bad. It was her stepmodder. She say dat her own two daughter is better dan Cinderella. But though she was in old, ragged clothes she was still much prettier dan de two stepdaughters.

"While she was at de fire wid her feet in de cinders she had no experience wid anyting dat was worthwhile, because she was all left alone by herself. No modder cared, because her modder died. So her fodder went and married anodder woman, and she brought home wid her two daughters.

"So while she was dere she said to him one night dat dere was a fair in a far away place. So dey want to go to de fair. He called de two daughters to him and de three of dem talked. He said, 'What do you wish?' One said, 'Beautiful dresses.' De odder said, 'Pearls and jewels.'

"He turned to Cinderella and said, 'What would you like?' She said, 'When you are coming home, bring me de first branch of a tree. Break it off for me.'

"And he did so. He came and gave de pearl and de jewel, de beautiful dresses and de limb of a tree. She ran so near to her fairy godmodder's grave and planted it on it. Den she watered de tree wid her tears, and it became a beautiful tree.

"And dere was a king named King Alexander. He said to his son, de Prince, 'Okay, we are going to provide a wife for you.' So den dey gave all de people in dat country an invitation. It say dat de fair will be on a Tuesday evening, or on a Monday, but it was a day in de week.

"Dat night everybody gone to get dressed. Cinderella was like, you know, so despaired dat she took her modder-in-law's dress and said dat she was going to de fair, too. But her fairy godmodder, (de dead woman you know), look at it and said, 'It is not right.'

"She den dreamed to her, and she got a lizard, a pumpkin and rat. De three lizard was de three horse. De pumpkin was de coach. And de rat was de coachmon.

"And when dey went to de fair, dey all were enjoying demselves. But Cinderella went in at de last, at twelve o'clock. So when de Prince did see her,

277

he left all dose girls now and cleaved to she, to Cinderella.

"She was told to go home at twelve o'clock to meet her fairy godmodder, so by dat time now, de duppy want to strip her. So she look at de clock and say, 'Oh my! It's late! I have to go!'

"So de Prince now run at her, but she was going so fast dat he could not catch her. He saw a mon coming, so he said, 'Who was dat ill dressed girl going on dere?' No one know, so he go back inside, but he was vexed.

"De next evening now dey all went off again, and she was sitting down washing de dishes, scrubbing de floor, doing all de house work, have to take out de tub wid de bath, and de rug dat dey bathed wid. One of de stepdaughters meanly said to her, 'You must take out dat!' And she did so, wid humbleness. Cinderella did not tink she could rise out of her slumber. She thought she had to be down all de time while dey were on top. And dem not pretty, you know. Dem ugly in de face.

"So den evening come and everyone sit down and enjoy demselves. De Prince and de coachmon come to de door. Dey all was dere. Dey want now to try on de slipper. So everyone try it on. Can't fit. De heel too big. Dey can't wind foot in it. While everyone try on de slipper, Cinderella began to clean de oven. De slipper not fit anyone, So de Prince want to know who is de girl in de oven.

"He insist she come out and try on de slipper. It fit perfectly and he just kiss her and hug her and say, 'You is my wife!' And every bit of dem dat had been mean to her come and bow down at her feet now, begging her pardon.

"She not only forgave dem, but said dat dey all could live togedder as brodder and sister in God's hands. So you see, she does have a nice clean, sweet mind even towards dose who does tings against her. She don't have anyting dat is rough, any hate. She have everyting dat is nice, de rat, de lizard and de pumpkin. And de nice, pretty Prince is hugging her and kissing her. She is Cinderella, de Prince's wife. God loves her. De message is true. You see? Never try to disdain a mon. Try to help him if you can."

As she told us this story, something in Adassa's eyes made me realize that she knows in her heart that she is Cinderella. She views life through the eyes of her spirit, not through the material realm. Her magic is felt by all, and it is very real. She laughs at her physical appearance, because she sees her soul when she looks at herself. She is one of the rare ones who actually knows who she really is. I am so blessed to have met this very special soul.

We talked on and suddenly heard a very eerie and mournful cry coming out of the hills. Adassa assured me that it was just a dog, but said that that particular cry signifies death.

She told me that she married when she was sixteen years old. Her marriage lasted for ten years, when her husband died. It was not a happy marriage though. She said her husband was a wicked man and ran around on her. Adassa is proud that she raised her twenty-five year old son all by herself.

"I am living in a house where I leased de place, but de owner did die."

"So who do you lease it from?"

"I lease it from a mon, but he's dead."

"You lease it from a dead man?"

"He was alive, but he died. I rented from a living mon, but he has gone home. So I live dere and nobody does come around to collect rent. But I need to go to de tax mon and talk to him because I can't pay all de taxes. But I can pay some of dem, and I do what I can. You understand?"

"Yeah. When did your landlord die?"

"He died a long time ago. He dead from 1975."

"Wow! And you haven't paid rent since then?"

"From den I haven't paid no rent. Last lease I had was up in 1976. And den Gilbert did come and blow away all de papers I did have."

"What happened up here when Gilbert hit?"

"Lord, he took off everybody's house! Three or four houses up and gone. De whole of dem mash up."

"Where were you when Gilbert hit?"

"In my house. And de roof go off and de ceiling! My son was wid me."

"We saw some rooftops laying around when we came up here."

"But nobody did get dead up here. De storm last de whole day. I got zinc and put up over my house, but it still leaks. But what matters is dat I can live in it. We have it very hard. Food, you'd better believe it! We have it tough up here."

"What was your childhood like?"

"When I was a little girl, I liked sewing. I made my own clothes. I had my own machine."

"When you misbehaved, how did you get disciplined?"

"Well, my modder told me dat I must learn to have manners to people. And you must know how to talk to bigger people dan yourself. And if you are doing anyting dat is not right and dey say, 'Don't do it!', den you mustn't do it. So I grow wid dat attitude, know how to talk, know how to move. I was told dat if you have morals, widout a penny, you will still live. But if you have money and no manners, God will know.

"De odder day I was at Halfway Tree, and a little boy went to buy someting for someone in jail. And de way how he speak to de Inspector of Police he have to go back out wid it! Because he don't know how to say 'No sir!' or 'Yes sir!' If he had got home training as a small baby, he would know how to talk to people. How do you like dat?

"I see modders today talk to dere child, 'Move your bumboclat!' We never get talked to dat way!"

Bumboclat is a very bad curse word in Patois, calling up darkness and impiety.

"When you treat de child wild, child must grow wild. My son come down here today and said, 'I don't have no money to get to work tomorrow. Nor is dere any bread or milk in de house.' I give him twenty dollars. You must talk to your child wid respect and love."

"Adassa, when you were young, what kind of things did you get punished for?"

"Well I tell you I love to romp. And sometimes when my modder did go to de market, I don't do what I asked to do. And she come home and flog me. And true, I grow up now and know dat it was not right. Now I try to do my work before I romp. I love to play marbles and ball.

"As a child, I had a big yard. I have pig to look about, fowl to feed, donkey to tie out, goat to tie out, cow to move, give dem water, horse. And I feed dem and carry water. I give dem to dose animal. And den I remove dem from out de sun and put dem under a shady tree so dat dey can enjoy demselves. And after dat, I came home wid wood in de hamper, and water also. And den I go to de market and take home my step-modder. I didn't grow wid my modder.

"Den I went to Panama, and my aunt died and I came back and I grow wid my cousin. And we had to go to de field and plant cocoa and banana, so we have food to get to people. Dat is how I got food and clothes to wear and could go to school."

She told me that Monday was wash day. Her step-father was a butcher, and Monday, Tuesday and Wednesday he would go out to kill. Thursday they would go out to the field and bring in food to go to the market and sell. She went to school from Monday to Thursday. On Friday, she would wash and iron her school clothes so they would be ready for Monday. Monday mornings she would get up early to do dressmaking before school. Sunday morning she would make breakfast while the others were at prayer meetings. Then she would go to Sunday School and come home and make dinner.

"Were you happy as a child?"

"Yeah mon! I was a very, very happy child. It was just nice. You know, sometime it rough wid modder and fodder and den it rough wid me, but den everyting gets alright again."

After telling us more stories, Adassa said, "So whatever you are doing, you must live wid love and wid unity wid your brodder and sister, until de day's end. If you're dealing wid a mon, don't try to do it in a trickery way. Just deal fair, you know. And let de mon deal fair, too. If anyting goes wrong, just remember dat de best of mon goes wrong sometime, and just live up to de friendship. It better dan to shut de eye and go away. Be fair, and de best of ability will happen to you. Be honest. God knows all. What you do will come back to you. Straight is de way and narrow is de gate to life eternal."

Deedra was cooking some soup over the fire now, and Adassa stopped her stories to go and help her. She was afraid that Deedra would burn herself. I was amused by the way Adassa mothered us.

Adassa commented that she could tell we were having a great time and that she feels we will come back here again. "But I don't know if you will see me again, because all has been left in de hands of de bigger mon. He's a mon dat you don't know when he's coming."

"So what do you think is going to happen when death arrives?"

"Oh, nice! Sweet! You don't have to tink about nutting. You come here widout nutting and you will go widout nutting. Just be happy and be nice."

We pondered her words as we sipped our soup. I asked her what she thinks of duppies. "Duppy dead. I see duppy. Duppies all about you. Duppy die and raise again, walks forty day and forty night. De dog will bark because he see, but you will not see duppy because you will be going about your business. De dogs, cats, trees see duppies.

"I'm going to tell you a story dat happened before I was born. Dere was two churchmon, live in Jackson Town in Trelawny. My grand uncle told me dis story." Adassa became so excited as she told the rest of the story that she lapsed into such heavy Patois that I couldn't make heads or tails of what she said. All I know is that whatever happened certainly made an impression on her!

"If any big dream of yours could come true, what would you want?"

"My dream is to tell de tidings of God, to speak about de tings dat is true. And to live clean and honest before mon and God. If you live dat way and have no fear, nutting can devour you. If you let God have his way wid you, you don't hunger, you don't thirsty, you don't naked.

"When Gilbert blew my housetop up in de air, I stood in de wide open in my house and look at de sky and say, 'God, when you take it away, where are you going to put me, sir?' And I see a housetop come back. And it put down. And I live in de house still and it only wet when it rains. But just beside my bed, not my bed is wet. I believe dat my God is a carpenter.

"I was raised in de Angelican Church, and I believe de sun and de moon and de stars are guiding angels for me. De same God rule Heaven and Earth."

We saw a dead guango tree and Adassa told us that the wood is used for making houses. She said we could probably buy that tree for $500 JA, a good deal. A delicious wine is made from guango fruit, breadfruit leaves, banana leaves and plantain leaves. Adassa said they boil it and then throw in a little spirits. I wonder if that's what our Roots wine was made of.

"He" had been sitting by the fire with us, but said he was going to bed now. It was midnight. Adassa teased him, reminding him that he made her stay and now he was already going to bed. She had all of us laughing hard. Then she said, "Go to your bed, my darling. You has to wake up early in de morning. We're staying here a little more and reason wid each odder as sister and sister and sister. I don't ready to sleep yet because you know I am not a sleepy head. So den, God bless you. Take care." Then she burst into hearty laughter. It was clear that she was also having a grand time tonight.

"He" didn't smile, but said angrily, "You talk too much, mon!" I was amazed. He was jealous of her! I realized then that he had figured that since he was a man he would get all of our attention tonight. He was acting like a spoiled two year old and I wanted to tell him so, but I didn't. He ordered her to stop talking so much, and she replied gently and lovingly, "Yes, I talk. God gave me a gift to talk and I will talk, because what I talk is right." He hollered "Bumboclat!" and stalked off.

Adassa said, "You know what is bumboclat? De snowy peoples live in bumbos. Eskimo peoples live in bumbos because dey live in cold land. And dey got to wear cloth to cover dere nakedness. So bumboclat is not a bad word." She said she knows that there are other meanings for it, but she refuses to see it as a bad word because she doesn't like to be cursed.

It felt good to sit around the fire and chat. The rest of the staff went home to bed, but we sat and visited for awhile longer. Finally Adassa looked around and said, "We had a nice time tonight. And may de God of Heaven be wid us until such time. God bless."

It was very late and we knew we had better call it a night. As Deedra put out the fire, Adassa said, "For de first time, you have been in Jack's Hill! You have seen joy, a happy night. Tank you very much for your kind hospitality."

I couldn't believe that she was thanking us. She's the one providing the hospitality!

Her eyes twinkled merrily as she said, "I believe dat you will remember me and remember my advise clearly." Then she broke into a happy folk song about the joys of life and her duppy going away to Ethiopia when she dies. We all laughed heartily when she finished.

"What do you think of dreams?"

"Well, I dream a lot. Sometimes I dream dat I can't remember my dreams. Sometimes I learn from my dreams."

Wishing each other sweet dreams, we all said good night and headed up the hill. It had cooled down considerably and dew covered everything.

Tuesday, March 13

We slept peacefully in our little tent last night and stayed plenty warm. I have an old down filled army bag that my father gave me. It was made in 1945 and I love it because it's like curling up in a warm, safe womb. It has traveled far and wide with me and I will never part with it.

Dawn came too fast for this girl, but I had to rouse myself because we had a guide waiting to take us hiking all day through the mountains. What a glorious day it was! We literally wandered through heaven. Mostly it was just us and nature, but we did pass a few villages. I couldn't help but wonder what it would be like to live there, so far removed from most of civilization.

While on what they call the "road," which is a rugged two foot wide trail, we met a beautiful little girl who was walking home from school. She told me that she rises at 4:00 AM everyday, takes a flashlight and walks alone two and a half miles down this incredibly steep trail to go to school. Then she has to climb back up it after school to get home.

We passed coffee plantations, all kinds of fruit plantations, and even headed into a rain forest where eucalyptus trees rose majestically through the cool fog and mist. The aroma was powerful and rejuvenating.

I can't begin to count the numerous kinds of trees, bushes and flowers we saw. Everywhere we turned the views were awesome. Tony, our guide, was great. At times we were so high up that we found ourselves walking in and out of clouds. It's exhilarating to look down on the clouds. We stopped to rest at a waterfall on Hope River. I felt like I could've stayed there for the rest of my life.

After hiking for nine hours with relatively few breaks, I am exhausted this evening. But it's worth every stiff muscle I have and every ache and pain. Opportunities like this don't come along everyday. The memory of this experience will live in the forefront of my mind for a long, long time.

We sat around the lodge this evening and talked with Sweet Pea and Hunter, who are guides at the lodge. Everyone was feeling silly and told lots of jokes. Sweet Pea told me that his grandmother used to walk to school barefoot, but everyone is civilized now and must wear shoes. "If you really check it out and look, you will see dat I always have on my socks and my crisp pair of shoes. I always like to be crisp, even when I'm going out wid de ladies. Even when I have dis beautiful lady beside me. Her name is Debbie.

"By de way, I love Debbie. I don't see no odder girl like Debbie. She's not even my girlfriend, but I know dat someday she will be. Is it true, Debbie?"

I laughed, recognizing the typical Jamaican come on. "No, mon!"

"Debbie say no, but I'm telling her dat I love her from de bottom of my heart." We all broke into laughter here.

I switched the subject to duppies, but both guys refused to speak of them. They seemed afraid of the subject.

I had hoped to have a serious interview, but soon had to abandon the idea as these guys were not in the mood for anything but fun and play. And that in itself is a good teaching. We all need more play time in our crazy lives.

Sweet Pea was so obviously enamored by women. His whole happiness seemed dependent on his relationship to women. I found that a bit refreshing. We women need to quit feeling responsible for men's happiness. We need to seek our own joy. In doing so, we will be a reflection for all they are seeking on a deep, emotional level.

Sweet Pea said that his grandmother always said, "Look somewhere and shook your head before you shook your crotch."

My own grandmother said, "Where is his brains? In his ass?" Same thing, really... .

I asked Hunter what his big dream in life is. "My dream? 'I have a dream.' Martin Luther King, you know. My dream is love. Me love everybody and everyting. I have nutting else to say."

Sweet Pea asked me to speak of myself now. "Debbie, what do you tink of love?"

"I think I feel so much love for people that it's unbelievable. Sometimes I feel like a flame that burns on this Earth, and I don't feel my body because all that I feel is love."

We spoke of things which are sacred and intimate in our own lives, and we ended the evening with mutual respect for one another.

10

THE FINAL HOURS

"I dance like this and I sing like this in a language that I was never taught. It's the language of my ancestors. The spirits taught it to me."
— *Jamaican Healer*

Wednesday, March 14

Last night after talking to Sweet Pea and Hunter, I went out and sat in a private spot in the mountains and prayed. And I wondered about life.

I needed and received time alone today. After hiking for awhile, I spread a blanket, laid down, and reflected, read, wrote and meditated. Soaking up my surroundings, the mountains, the cows, and all the tropical vegetation, I transcended time really, as I journeyed beyond the present, into my future. I sensed that my road won't be easy, but I'm ready to face the challenges.

I stayed out there until dusk, when I found my way back to the lodge. After having a scrumptious Jamaican dinner cooked by Adassa, we built another bonfire and sang with some Canadians who had just arrived. Deedra and I finally found our way back to our tent, and after enjoying the big moon and mountains one last time we drifted into a peaceful slumber.

Thursday, March 15

It was difficult to make the shift from the mountains back to the city today, but it was time. Deedra and I finally managed to track down Olive at the Institute of Folklore and Culture.

I was embarrassed about my appearance and hygiene. I definitely looked and smelled like someone just coming out of the wilds. Also, since we had arrived unexpectedly, I was surprised that Olive had time to see us.

Ms. Lewin is a beautiful woman, both inside and out, and very refined. I spoke with her about this project, and then with her permission I turned on my tape. We were talking about modern medicine versus traditional, and cultural reaction to it in this day and age.

As I turned on the tape, Olive was saying, "They wanted to blend the two, because they realized that the traditional healers had to heal. That's the only way they remain as traditional healers. And these are not idiots! If you have a bad sore and somebody heals it, you know when it's healed. If they don't heal it, you know they're not healers.

"Okay, I told them I couldn't blend the two. When they asked why, I told them that in Jamaica there is a lot of confusion in people's minds about what is a healer and who is an obeah person. Because you know, this is how we have been brought up. If Father does an exorcism, that's okay. But if a Revival person does it, it's obeah. See, if there's a laying on of hands in the church and people are healed, then it's wonderful. The Lord has spoken.

"But if somebody in the traditional, who does not speak the Queen's English, does it, then it's obeah. They are not healers. So I couldn't expose them to being accused of obeah, being obeah people, because that is punishable by law. Get me?"

"Yeah. Do they still uphold that law in Jamaica?"

"It is a law. I mean it's not a matter of upholding it. It is a law! I read recently that a lot of people still go to obeah people. I wouldn't be surprised. I, personally, wouldn't go to an obeah person with a problem to do with health. But I believe we have a lot of very efficient and effective healers.

"Talking like this will damage my credibility amongst the intellectuals. You know that. And so I have not talked like this a lot because I think I must pass on a lot of other things that depend on my credibility. Okay? But the island people trust me. They know that I respect them and so on. And I have a lot of experience when it comes to dealing with spiritual things.

"I have no problem with not being able to understand everything. I do not understand how I see. I do not understand how one thing that I eat nourishes my skin, and another nourishes my blood. I don't expect to understand it! I can read the explanation. Do you get what I'm saying? And I understand about lenses and so on.

"But there is something else to it that I do not understand. And when I look up at night and see our magnificent skies, I don't believe that man can understand everything. You see? There are no problems with that.

"But then again, I suppose that's not very academic. Get me? And our people are very conscious of that. May I give you an example of how they protect themselves? An eminent West Indian scholar wrote, in one of our very good publications, ideas presenting our traditional folk and festivals and so on. I was asked to comment, and I said that our real traditional people are capable of protecting themselves. You see, society has this feeling that if a person has not been to school or college or university they have to be stupid.

"Just the opposite is true. Such people have had to learn to cope with life as it is. They solve problems. They have to! They have always had to!

"We don't. We run for a psychiatrist. We run for a cigarette. We take a drink. They cannot do this! They have to know how to feed their child. They have to know how to solve that problem, how to cure that ill.

"And they have a different belief, because they see healing as having to do with a lot of things that we don't. We think so physically and materially that we don't see that health means mental health. It means the health of the community. It means the health of the environment. Right?

"A traditional person says, 'Don't trouble de waters now.' Others say, 'Oh, nonsense!' See? But eventually, ecological studiers will tell us that at that time the fish are spawning! Traditional people do not put it like that, but they know that if they fish now they are robbing themselves of life giving food.

"Okay. I am a Jamaican, born and bred from the country, and from so high, I have loved Jamaica! I love the stones. I said, 'Papa, what stone is this?' He said, 'My dear, that stone has had a lot of impression. This stone has been washed by water.' And he say, 'You know, you see that tree? That tree was brought here by so and so. And you know the pointsettia is named after—'

"Everything was very interesting! Sometimes we thought it was amusing. He would stop the car and scoot out of it to see. 'Ah, yes! Come children,

289

come!' And we'd all stream out of the car and he'd say, 'Here you see—' and we'd see some scratches and he'd say, 'Those are Arawak carvings.'

"So I mean, at the time it didn't mean anything to us. But it was sensitizing us to our environment. So when I see bulldozers bucking it down I want to bound them! You see? Because ten years time somebody comes and tells us, 'Oh, the Arawaks used to do so and so.' Right? And it's a battle that we fight all the time.

"People like me are thought to be paranoid, right? Anyway, so I am genuinely, I am telling you because you don't know me, I am genuinely a Jamaican lover. I know we have a lot of things that are terrible now, but I still feel that the center of Jamaica is beautiful and clean.

"I think we are suffering from a clash of cultures. I think we are suffering from people leaving the values of our old folk behind, running after values that don't apply! You know, they feel they can buy happiness. You can buy this. You can buy that. And it's a race that never ends! You have one car and then you want two. And then you want a boat. And then a plane. And you're never satisfied!"

"That's right! Sounds like the American value system. I believe that it's very screwed up!"

"Well you see, we have learned it. We are now becoming developed. You see?"

"That's why I wanted to go back to the people who haven't been exposed to this so much, the people that live in the country and small villages. I wanted to talk with them because I knew they would have much to teach me."

"Well, I appreciate that. I hope they sensed your sincerity and spoke honestly with you."

"I feel blessed. I am amazed by what they told me. I asked questions like, 'What is your big dream in life?' In America, most answers would be based on materialism. Jamaicans would ponder this for a second, or sometimes not at all, and then they'd say something like, 'Well, what I would like to do is to take a walk with God in his garden.' To me, that is so wonderful! After talking with them for awhile, I felt like I understood why they are as happy as they are."

"Exactly! Now you see, a lot of us don't understand. We think they're stupid. You see? And I tell them that when you give one of those old people something, she says, 'God bless you.' She doesn't say, 'Thanks.' It's not because she doesn't have any manners. It's because she knows that he owns nothing, only the hand of the Creator. That's what she's saying. She cannot put it into the language that's accepted, but it is there.

"And for us, who think we are so educated and learned, to understand! They understand us! It's we who don't understand!

"Anyway, let me tell you about this. I won't identify the person, but she is a healer and a head of the cult. And I learned long ago not to betray trust, because they tell me things that are very precious. And I never know what I should say and what I shouldn't!

"So if somebody says, 'Please come and we want you to give a talk on XYZ television', I say, 'Okay. May I bring Mrs. So and So?' Because then what I do is interview Mrs. So and So. And I tell her, 'Now if I ask you something that you can't say, just tell me that you can't say. Don't make it up!' Because they are very good at making things up. See, this is what I was saying about your questioning them.

"So they understood it and they knew that I respected them. People would ask me to repeat what I've been told, but instead I would invite the person in question to come with me and give her own answers.

"This happened with our broadcasting station. I invited the lady and she answered the questions. And I showed a film clip that I had done of her, singing and dancing. It was electrifying! And of course she said, 'I dance like this and I sing like this in a language that I was never taught. It is the language of my ancestors. The spirits taught it to me.'

"And she speaks the language. People have identified the words. And she did not come straight from Africa. Nor, she said, did her parents teach her. Her parents were staunch members of a church, so they were into the, how should I say it, the 'accepted' society. They don't speak African either.

"Anyway, that was only one of many interviews. And afterwards one of the interviewers said to me, 'When are you going to any ceremony that this lady is having? Please take me with you.'

"Now, the first thing is she should have spoken to the lady, not to me, right? So I said, 'Let me introduce you to her.' And I did.

"And the lady suddenly became very meek and somewhat intimidated. And this is how we are. We live on two levels. We've had to, to survive! And she said, 'All I want to do is come and visit you when you are having something.' Mrs. So and So said, 'Yes ma'am,' 'Well then, how can I find you?' She said, 'Let me give you the address.' And she got a piece of paper and gave her an address.

"Later I said, 'Why did you give her the wrong address?' She said, 'She is looking for a dance and she has seen it already. I've always told you to teach that you must be as gentle as a dove and as wise as a serpent.' You see? She realized that she was ahead of me, okay? So that's what I'm telling you."

"I don't know. I really feel like the people I talked to opened up to me. They knew that I respect them."

"Yes. And the thing is that we - I'm ambitious enough to say 'we' - we sense things, and we can sense sincerity. But the point is, if we sense that it is not sincere, we still cooperate. So the person who comes and questions will still get answers. The quality of those answers depends on what we sense about you. And I so hope they sensed your sincerity you see, in which case I don't have to say this at all."

"I lived here for two years and worked in tourism. And I really made a point of getting away from the tourist areas whenever I could. I developed good, solid friendships with many people who live in the country and small villages. Many of them I've known for about four years now. I also made a point of letting people know that if they didn't wish to answer a question I would respect that. So what you have just told me merely reaffirms what has happened."

"Well, I hope that it was very useful and informative, and that it will teach us a lot of things. Because this is what we are trying to do. We are trying to glean the memories and the beliefs of our senior citizens, or it will be too late! You'd be amazed how many people don't understand that!"

"I agree. In my mind I saw what was happening to Jamaica as far as the value system changing. That's why I wanted so much to do this now, before it changes any more."

Deedra piped in, "Especially in the tourist areas!"

"Yeah. The tourist areas are so different from the rest of Jamaica. I wanted to capture as much of old Jamaica as I could. I think the people have so much inside of them to share, and so much to teach us, and it's important."

"Please read my article in Sunday's *Gleaner*. I've been doing an article for eleven years. But I'm really very steamed up right now. I think that in order to save us, we need to concentrate on the children. And it needs a linking of old values to the youth. And it means that research must not be used academically, because we plough back into life.

"And we must recognize experiential knowledge of these people as being of use to everybody! And perhaps to America, and to Germany and to England. We must share it! But we can't share it until we have collected it. We have to collect it and then respect it.

"I have a Jamaican friend who went with me to an International Conference in East Berlin. She seemed almost embarrassed by my behavior and said to me, 'Boy you come on strong!' I said, 'My darling, how many people like us do you see here? We have got to talk!'

"And I tell them I say, 'Look, poverty is comparative. There are many times of which we are poor materially, but spiritually and culturally we are very rich.'

"And as far as your standards are concerned, even I fall below the poverty line. Do I look impoverished? I said to my friend, 'You have to do it! You cannot just say that we're not really poor, you know. You have to make the point!'

"We were in a hall with three hundred people, of which you had only two people like me. So if we sat there acting dignified and not doing anything, then nothing would ever be accomplished. People don't mean to be wicked. They just don't understand. We mustn't be afraid to speak up just because some of the people we speak with won't get the point. So those of us who have had the privilege of learning from them, and from civilized parents, must share it."

We had to end the interview here because Olive had a meeting to attend. She said that she really wanted to meet with me again on this, but when we tried to make arrangements I realized that it wouldn't be possible. I had to get back to Montego Bay now, and I'm going back to the States in a few days.

Friday, March 16

Our journey back to Mo-Bay yesterday was tiring. We had to transfer minibuses several times, which was no easy feat considering all the gear we were carting around. But we made it, and a cold shower never felt so good! Then we treated ourselves to roasted breadfruit and plantain.

We slept in this morning and then each of us took care of personal business. I did some laundry and then started packing for Wisconsin. It's hard for me to believe that I'll soon be going home. Somehow it doesn't seem real. I have mixed feelings about it. Jamaica is also home to me, and the thought of leaving is too painful to dwell on. Yet I am also looking forward to all that awaits me in Wisconsin. That's when the real work on this book will begin. It will take commitment. I know that I can't expect anyone there to be excited about it, so I'll have to be my own cheerleader.

These last few days I've been bleeding unnaturally again. I'm frightened. I'm facing the truth that physically I will die sometime.

Saturday, March 17

Today was special indeed! Deedra and I had promised Harris's children that we would have a party with them before we left the island. We had arranged to meet them on Sam Sharpe Square and when I saw them, my heart melted. They were standing quietly in a group, all dressed up in their Sunday best, their eyes and smiles shining brightly.

Walter Fletcher Beach

We walked them down to Walter Fletcher Beach and spent the whole afternoon swimming and picnicing. I was amazed to discover that they have only been swimming there once in their lives. They aren't allowed to swim alone, and Dawn and Harris are always working.

What a shame, because swimming is such good exercise. And they were all so comfortable in the sea. It was obviously a very thrilling experience for them. We laughed and sang and splashed merrily in the waves, and rolled around in the sand until we were all the same color.

They are so well behaved and it was a joy to be able to treat them. I soaked up their innocence and the love they so freely showered onto me. My little darlings! How can I bear to let them go?

Later we bussed them back up the mountain and visited with Grandma and Grandpa. Then we went to tell Daniel God good-by. He lit a kerosene bottle and made a ceremony of giving me some of his drawings. He also gave me some tamarand and grapefruit off of his trees. Then he took our hands and prayed for us. Our last stop was to say good-by to Harris, Pauline and Kimoy. It was terribly difficult for me to leave that mountain, not knowing if I shall ever return. I want to, but who knows what's in store for me?

Sunday, March 18

I woke up to the thought that I had to rouse myself in time to get down to Pier One to go snorkling and sailing on the Calico. This was a day of intense joy and a celebration of life. The Calico is an old wooden sailboat. I've spent many a day sailing with Captain Brian and his crew. It was so much fun to see them again. The real riches of life lie in friendships.

Mother Nature blessed us with perfect weather today. The sea felt warm as I romped with the colorful fish, admired the reefs, and danced around the jellyfish. There is an incredible world beneath the surface of the water. It amazes me to realize that many people never even experience it. How much else is going on in our great world that we never see? It made me wonder.

Death didn't, couldn't exist in the world I was in today. The warm sun and tropical breezes reenergized me. A thrill rose in me as the boat keeled way over and the sea sprayed against me. I have never seen water this color anywhere else. It is here that I am most at home on this planet. My gypsy soul was one with the elements. I give thanks, intent on enjoying my last few days in Jamaica.

Monday, March 19

I'm feeling very sad today. The awareness that I'm really leaving is hitting me in the gut and knocking the wind out of me. Right now I'm in the transition stage, half here and half there. I'm going to try hard to remain in my spirit and not be materially attached to things. My emotional body is threatening to do me in.

Deedra and I spent the day on the beach. As we were leaving, we ran into Captain Brian. He told us something that spooked me. My beautiful sea had just claimed the bodies of three American tourists and a diving instructor friend of mine. His name was Nigel and I had dived with him in Ochi.

I can't figure out what happened. No one can. We're all kind of in shock. They were all doing a deep dive, going down a sea wall. Normal sport diving recommends never exceeding one hundred and thirty-five feet. Somehow they all became disoriented and ended up over two hundred feet down. The air tanks of the Americans all blew up. Nigel dumped his empty tank at two hundred feet, but he surfaced far too fast. This caused his lungs to burst and his body to blow apart when he took his first breath of air.

I knew a diver from Trelawny who also died in a diving accident. Unfortunately, many people don't take the rules to heart. I am very strict about that when I dive. This is one time when I believe wholeheartedly in rules. I love diving, but take it very seriously. We must respect the sea.

Before we left, I had to sit for a bit by the sea and reflect on what I had just heard. I prayed for an easy transition into the light for those who had just left their bodies. More than ever, this is awakening me to the truth that my time on this planet is limited. And to the truth that I am more than a physical being.

Howard works at Sandals Royal. This evening he took Deedra, Gary and me there for dinner and a show. A magical event.

Tuesday, March 20

Well, this is it, my last day in Jamaica for who knows how long. Deedra and I spent most of the day on the beach. On the way over there, I stopped to talk with a lady I have known for years. Her name is Enid and she's a higgler who has a shop right under the office of the tour company I used to work for.

Enid is a large, gentle, loving lady. She has eight children, seven of which still live with her. The eighth one is married and living in Australia. Enid had a rough childhood and because she was needed at home, she never went beyond third grade in school.

For awhile she earned a living doing laundry for people. But then someone helped her get her little business going. It's not going well for two reasons. The first is lack of tourists right now, and the second is because the police are trying to eradicate higglers.

Enid told me that she practices no particular religion, but she has a strong personal relationship with God. She's living the best way that she can so that she will go to heaven when she dies and not have to work anymore.

She believes in obeah and thinks that someone has thrown a spell on her. That's why her business is so slow right now. I asked her if she has ever seen a duppy.

"One time. I can't see it again, but I know when it is around. You feel different, and your head grow like dis. You know, when your head grow big, he is around. And you smell different tings like yodiform."

"What is yodiform?"

"It smell bad. You call it a yodiform."

"Oh. And what do you think duppies are?"

"It's an evil. He is an evil. It's a spirit. If dey set out to hurt you, dey will hurt you. But if it don't set to hurt you, not going to be."

"Tell me how you felt that time you saw the duppy."

"Dizzy and frightened. It last a long time, happened at home about two years ago. And you can see it in different tings. You had frogs, you can know it different. Yes, frog. You know you can know a bad frog from a frog dat don't bad."

"How?"

"If dat frog is evil, it doesn't move. Anytime you see a frog it always tries to jump away from you. Dat evil frog doesn't try to jump away from you. Just staring at you. Such as de lizard. An evil lizard, he doesn't run."

"That's interesting. Let me ask you something. If you could do anything you wanted in your whole life, and nothing mattered — I mean if you had all your health and as much money as you wanted and you didn't need passports or anything — if you could do anything in your life, what would you do?"

"I would be happy."

"You would be happy?"

"Yes, and pray to my Lord."

"That's wonderful! Do you have anything else you would like to say? Any message you would like to leave with the world?"

"I would like to tell de people to love one anodder. Put down dere gun, knife, and machette and unite wid each odder. Because I know God is coming soon, soon, and very soon. So let God come and see we is happy wid one anodder. Ohhh... oh tank you, Jesus! Tank you, Jesus! Praise God! Tank you, Lord! Tank you, Jesus! Tank you. And Debbie, I want you to love each and everyone. Pray for us, and odders will pray for you."

Here Enid lapses into a song, thanking Jesus for everything. She is in a world all her own and her soft voice is coming straight from her heart. When she finished, she whispered, "Tank you, Lord!"

I thanked her and gave her a big hug, assuring her I would remember her in my prayers. She was humming joyously as we moved on.

Going away party
We enjoyed our day at the beach and at sunset we headed over to a local

beach for my going away party. Gary, Morton, Brian, Linda, Howard, his brother and niece, and a bunch of local boys joined us for the celebration. Mother nature provided the most spectacular sunset I have ever seen. We built two fires, one in which to roast breadfruit, yams, fish and plantains in, the other just a huge roaring bonfire.

I was so happy to be sharing this feast with all these people who are so very dear to me. It was fun and yet painful simultaneously. At moments like this, I want time to stand still. We sat around the fire for hours, telling stories and enjoying the stars and sea and warm night.

So much has happened to me these past few months. It will amaze me even more when I get home and review it all. I feel rich indeed, to have been blessed with this incredible journey. Thank you, Jah, for my good friends and my great life. I am so full of love that I can't contain it. It's pouring out of me like the thundering water of Dunn's River Falls.

Wednesday, March 21

This is it. I'm going back to Janesville, Wisconsin today. All I can say right now is that this airplane may be able to take Debbie out of Jamaica, but nothing has the power or ability to take Jamaica out of Debbie.

EPILOGUE

I believe that the people in this book represent the true spirit of Jamaica. Sixteen years have passed since this journey, but I still spend time in Jamaica every year. Although I have physically lost touch with several people in this book, they all live on in my heart.

Here is what I do know about some of them:

In 1999, I traveled up to Farm Heights and Rose Heights. I was amazed to find no trace of either Daniel God or his Garden of Eden. It left me with an eerie sensation that I had just dreamed the whole experience I had with him. I asked around and a few people remembered Daniel. "Him got dead."

"How?"

"Me no know. Him old."

I asked about Mother Heart. If anyone did know her, they weren't about to admit it. As for Harris and the families up there, I experienced much the same thing. The children are grown up now. Last I heard, Coretta had a pickney of her own.

Bibsey had another son named King. She, King, Devon and Steve live in Florida. Mr. Lindsay has passed on. I'm sometimes conscious of Mr. Lindsay and Daniel God watching over me still.

Last I knew, Sunshine had made it to the States also. I wonder if she ever pursued any of her career dreams.

Keith Foote and Baldie are still running the Little Pub in Ocho Rios, although it was badly damaged in a fire and had to be rebuilt. When I visited this year, Baldie once again sang me the *Coconut Woman* song. He told me that Dennis Malcolm is also still singing.

Howard moved to New York City and started a catering business. He does the cooking from his apartment and has the food delivered via taxi.

Deedra is now married to a real estate agent and has a pet sitting service. She and her husband live in Florida with their dog.

Birgitta is also married and is a stay at home mom, busy raising two beautiful little daughters. The family lives near Chicago.

As for me, my finger healed, but I'll never be able to bend it. My bleeding turned out to be nothing more than a hemorrhoid. I am now happily married to a man named Keith who shares my passion for Jamaica. I am currently working on a five book fiction psychic romance series that takes place in Jamaica. (Where else?) My island will forever call me home.

Jamaica, Jamaica, Jamaica, land we love...

GLOSSARY

ackee and codfish: the national dish of Jamaica. Ackee is the national fruit of Jamaica. It grows on trees and is red with a yellow interior. The pod must be allowed to open naturally in order to dissipate an otherwise poisonous gas. When cooked, ackee resembles scrambled eggs.

Arawak Indians: the original inhabitants of Jamaica. They were a peaceful, gentle people who were totally wiped out after the arrival of the Europeans.

Babylon: In the context of this book, Babylon refers to governing by evil, corruption, greed and all that is not in the best interest of the whole.

Bob Marley: the father of reggae music. Through his music and example, Bob did much to uplift the people of Jamaica spiritually. He believed in peace and the power of love and instilled hope in weary hearts. Mr. Marley passed on May 11, 1981.

calalu: a green plant whose leaves are cooked and eaten as a vegetable. It is a main ingredient in pepperpot soup, and is also known as Ital food.

Cumina: (also spelled **Kumina**) a religious cult brought over from Africa. Rituals consist of a lot of singing, dancing and drumming. The drums call up spirits which possess the dancers during the ceremony.

currency: In 1990, $1.00 US = $6.35 JA

dreadlocks: hairdo originally worn by Rastafarians, but now popular all over. Hair is never combed or cut, but twisted into ringlets as it grows. Rastafarians believe that much power lies in their hair. Hair is like an antenna that connects one to the realm of spirit.

duppy: spirit of the dead or Jamaican ghost

303

ganja: marijuana

Haile Selassie I: the late emperor of Ethiopia. Some Rastafarians consider him the Black reincarnation of Christ.

higgler: a Jamaican vendor or peddlar

Irie: Jamaican salutation meaning "Everything is just cool, wonderful, excellent."

Ital: health food, unprocessed with no preservatives, cooked and eaten by Rastafarians and others

Jah: the Creator

jerk food: meat and fish which is prepared with a special, very spicy seasoning and grilled slowly over an open pit

karma: What we put out comes back to us. Our behavior here and now determines our destiny in the next existence.

Leaf of Life: a succulent plant with many medicinal properties

Marcus Garvey: evangelist whose teachings provided an inspiration for the Rastafarian movement

mongoose: small, furry brown animal brought to Jamaica to destroy rats. Unfortunately, the mongoose also destroyed many other things which are important to the balance of nature.

natty dread: a term used for someone sporting a dreadlock hairdo

obeah: mostly thought of as Jamaican black magic or sorcery. Obeah was originally brought over from Africa and even though it is illegal in Jamaica, it is still widely practiced.

Parish: a geographical area of Jamaica on the order of a county in the United States

Patois: local dialect of Jamaica. English is the official language of Jamaica.

pickney: Jamaican child

Pocomania: Jamaican religious cult group, branch of Revivalism

Rastafarianism: peaceful cult which originated in Jamaica. It holds two basic doctrines, (1) the belief that Haile Selassie I is the Black reincarnated Christ, and (2) the goal of redemption through repatriation to Africa (Ethiopia) which is seen as the spiritual home of black people. In this cult, ganja is considered a sacred herb and is used by many to gain insight and communicate with God (Jah).

reggae: music which originated in Jamaica and became popular in the late sixties. The theme often invokes unity, love and the beauty of life.

Revivalism: Jamaican religious cult which combines African and European beliefs. Some of the services incorporate trance dancing, which brings about spirit possession in the worshippers. Some branches, such as Zion, deal only with heavenly spirits such as saints and angels. Others, such as Pocomania, deal with ground spirits, dead humans and fallen angels. Some of the leaders are obeah practitioners.

spliff: big, fat marijuana (ganja) cigarette

RESOURCE

Senior, Olive *A to Z of Jamaican Heritage* (1983)

ABOUT THE ARTIST

"Angels Appear"
by Rita Genet
from the private collection of Evita's Restaurant
Ocho Rios, Jamaica, West Indies

The visual splendor of the Caribbean Islands has been a continuing source of inspiration for RITA GENET, who lived in Jamaica for twenty years A native of Milford, Connecticut, she received a Bachelor of Fine Arts Degree in painting from the school of Visual Arts in New York City.

Over the past thirty-five years her paintings have been exhibited in fifty group shows in the United States, Europe and throughout the Caribbean. She has had eight one woman shows, the most recent being *Angels in Jamaica.* The artwork of RITA GENET has been used for Christmas cards, for UNICEF, corporations, hotels and many charities. She currently lives in Asheville, North Carolina.

ABOUT THE AUTHOR

Debbie Smoker has lived in Jamaica off and on for over thirty years. Her work has been published in several magazines and she has written two novels, *Turn on your Magic Eyes* and *Joy of Jamaica*. Debbie is also an international speaker and has appeared on several radio and TV shows in Jamaica and the United States. Side careers include being a hypnotherapist, a professional tarot reader and a stained glass artist.

For relaxation she camps, bikes and boats with her husband Keith. Her philosophies: Fun with a purpose and education through entertainment. Her heroes: Walt Disney and Bob Marley. Jamaica and Wisconsin are both home to Debbie. *www.dsmoker.com*

EXCERPTS FROM DEBBIE SMOKER'S OTHER BOOKS

From *Turn on your Magic Eyes*

Entering a narrow passageway, I feel my way along the stone walls. The path curves sharply and I'm suddenly in a clearing. I gasp. There in front of me is a crackling fire and in the glow of light surrounding it sits the old woman I saw in my dream last night!

Now I'm spooked and I want to run, but I find myself paralyzed to the spot. The woman's brown eyes bore into me and I hear a deep chanting coming from her mouth. I don't understand the chant but somehow I hear a duo voice coming from her. One is of a higher pitch and speaks perfect English.

"Welcome, Paul. I've been waiting for you. You've been seeking me for a long while now but you weren't aware of it on a conscious level. Sit down here by the fire. I have much to tell you."

I sink down, convinced that I'm hallucinating. It must be an after effect of all the ganja that I smoked yesterday. I silently curse and promise myself that I'll never smoke again if I get through this ridiculous dream.

From *Joy of Jamaica*

Eventually we come to a small clearing. A single wooden room much in need of a paint job is nestled here. We climb up some creaking steps and onto a rickety porch. Turning to me, she says slowly, "I have something you want."

My heart is pounding wildly as we enter. The room is filled with lotions, potions, herbs, skulls and books. Odd looking symbols are painted all over what appears to be some kind of altar.

"Who are you?" I ask, frightened now but determined not to show it. My skin crawls because somehow all of this looks too familiar.

308

TO ORDER:

Turn on your Magic Eyes $10.95 + $3.00 S&H

Joy of Jamaica $10.95 + $3.00 S&H

Adventures of Coconut Woman $15.95 + $4.00 S&H

Wisconsin residents: add 5% sales tax (80 cents)

SEND CHECK OR MONEY ORDER TO:

Joy Won Publishing
7857 E. Oakbrook Circle
Madison, WI 53717

Questions or comments, e-mail:

joywonpub@tds.net